THE
CUTTING
GIRL

m
B

MIRROR BOOKS

1

Published in Great Britain and Ireland in 2025 by
Mirror Books, a Reach PLC business,
5 St Paul's Square, Liverpool, L3 9SJ.

www.mirrorbooks.co.uk
@TheMirrorBooks

Print ISBN 9781915306999
eBook ISBN 9781917439275

Design and production by Mirror Books.

Printed and bound in Great Britain by
CPI Group (UK) Ltd, Croydon, CR0 4YY

Cover image: Alamy
(Posed by model)

This book was printed using
FSC approved materials.

MIX
Paper | Supporting
responsible forestry
FSC® C013604

SLAVE GIRLS

THE CUTTING GIRL

Louise Allen

with Theresa McEvoy

MIRROR BOOKS

Author's Note and Warning

People who are unfamiliar with the workings of County Lines and trafficking gangs may be shocked to read how quickly this can happen. In my experience, the whirlwind process of approaching, befriending, grooming and then blackmailing vulnerable young adults can be frighteningly fast, giving victims no time to take stock, seek advice or speak to a trusted friend or adult before it seems, to them, that their situation is hopeless.

The more we all learn about how to spot the tell-tale signs of a criminal gang's influence, the faster we can check in and potentially prevent a catastrophic turn in someone's life.

There are links to further help and advice at the back of this book.

This book contains descriptions of self-harm, sexual abuse, suicide ideation and eating disorders.

Foreword

I spend a great deal of time working with and writing about vulnerable children.

Inevitably, that means that I also find myself writing about those who are out there waiting to pounce on them.

It used to be that kids in care were the primary target for County Lines gangs: easy marks whom nobody was looking out for. The National Society for the Prevention of Cruelty to Children (NSPCC) definition of a County Line is an organised criminal network involved in exporting illegal drugs into importing areas using dedicated mobile phone lines or other form of 'deal line'. They are likely to exploit children and vulnerable adults to store and move drugs and money and will often use coercion, intimidation, and violence, including sexual violence and weapons.

This kind of activity has gone on for years amongst the *most* vulnerable of our children, those who, for one reason or another, find themselves without parents to look out for them: those caught up in the care system. Consequently, there are plenty of children's homes that have been infiltrated by County Lines gangs, especially unregulated homes that aren't scrutinised too closely by local authorities – who are over-stretched and desperate to place children in shelter.

But markets have changed. There are only so many kids in care that can be recruited and, since awareness of County

Lines has improved, training has improved too. As a foster carer myself, I have encountered too many children ensnared by the debt bondage and threats that characterise County Lines involvement. Most foster carers and children's homes are fully aware of the operation of gangs and are far more clued up than they once were about how to protect their children from them.

So, surprising as it may seem, gangs from different lines, already established in state schools, are moving in on private schools. It's big business. Because society doesn't perceive the situation of children in private schools as one of obvious neglect, it's easy to recruit them.

A huge number of children go missing in the United Kingdom: over 100,000 of them every year according to the National Crime Agency and the UK Missing Persons Bureau, although it's difficult to establish exact figures.

Again, those in the care system fare worse. The statistic that one in 10 looked-after children are reported missing, compared to one in 200 children in the general population, is a frightening one. Tragically, not all are found. Around 1500 children every year are labelled as 'long-term missing', which in reality means for more than a month. Again, as unbelievable as it might sound in the civilised 21st century, some are trafficked and sold, and experience unimaginable horrors on the way.

You're about to meet Charlotte, The Cutting Girl.

Her name has been changed, of course, and elements of her story have been fictionalised to disguise her identity. But, sadly, Charlotte's story is not unique.

I only wish it was.

Prologue

'Bye, darling!'

There is a flurry of bags and movement in the hallway, and hurried hugs, as the dreaded moment of departure arrives.

In a sudden fit of panic, Charlotte throws out her arms and clings onto her mother's legs, wrapping herself around them and pressing her forehead into her mother's knees as if she might somehow be able to stop her from walking away. She feels as if she might not be able to breathe if her mother takes another step. But the gesture is futile. Her mother moves forward, dragging Charlotte a few inches with her as if trying to shake her off.

'Don't be so dramatic, darling. Dear me. It's not as if it's for very long. And Daddy's here. And Nanny and Bob to look after you. The time will pass before you know it. Your brothers were never like this! For goodness' sake, don't be such a cry-baby. We've been through all of this already. There's no need to make such a fuss. I'll be home again before you know it.'

For a moment, her mother is framed in the doorway. The bright sunlight behind her makes her red hair look as if it has a halo around it, as if her mother is an angel. Then the giant wooden door closes and the hallway suddenly looks much bigger without a mother in it. Charlotte is six years old. She looks down at the black and white diamond pattern on the hallway floor, which seems like a giant chessboard. Nanny has taught her to play chess recently. But in this game, she is only making wrong moves.

'Come back, Mummy!'

The words thud into the back of the door and, just for a second, Charlotte thinks it might reopen. When it doesn't, the silence is loud. She fills the terrible quiet with a wail.

It's the first time that she is conscious of being left, though later she will learn that it's happened periodically since she was born, given the nature of her mother's work.

At seven years of age there is more upheaval. More tears. More protestations. As ever, they are to no effect. Her parents have decided on boarding school.

This time it is Charlotte who leaves, her parents waving her off in front of the impossibly large oak doors. Only it isn't her choice to go. She can't believe she is being abandoned again. She resists the urge to turn around and run back into their arms. She knows only too well what will happen.

'It's just school, darling. Everyone does it. It's the law.'

The first term is the hardest. After that she gets used to it. The loneliness. The dread of not making friends. The terrible feeling of not belonging.

At Christmas, at the end of that first term, Nanny gave her a teddy bear to take back to school with her. She has a collection of toys that her parents have given her over the years, but nothing like this. Her parents have always chosen expensive Steiff teddies, which sit on a shelf in her bedroom because they are stiff and 'investments' are hard to cuddle. But Gertie is soft and squidgy, almost as if she doesn't have quite enough stuffing inside her. Gertie comes back with her to boarding school in the new year.

There have been many more goodbyes since.

Today, 13-year-old Charlotte is experiencing the dread of parting again, along with a distinct feeling of déjà vu, although this time her mother is not going away for work. It feels much worse than that. Charlotte is being left out of a family holiday. Her father and older brothers also have their stuff piled up in the hall. The atmosphere is merry: school's out for summer. A flight is booked and, with it, all the joyful anticipation of vacation pleasures to come – but without her. The excitement of everyone else is palpable in the last minute checking of passports and tickets and have-you-remembered-this and have-you-packed that which echoes around the hallway as the rest of her family charge around before departure.

'Oh, don't look so glum, Whoopsie. You know you won't enjoy it! You'll have a lovely time here with Nanny and Bob. A *better* time. We've been over this. You hate the sea!'

There is no point wrapping herself around her mother this time, because she will leave anyway. She always does. When the door closes it no longer looks as enormous as it did when she was younger, but the hole in her heart is just as large.

At least Charlotte has Napoleon and Julius with her, the two large Wolfhounds that are the family pets. She misses the comfort of their warm fur and their unconditional love when she's away at school. Because she is staying behind there's no need for them to go into kennels. She buries herself in Napoleon's neck and sheds tears that she knows are futile but can't stop.

Charlotte is different from her family in so many ways. Her pudgy frame means that she is very definitely not sporty like her brothers. Neither is she academic like the two eldest, Henry and Edward. She likes art and animals. Maybe a little bit more like Oliver. She doesn't like school, or books. And she definitely doesn't like to be on board a boat. She knows that she lets her family down on every front, especially this one. She hates sailing. She finds it boring, mainly because her mother is right; she has no sea legs and gets seasick very quickly. It's embarrassing and unpleasant. Her family quickly get fed-up with having to turn around – or one adult having to stay at home with her when both her parents love being out at sea. So this is the best solution.

In which case, why does it feel so horrible?

Charlotte reaches for Teddy Gertie, even though she's getting far too old for soft toys these days and Gertie's fur has begun to wear away.

It's also true that Charlotte is very fond of Nanny and her husband, Bob, even though she doesn't see them so much these days, now that they've moved to Bath and are no longer on the doorstep. The drive is too much for Bob who is getting on a bit now. In Charlotte's memory, they have always been there, in the background, like part of the furniture. And, although she understands that they are paid by her parents to look after her, the closeness she feels towards them makes them more like family than her actual parents. The smell of Nanny is warm and familiar. It's the smell of flour and apples and jam tarts and Oil of Olay and lavender bags all mixed up.

And, while Charlotte is at home and sleeping in her own bed, Nanny finds ways to turn the days into a little holiday. They soon settle into a rhythm of walks, day trips out and evenings spent playing board games and eating the food that nursery-aged Charlotte used to love: cottage pie or fish pie with carrots sliced to just the right thickness, and peas that she can chase round the plate; apple pie with thick crust and custard and no reproving look if she takes a second helping.

In the mornings, Nanny makes sure that the inside of the egg is runny, and cuts the toast into soldiers, even though Charlotte is far too old for them.

For this week, Nanny and Bob have brought their little dog with them, Rolley the Tibetan Terrier. In some ways Rolley is more fun than Napoleon and Julius, even though Charlotte loves the 'beasts' as her parents call them. On the first night, Nanny lets Rolley sleep on Charlotte's bed. Napoleon and Julius are far too big to do that.

Charlotte speaks to her family several times; short facetime calls when they remember her and there's enough signal. Of course, they are having a wonderful time and the sailing has been marvellous and the seas are divinely blue and they have found some great spots for snorkelling and Henry, who loves scuba diving and has done a night dive on a wreck in the Mediterranean, now thinks he's James Bond.

'But you'd hate it, darling.'

The frightening call comes midway through the week, late at night.

'Whoopsie, darling, I don't want you to worry, but the boat's in trouble. There's been a little fire. We're awaiting rescue.'

Her mother, never ruffled, sounds panicky.

Nanny puts her arms around Charlotte as Charlotte takes the call. How can Charlotte not worry?

'I'll make some hot chocolate,' Nanny says. And bedtime rules are relaxed for a night as they wait up for a tense few hours, until news reaches the UK that the rescue has taken place.

Charlotte hears the details a thousand times afterwards as the story is told repeatedly. The 49-ft sailing yacht her parents chartered for the family to sail around the Ionian islands ran into trouble when the air conditioning system caught fire between Corfu and Kefalonia, and the boat actually began to sink.

'We had to step up into the life raft,' her mum, Kirsty, tells her when they have enough signal to Facetime.

Charlotte knows from her limited time in the sailing community that only happens when things are really bad on board the boat.

'But it's alright, darling. We're all a bit shaken up, but your brothers were totally brilliant in a crisis. You should have seen them!'

Of course her brothers were brilliant in a crisis, because that is what Henry, Edward and Oliver do.

'Anyway, all's well that ends well but we're coming home early.'

Charlotte isn't sure what it is she feels as she hears that news. Part of her is, of course, relieved that everything is alright. That her family has not been harmed. Part of her doesn't know if deep down she would rather enjoy the holiday with Nanny and Bob to herself.

And part of her, a part she tries to suppress, can't help but wish that they'd all gone down with the stupid boat.

PART ONE

Charlotte

I

'Darling, are you nearly ready for a little top-up?'

James Ashman smiles back at his wife, Kirsty, and lifts up his champagne flute so she can pour another half glass in.

'Just a splash,' he nods, 'I don't want to go too mad before the other guests arrive. But there's so much to celebrate. I'm so proud of you, my high-flying surgeon-wife.'

Kirsty is, indeed, a success story. She's already completed more tours as chief surgeon in the forces than most men, let alone women, in a space where women are still under-represented. Originally from Scotland, she has spent time in different parts of Africa, in Brunei, Oman and across Europe, most recently in the Netherlands, France and Germany. After a big decision to leave that behind and become more rooted, she is about to join a team in a top private hospital in Switzerland.

'I won't offer you a top up, Whoopsie. One glass is enough for you, don't you think?'

Charlotte has never understood what's so special about champagne, but takes a dutiful sip.

They're taking a final break in James' family home in Cornwall, inherited when his father, Charlotte's grandfather, died a decade ago.

Kirsty places the premier cru down next to a photograph of James' father in full military regalia, back when he was a commander in the Navy. It's a picture that fascinates Charlotte. She doesn't remember much about her grandfather; a remote, intimidating figure – but in the photograph, it looks like he comes from another age. James followed suit, entering Sandhurst and becoming a senior ranking officer in the army. Kirsty, too, was born to an army family. The military is in their blood. Though somehow that gene skipped Charlotte.

'To pastures new.'

There are big changes ahead for Kirsty – and lucrative ones at that. She is at the top of her game and Charlotte is in awe of her mother. She wonders quite how she'll ever be able to match up to all her mother's achievements. More still are planned. Kirsty has never been one for standing still; this is the start of her trajectory towards a goal of early retirement and eventually running her own charity. Tonight's party is all in her honour.

'They're lucky to have you.'

'*You're* lucky to have me!'

'And don't you like to let me know it!'

The banter is flirtatious, even after a quarter of a century of marriage, and Charlotte, as always, feels excluded.

Kirsty's eyes alight upon one of the many splendidly-framed photographs of their three sons: Henry, Edward and Oliver, back when they were still in school together. She picks it up. The boys are all carbon copies of James: dark-haired and dark-skinned. They were all sent to different boys' boarding schools that matched their strengths and interests: all three are accomplished sportsmen; Henry, in particular, was captain of the first XV and has carried that over into his university rugby days. They are all the things that Charlotte will never be.

'A shame that the boys can't be with us tonight,' her mother says.

Charlotte's practically grown-up brothers all have their own summer commitments and Charlotte knows only too well that their company would be preferred to hers. She'd like them to be here tonight, too. Especially Henry, who always has a kind word for her.

Kirsty turns towards the windows and sighs.

'Look at that view.'

They've all seen it a thousand times before, but it's never exactly the same each day. Outside, the sun is dipping on the horizon beyond the curved bay. The garden, filled with hydrangeas and easy-to-care-for shrubs – neither Kirsty nor James has any time or interest in gardening or domestic life – still manages to look bold and impressive. Beyond the garden, their private jetty disappears into the estuary, with a view of the sea beyond. It is a striking vista at this time of day.

'I never tire of it. But I'd rather look at you.'

Kirsty pushes his shoulder playfully. 'I'm awfully glad we never sold this place when your father died.'

'It's a luxury we can afford,' James assures her.

It's also where they spend a great deal of time socialising, sailing and relaxing.

'Because we work hard,' Kirsty reminds him.

James left the army some time ago, retiring at 40 after considering that he'd done his time. He was also dissatisfied and frustrated with his community from both within the service and also as a citizen. And, although perhaps not as driven as his wife, he wanted to make sure that he gave something back to society after his career.

Retirement came with the Early Departure Payments (EDPs) unique to a career in the forces and, despite being personally wealthy, James was entitled to a tax-free lump sum plus regular monthly payments. That level of financial security enabled him to embark upon a political career for the last decade, recently entering Parliament.

The early evening light filters between trees, falling through the windows and illuminating Kirsty's mass of hair into its distinctive, fiery red halo. She looks beautiful. Charlotte has inherited her mother's fair, highland skin, but not her beautiful red hair. She fingers her own mousey-blonde locks, which she sees as nondescript and ordinary. It's not so much that she envies her mother, more that she feels a kind of disgust at her own inadequacy by comparison.

Perhaps Kirsty notices the gesture.

'Run along, Whoopsie, and do something with your hair before the guests arrive.'

She has been dismissed.

Charlotte puts the champagne glass down on the coffee table with a nod. But she lingers a little behind the door.

'I'm still worried about her,' Kirsty admits, returning to a conversation they began just before the champagne came out. Whoopsie is their pet name for Charlotte, though Charlotte makes no secret of the fact that she hates it. When Oliver was six years old and heading off to prep school, neatly two years behind Edward, himself two years behind their firstborn, and everyone was where they should be, Kirsty fell pregnant with Charlotte. She has been affectionately known as the 'mistake' ever since. 'Whoopsie' has stuck.

'Darling little Whoopsie,' James sighs.

'You baby her!' Kirsty accuses. 'If you'd just treated her the same as the boys, everything would have been fine.'

'You're too hard on her!'

'I'm hard on her because she needs to toughen up.'

It's a well-worn argument. Kirsty is the epitome of independence and resilience, and Charlotte's helplessness continually frustrates her – a situation that Charlotte is only too aware of. Not only does she seem unable to succeed at school, resulting in yet another move on the horizon, but she is neither beautiful nor charismatic enough to charm her way into the world, the way the rest of her family are able to.

'Don't be so disparaging. She can't help being the way she is.' James always defends his daughter. 'She's just at a difficult age. Things will iron themselves out and she'll be fine. How could she not be fine with parents like us?' he says, only half in jest.

Kirsty smiles and looks down at her watch. 'I hope so. Right. Guests will be arriving soon.'

'That reminds me, Martin will be one of them. I know he's not really one of us these days, but I thought it better to invite him than not, under the circumstances. Is all the paperwork sorted out for Whoopsie's school?'

'Thank God for the old boys network, eh?'

'Well, sometimes a lefty idealist is what you need.'

'Hmm, if you say so. But yes, I've done all the admission forms and it's all gone through, no problem. She can start afresh in the new term.'

James' old pal from boarding school is now a headmaster. Significantly, he is headmaster at Hickman's College, a former independent boys' school that recently became co-educational, and the place where Charlotte will be starting in September.

Kirsty is not a fan of the kind of school that Martin now runs: a boarding school that takes the kids that other schools might not be so keen to have, whether that's related to academia or behaviour, but his establishment is just about the only option left for Charlotte. That or a state school, which neither James nor Kirsty can contemplate with their current plans, neither willing to put their careers on hold to look after Charlotte.

'Good. And then we can just draw a line underneath everything that's gone before.'

Charlotte feels sick at the thought of starting at another new school, having to try and make friends with more bitchy girls she has nothing in common with. She wishes she could just 'draw a line' under everything that's happened, under all her flaws and failings. But she is still the same person who will fail again, no matter how much money they throw at her education.

The doorbell rings to signal the first of the great and the good to arrive at the soiree. Charlotte darts up the stairs so she isn't caught listening in the hall. She delays as long as she thinks she can get away with. When she comes back down, a clip pinning back her hair, the room is already filled with people.

Charlotte lingers awkwardly by the table with the photographs and watches the room. She notices how her mother tilts her head to one side while talking to each guest to indicate how intently she is listening to whatever they have to say. She is wonderful with people, and so many guests today are influential – or need to be influenced. Kirsty has made a beeline for Martin, the man who is about to become her headmaster. Charlotte cringes inwardly to think that they'll start talking about her. Thankfully, from what she can hear, her mother seems to be keeping the conversation quite general.

'How are things shaping up for the new term? Do you have much to do over the summer?'

Martin launches into an explanation about all the work that has to be done in relation to the exam results, plus all the building work that's been going on at Hickman's while they haven't had students on site.

'And how's Charlotte looking forward to starting at Hickman's?'

'Oh, usual nerves and trepidation. You know. Speaking of the site, don't you mind living and working on site all the time?' Kirsty asks Martin. 'Is there ever any downtime?'

'You get used to it,' Sarah, Martin's wife, answers. 'And it gives us a bit more space at home in the evenings because our own boys actually sleep in the dorms with the other children.'

'Built-in babysitting!' Kirsty jokes. 'Lucky you.'

'Yes and no,' Martin smiles. 'Sarah is one of the five house mothers who take care of the children's needs, so she's actually on site taking care of a lot more than just our kids!'

'Do you ever miss nursing?' Kirsty asks, remembering that Sarah trained as a nurse before she went into education with her husband.

'God, I don't have *time* to miss nursing!' Sarah laughs. 'I look after the welfare and personal development of the students, supervise and coordinate their activities, maintain discipline, standards of behaviour, manners, dress… you name it, I'm on it!'

'And all that other unpleasant business is forgotten about now, I expect? The press can be so insensitive, can't they?'

Kirsty is referring to a suicide at the school the year before. It was hushed up, but the press found out about it and blamed the school. Charlotte has read about it online.

'Yes. Yes, they can.' Sarah isn't laughing now.

'It's so hard to choose a school, but I'm really pleased that Charlotte will be with you both.'

'And we're looking forward to welcoming her!' Sarah smiles enthusiastically. They all glide over the fact that the reason Charlotte is having to start at a new school is because she was asked to leave her previous one, due to continually 'under-achieving'.

Charlotte knows a little about how all this networking rubbish works. Martin and Sarah are, apparently, old friends of her father's, but only recently have they been included in parties and get-togethers, welcomed back into James' world because Kirsty and James need to put Charlotte somewhere and Martin is happy to oblige. His admissions numbers were probably down after the suicide and, since he's effectively running a business, he needs the money and contacts just as much as Kirsty and James need his school. The whole thing makes Charlotte sick.

'How are the boys getting on?' Martin asks.

'Well, Henry finished in the summer and is off to Sandringham.'

'A chip off the old block!'

'And Edward is off to the US in two days' time to begin his scholarship.'

'Ah, yes, the mathmagician. How did that come about?'

'He's been very lucky. His head for numbers caught the attention of an American maths organisation and he was offered a scholarship. James is going to head out there with him so they can have a little holiday together, and then he can settle him into his dorm.'

'And Oliver?'

'Well, Oliver is our little artist, as you know. He wants to pursue sculpture at St Martin's School of Art, but we'll see!'

'How does that sit in your military world? I imagine it's not what James would have chosen, knowing James as I do,' Martin says, with a wink.

'Oh, you know. You have to let them do what they want to do, don't you?' Kirsty says vaguely. 'Back in a mo. I'd better circulate for a bit.'

The truth is that both Kirsty and James do struggle a little with Oliver's bohemian ethic, but he's in the best school for the arts, or at least the one that boasts the best facilities and connections in the country, so Oliver will do well. It's Charlotte whose prospects look less promising, given that she doesn't share any of her brothers' talents. On paper it seems that she isn't very good at anything, nor does she seem to have any particular interests.

The party is full of chitter chatter and introductions. 'Darling, come over here, you simply must meet…'

James and Kirsty are experts at social steeplejacking, Kirsty in particular.

'*There* you are, darling!' She stands next to Charlotte and puts her arm around her while she talks to a political hack who freelances for the nationals; no doubt someone that her mother and father need to 'keep sweet,' a phrase that Charlotte is well-used to hearing. As Kirsty talks, she idly strokes Charlotte's hair with one hand, while holding a champagne flute with the other. The gentle summer breeze moves Kirsty's jade scarf a little – a favourite colour, picked to set off her hair. A paler linen tunic is draped over white cotton pedal-pushers which look casual, but Charlotte knows will have cost a fortune. Her mother's toenails, encased in silver sandals, are well-manicured and painted to match her outfit.

By contrast, Charlotte is pasty and pale, having spent most of the summer indoors hiding from the sun, and missing out on the family's two weeks of sailing in Greece.

She is bored at this party, just as she was bored when her family were abroad. But she knows the drill and goes through the motions. She has made sure that she looks the part, wearing the clothes that Kirsty laid out for her: a pink dress and white pumps, even though they don't come anywhere close to her own taste.

'Did you enjoy the summer sailing, Charlotte?' the journalist asks.

Charlotte thinks that she vaguely recognises him. Perhaps he's been on TV. At boarding school, they watched TV after dinner in the common room. Actually, come to think of it, there are a few faces that Charlotte recognises from the TV as she looks around.

'Oh, Whoopsie isn't the greatest of sailors. She doesn't quite have her sea legs like the rest of us, do you darling?'

Charlotte waits a moment before answering. She's not sure which bothers her the most: the use of the stupid nickname in front of strangers, the fact that her mother answers for her before she has a chance, or exposing another of her 'flaws' in public. Still, it's better than 'Whoopsie-dozy' which is another, supposedly affectionate, variation.

Before she has a chance to explain that she wasn't on the summer trip, the journalist picks up on the hated nickname. 'Whoopsie?' he repeats, the corners of his mouth turning up into the hint of a smirk.

'Our darling little mistake − she came along unexpectedly after we thought we were finished having children,' Kirsty laughs. The journalist laughs along with her.

Charlotte swallows. It still hurts, even though she's heard it a thousand times before. She knows that she lets her family down on every front. She will always hate sailing, even the thought of it. She finds it boring, mainly because her mother is right about the lack of sea legs and getting sea sick. But she doesn't have to tell every single person they meet about her lack of sailing ability.

'We did have a bit of a drama while we were sailing in the Ionian Sea,' Kirsty trills on. 'We had a problem with the air conditioning and the whole thing caught fire. We wondered if we'd actually make it. Terrifying to be on board a sinking ship at night. It was so treacherous.'

'How did you cope with that one, Whoopsie?' the journalist asks, politely trying to bring her back into the conversation.

Charlotte winces inside at the way he has casually picked up the name and evidently now feels he has the right to use it.

'Oh, well, happily I wasn't on that trip!' she says carefully. She doesn't want to be rude. It isn't his fault. He's trying to be kind.

But she really doesn't want to talk about the summer. She is sick of hearing about the drama that only seemed to have brought the rest of her family closer to one another while further excluding her. That trip has managed to become quite the family legend in a very short space of time. How they argued about whether or not to go for a boat with air conditioning in the first place. How Henry was so brave. How Oliver and Edward got their parents into the life raft first. How they all had such a bloody marvellous adventure. It sickens her.

The chat continues awkwardly. Charlotte is nauseated by the way her mother crawls over the journalist, trying to impress him. Her mother has explained countless times the need for networking, how important it is – especially to her father's career. But it doesn't make it any easier to watch.

Thankfully, it doesn't take long for the party to reach full swing, when Charlotte knows that she can disappear and hide in her room.

In the kitchen the caterers are busy clearing up. They barely notice Charlotte as she pulls a dinner plate down from the rack next to the sink. She takes a moment to select a pile of canapes and little cakes, along with a can of Diet Pepsi from the fridge, and heads upstairs. Her room is at the top of the house. It's the smallest room and out of the way of the rest of the family. As she mounts the second flight of stairs and passes an open window, she can still hear the laughter and chatter from the guests below. They must have spilled out onto the lawns for the fine evening. She keeps on walking until she is safely in her room.

No one will even notice she's gone.

II

By the end of the week the Cornish part of the summer is done and her family have all returned to the 'big' house in Surrey. As if the one in Cornwall were small. There isn't much time to spare before they will all be separated once more. Once again there is a flurry of activity and packing, everyone getting ready for a new adventure.

'Keep a separate case for Washington,' James advises his middle son. They will stop off there before they reach Ed's university. James has a few political friends who work in the White House he wants to catch up with.

Edward reveals that he has been two-timing his girlfriend and might continue to 'play away' while he's in the US. Charlotte is astonished that everyone, even her mother, seems to think that's funny. Oliver is smoking weed with some old school friends. Kirsty and James turn a blind eye, which doesn't seem fair. Charlotte has heard them say to each other that it's 'a phase' and he'll grow out of it.

Kirsty is about to start her new job in Switzerland. She's going over a few days before the official handover so that she can settle into the Geneva house that comes with the job as part of the generous relocation package. She has treated herself to a whole new wardrobe. Charlotte tried to help with choosing things, but Kirsty ignored most of her suggestions on their girls' shopping day in Guildford and has ended up ordering most of it online at Sahara London. Charlotte got some new things out of the day though: civvy clothes to wear at weekends at Hickman's, as well as new uniform. To give her mother her due, Kirsty is doing her best to sell the idea of a fresh start and be optimistic about it all.

'We can give you a bit of a glow-up, darling, all ready for your fresh start.'

This is part of what makes it all so confusing for Charlotte. On the one hand being known as Whoopsie has, over time, eroded all her confidence and makes her feel unloved. On the other hand, Kirsty spends money on her and has moments like the Guildford trip when she really does *seem* to care, helping her to choose clothes and being interested in how she looks. If Charlotte ever tries to talk to her about how she feels, her mother is effusive. 'Of course Mummy loves her little Whoopsie!' But Charlotte isn't convinced.

But for now, she has a list of things for a new school that she needs to pack into the large burgundy trunk with silver buckles. It has shoes, three towels and some games and mementos from home, including a picture of Nanny and Bob from the summer. Then there are her new clothes which are mostly from JD Sports, along with the new uniform that she already despises. Burgundy is worse than the green of her last school, if that's possible. A large suitcase is also open on the bed. Inside this one is her underwear, night clothes, her new dressing gown, a hand towel, make-up, sanitary products, hairbrush, scrunchies, mousse.

Packing up again makes her sad, but she doesn't resist the move. There's no point. And she knows she's being given another chance.

Kirsty comes in to check on progress, repacking anything that doesn't pass muster.

'Can I take my onesies?'

'Best not, Whoopsie, it'll only give the other girls a reason to laugh.'

The onesies go back in the drawer.

If only she could find a way to win her mother's approval. Once the packing is complete, she follows her mum around the house like a puppy.

'Can you stop getting under my feet? You're too old for this, Whoopsie.'

Now Kirsty sounds frustrated, and that upsets Charlotte. It doesn't matter what she does, she always seems to irritate people.

And she is too old to be so clingy. Her mother is right, as she always is. She will soon be 14. Her birthday is in October, when the boys will all be at school and university. Ed will be in the US. Kirsty and James will have to wait and check their diaries to work out if they can whip up to Hickman's and take her out for lunch on the Saturday nearest to her birthday.

'But the good news is that there's a Michelin-starred gastro pub not a million miles away from Hickman's which I'd love to try out,' James reports. 'So, if we can get your mother back from Geneva for the weekend – it's a plan!'

Once James and Ed have left for America, Charlotte feels numb, and a little lost.

The day comes for Kirsty to drive Charlotte to school. Charlotte talks incessantly on the journey, well aware that her mother will consider it wittering on, but unable to stop herself. All too soon they reach Hickman's. They turn off from a roundabout up a long, winding drive – perhaps a mile or more – before the main school building comes into view. It's Hogwartsy enough to be intimidating, with an imposing bank of unblinking windows beneath dark turrets and brick crenellations.

Don't leave me here, Charlotte thinks, as a wave of panic sweeps over her. But she knows that any appeal to her mother will fall on deaf ears.

She swallows hard.

Soon they are parking the car, heaving the trunk from the boot and finding her room.

Charlotte is dismayed to find that her roommate is already there, sitting on the bed while a woman, presumably her mother, helps her to unpack. 'Hi. You must be Charlotte,' the girl says.

Charlotte notices that she looks a little overweight and is strangely reassured by that. 'Hi,' she says, shyly, wondering if it's possible she might make a friend.

'I'm Kirsty.'

'Oh, isn't that nice, Whoopsie! Not only is your roommate polite, she has the same name as me!' Charlotte's mother laughs. 'I'm Kirsty, too.'

'Isn't that funny,' Kirsty's mum laughs and introduces herself as Aoife.

'Whoopsie?' student Kirsty pounces on the name and smirks. 'Is that a nickname?'

'Mum!' Charlotte is mortified that the hated moniker is already out of the bag.

'What, darling?' Adult Kirsty is oblivious to the *faux pas* she has just made.

Charlotte wishes she could just walk out of the door, rewind the scene and start again. Why does everything always go so badly? she wonders.

'Perhaps you should call me Kirst, for short,' child-Kirsty says. She is a large, insecure girl.

'Kirsty was bullied at her previous school for her weight,' Aoife says. Now it's Kirst's turn to look uncomfortable as her secret is out of the bag. But actually, Charlotte warms to her even more. Still, just when Charlotte wants time alone with her mother, they are plunged into a conversation about Kirst's eating habits.

'I'm worried that she's developing an eating disorder. You know, binge and purge. But the school has been marvellous about coming up with a solution. Kirsty will be on a strict diet while she's here. So I hope there's nothing naughty in that trunk, young lady.'

The other mother waggles an accusing finger at Charlotte.

It's not the most auspicious start she could have imagined.

'We've come from Anglesey,' student Kirst says, breaking the tension and attempting to steer the conversation away from her weight and diet. 'We came up last night and stayed nearby. So Mum's leaving soon because it's a long way.'

'Right,' says Charlotte.

'Splendid! Well, in that case I won't stay long either,' adult Kirsty says. 'I'll have a quick tour of the facilities if Martin is around and leave you two to get to know each other. But, Aoife, we should exchange numbers, so we can stay in touch over our girls!'

'Er, yes, I suppose so.'

Charlotte can't help noticing that Kirst's mum doesn't look as keen as her own mother does, but they swap numbers nevertheless. Just as they are at the end of the exchange, her mother's phone rings. She looks down at the display and then says to Charlotte, 'Sorry, but I have to take this, Whoopsie. Be a good girl now. Speak soon.'

They don't even get to have a proper goodbye, and suddenly her mother is gone from the room. Charlotte feels sad and a bit sick. She just wants to be at home with her mum.

Charlotte runs out after her, hoping they can have a proper hug in the car park, but her mum is preoccupied with whoever it is on the phone. The feeling of losing her mother once more is almost too much to bear, even though she knows she should be used to it by now. How is it that her mum can't ever be fully present, even in a moment like this which, for Charlotte, is filled with monumental importance?

Charlotte watches as her mum drives off, seeing her manicured hand wave briefly out of the car window. She walks back up to her room, reluctantly, but where else is there to go? Kirst's mum is still fussing around, helping her daughter to unpack. Kirst has so many lovely things. Personal things that she arranges carefully in a little display. Photographs of friends, and nick-nacks that have been carefully selected and have a history – 'the pebble from the beach in Scotland' and 'the ornament that my friend Lulu made at the end of primary school' – rather than the random stuff that Charlotte seems to have brought with her. Kirst gives a running monologue as she goes. Kirst's mum seems to be delaying the inevitable goodbye, while it's clear that Kirst herself is very ready for her mother to depart.

Eventually, Sarah knocks on the door to say that it will soon be time for the children's dinner. She doesn't make a point of acknowledging Charlotte, even though they were at the same party in Cornwall less than a week ago. It could be the fact that Sarah is being professional and not making a point of singling her out, but it only helps to reinforce the fact that Charlotte is invisible and unimportant.

Kirst's mum seems to be fighting back her tears as the time marches on. Charlotte watches Kirst hug her mother. It's a tight warm hug, exactly the sort that Charlotte herself wished for and didn't get. Kirst's mum makes Kirst promise to call her and let her know how she is.

Once her mum has left, Charlotte asks Kirst what her mum does, wondering if perhaps it's because her own mum works so much that she seems so emotionless.

'She's a civil servant in Ireland,' Kirst says. 'She commutes from Wales during the week, which is why they've sent me here.' There is a short pause and then Kirst asks, 'Why does your mum call you Whoopsie?'

Charlotte stares down at her feet dangling from the bed. 'Because I was a mistake,' she says, without looking up.

'Oh.'

Both girls sit on their beds quietly until they hear the clamber of other footsteps heading down the stairs to the dining hall and there is nothing for it but to follow.

III

After dinner, there is a 'special welcome assembly' to be endured. Hickman's College is a 'special place', based on an international model and very different from other schools, Martin explains to the students. Although she must remember not to think of him as 'Martin' any more. Now Charlotte must call him 'Mr Whitney'.

'Here at Hickman's we welcome students from all over the world,' Mr Whitney continues. 'And one of the things that makes Hickman's unique, is that we treat all our students as if you are adults as we prepare you for life in the wider world.'

There are school rules and protocols explained. At weekends, once Saturday morning lessons are complete, the children can sign themselves out for the whole weekend. They and their parents have each already signed an agreement that when they do this the students are expected to take full responsibility for their actions and behaviour.

'But that privilege can easily be taken away,' Mr Whitney declares. 'And, if it does not go well, there are consequences.'

He does not explain what those consequences are, apart from losing the right to unsupervised leave.

A nice insurance manoeuvre, as Charlotte's mother observed when they were looking at the school policy.

Martin's catchphrase, which he repeats several times during

the assembly, is, 'We have a global outlook in an English country setting.'

Most of the words wash over Charlotte. She doesn't care about 'leadership skills' or 'creativity' or 'academic rigour' or the 'excellent tutorial system' or any of the other educational buzzwords that pepper her new headmaster's introduction.

Back in their room, Charlotte relaxes a little. She could have had a much worse roommate. Kirst is nice. They're going to get along well enough. Whoever has matched them up – probably Sarah – has done a good job. Both girls feel nervous and a little lonely, but it's clear that they recognise their need for one another. Kirst chatters on and Charlotte finds her Welsh lilt soothing. Charlotte notices that Kirsty has her teddy with her. Charlotte's teddy is still in her trunk. She wasn't sure if Teddy Gertie would be seen as babyish. Charlotte decides that tomorrow she'll fish Gertie out of her trunk and put her in the bed, ready for cuddles at night. That will help her to feel less homesick.

Lessons begin the next morning. The school feels like a bit of a rabbit warren. There are corridors everywhere and although there are only 600 students on roll, it feels vast. What doesn't help is that Charlotte is separated from Kirst for most of their classes – presumably as a way of forcing students to get to know more people. Why is it that adults always seem to want to make things harder in the name of 'helping'? Most of the students were here last year, so already know each other. Being separated from Kirst just makes her feel isolated.

Charlotte is surprised to see that some of the teachers wear jeans during the lessons which makes it feel a little more relaxed than other schools that Charlotte has been to. How her mother would hate that! Although there is a uniform, that too seems a little more casual than at other schools. Charlotte sits quietly, hating the moment when the maths teacher draws attention to her by welcoming her and another new girl, Lia.

Lia goes red when her name is mentioned, too. They share a smile of mutual understanding. Perhaps the seed has been sown for another friendship. Lia is also in her English lesson, so naturally they sit next to each other. With around 15 students in a class, there's nowhere to hide, but because there are lots of introductions and explanations of what they will be doing as term goes on, there is little actual work to complete and Charlotte's academic failings remain unexposed for the time being.

At lunchtime in the dining hall, where a healthy display of food is on offer, along with a choice of lighter snacks or hot lunches, Lia and Charlotte queue up together holding their trays. How are they even supposed to know where to sit? Is it just a free-for-all? There is a big table where staff are sitting and eating together at one end, but a few members of staff seem to be sitting with students.

Charlotte is not used to this sort of attitude and it feels very alien; her old school was quite clear about where the students and staff sat and who spoke to whom. This seems a little friendlier. Maybe things really can be better here.

Slightly overwhelmed by the food and drink choices on offer, Charlotte's response is to select the same meal as Lia: a mozzarella panini and some salad, a glass of mango juice and a bottle of water. They sit down together and watch who comes in and walks around. When some older students walk through the double wooden doors into the dining hall, Charlotte notices how trendy and good-looking a few of the boys are. They have that confidence that only money can buy. Lia and Charlotte carefully watch how the older students behave. One of the teachers high fives one really good-looking boy, who has somehow managed to take the basic school uniform to the extreme. Everything about him is cool, from the way his shirt sleeves are rolled up so that it looks as if his biceps are about to tear the fabric, to the way a floppy bit of fringe hangs down over his eyes. Charlotte wonders what must it be like being able to go through life so effortlessly.. She's forced to look away at one point when she realises that they have caught the attention of the boys. The group are looking in the direction of Lia and Charlotte, and though she can't hear what's being said, she knows it's about them.

She looks down at the half-eaten panini and then at Lia to see if Lia has noticed that they are, for whatever reason, the centre of attention. Suddenly she isn't hungry anymore. But the little fluttery feeling in her stomach is excitement. She's always been the girl who's ignored: plain features have never attracted the attention that her mum's looks have, or the 'three bears', Henry, Ed and Oliver. It's rather nice to be pointed out and talked about, even if it's probably just because they're new.

The afternoon goes surprisingly well, and Charlotte feels safe. She has Lia in most of her lessons and then Kirst back in her room. Teddy Gertie is now nestled in pride of place on her bed. Kirst has had a good first day, too, even though Charlotte has barely caught a glimpse of her at any point through the day. During the period before dinner when the girls are in their room, Sarah – Mrs Whitney – knocks on the door to see how they are, and how they are settling in.

Mrs Whitney is nice, Charlotte decides. There is something genuinely warm about her. She has a Lancashire accent that is so different from the people Charlotte is usually surrounded by when at home with her parents.

'Don't forget that our quarters start just beyond the end of the corridor. If there's a problem in the night then you are to come across and knock on the door, but don't wake up the other students, and only knock if it's urgent.'

She smiles her kindly smile. 'And I know that you are probably already feeling a little homesick – that's only natural, and you're still of an age when you might have bad dreams. But neither of those things are urgent, they are perfectly normal. So, remember, I don't need my sleep disturbed over a bit of homesickness!' She says it with a wink and feels like someone you might actually be able to go and talk to if you needed to.

Charlotte doesn't see Lia at dinner, but there are different sittings, and anyway, she has Kirst. There is an hour of prep to get through and then it's time to be getting ready for bed. Charlotte has survived a full day.

Sarah walks around with a box and collects all the students' phones just before lights out. 'Goodnight girls. Time for sleep.'

But of course, there is too much to discuss. Charlotte and Kirst lie in their beds and chat about the other students.

'Did you see those older boys?' Charlotte asks.

Kirst immediately giggles. 'Fit!'

After a bit of chat, both girls start to drift off towards sleep, tired after their first full day at their new school, and barely notice when Sarah checks on all the girls at 10.30pm just as she prepares to go to bed herself.

Half asleep, Charlotte decides that tomorrow she will try to find out the name of the *really* good-looking boy. Not that he would be interested in a mouse like her, but still, everyone can dream. She smiles in the darkness and allows a crush to begin.

IV

In the morning, Charlotte's first waking thought is the handsome boy.

There is no sign of him or his little posse in the dining room or in any of the corridors between lessons.

Lia is in a different science class from Charlotte, just about the only lesson they don't have together.

'Got news,' Lia says, when Charlotte slides into the seat next to her in English. 'They're all out on a trip today. And the one you like is called Bruno.'

Bruno. Bruno. Bruno. The sound of his name is strange and beautiful, and Charlotte finds herself mouthing it silently from time to time. Still, knowing that she can't bump into 'Bruno' at any point today actually allows Charlotte to settle down a bit and concentrate better on her schoolwork. She still finds it hard to listen to what the teachers have to say all of the time, but then she always has. And it's a relief to discover that Lia isn't brainy either; she's in a similar position to Charlotte and has found herself at Hickman's because she also didn't make the grades in her last school.

At lunchtime, Charlotte finds out more about her new friend's family. Lia's father is an architect who is also something in media and has been on TV a few times.

'That's cool!'

'Yes and no. On telly he comes across as whacky and fun,' Lia confides, 'which is a total lie because at home he's mostly grumpy.'

Charlotte nods, unsurprised. She can relate to the idea of a facade of a perfect family. Lia's mum works 'in PR' which neither Charlotte nor Lia fully understand. 'I think PR actually stands for 'Permanently Running. She's always busy.'

Charlotte nods once more. Then laughs. She has a different version of a mother who is permanently running. And actually, hers does actual running, in Lycra and at the gym.

'Mine's always on the train to London early in the morning and home late after some do or another.' Lia makes a mock-haughty face and says '*daaarling*' in such an exaggerated way that both girls laugh. They each know this world well.

For the rest of the day Charlotte and Lia speak to each other in an exaggerated version of Estuary English that they know their parents would hate. The more 'Essex' they can get, the more they collapse with laughter.

School might not be such a terrible place after all. She has not one, but two friends and even the schoolwork isn't that bad.

In the evening, Charlotte introduces Gertie to Kirst's teddy, who is, inexplicably, called Mushroom. They sit on Kirst's bed together with their teddies like little girls, as though they are far younger than 14 years old. They both text their parents with updates about the start of term. Charlotte is still waiting for a reply by the time Sarah comes around with the mobile phone box. It takes Charlotte longer to fall asleep because she lies there for a while wondering what her mum and dad are doing. She's not sure what the time difference is between here and Washington, so maybe her dad hasn't seen the message yet.

But even if her mum is already in Switzerland, that's Europe. Charlotte's travelled enough to know that it can only be an hour or two maximum.

When she cries she tells herself it's normal to feel homesickness. Didn't Sarah say so? She consoles herself by thinking about Bruno.

On Wednesday, Bruno and his little posse sit near Charlotte and Lia.

'Don't look now but he's looking at you,' Lia says.

'He is not,' Charlotte replies, turning pink and excited by the thought of it.

'I reckon he fancies you.'

'Don't be daft.' The words might be dismissive, but the seed takes root in Charlotte's mind. Could it be that Bruno is interested in her? No one, especially no one male and good looking, has ever paid any attention to her before.

In the evening, Charlotte's mother gets in touch. It's bad news. Nanny passed away. She died peacefully in her sleep of an aneurysm. 'It happened last week and I didn't want to tell you straight away because I needed you to be in a good place to start school.'

'You didn't tell me? Mum!'

'I didn't want to upset you. But, you know, she had a jolly good innings. And I'd choose that way to go if I could, so there's no need to be sad about it.'

Kirsty is very matter of fact about it, but Charlotte is heartbroken.

How can Nanny, who just a couple of months ago was living and breathing and cooking her nice meals and playing Rummikub and Ludo, be gone? It doesn't seem possible.

'Of course I'm sad!'

'I don't know why you need to make such a drama out of everything.'

After a pause, Charlotte says, 'Can I go to the funeral? When is it?'

'I don't know, darling, but do you really think that's a good idea? You've only just started at the new school and it will be disruptive so close to the start of term. I don't think Daddy and I are planning to go. I won't be able to get back from Geneva. You don't really need to go, do you?'

'Of course I need to go! I have to be there. Where is it? I'll get there myself if I have to.'

'Don't be silly, Whoopsie.'

She hears her mother sigh down the phone, but for once she doesn't care that she's saying the wrong thing or disappointing Kirsty. This is too important.

'I'll go on the train if you won't take me.'

'I'll see what Sarah and Martin say if you're going to be so difficult about it. But I really don't see why it's such a big deal. You didn't see them that often.'

'I was staying with them this summer while you were on holiday!'

Charlotte is furious with her mother. Kirsty never understands what's important to her.

Sarah is more sympathetic, and lingers in the room at bedtime to check that Charlotte is okay.

'I'm so sorry this has happened, Charlotte. I know how upset you are, and I understand that Nanny was a very important person in your life. I've spoken to your mum and I'm sure something can be sorted about attending the funeral, if that's what you want to do. It's taking place on Friday.'

Charlotte nods. It feels like her world has ended.

She cries herself to sleep, dreaming of being consoled by Bruno.

In the morning she wakes feeling empty, unsure why at first, until she remembers about Nanny and the weight of grief washes over her again.

Sarah helps her to book train tickets and liaises with Kirsty over releasing her from school. Charlotte cries, alone, on the train. She is only able to hold it all together because of being on her own and needing to concentrate on the journey and where to change trains. Her parents have given her money for a taxi from the train station. She hugs Bob, who is there with Rolley. The funeral is a small affair. She doesn't really know anyone apart from Bob, and Merv, a gardener who also used to work for her parents.

'That's sweet that you've come by yourself,' Merv says, and sits with her in the church. He gives her a lift back to the train station when it's all over. Bob is going to sell up and move into an old people's home, so even their cottage won't be there anymore. It feels to Charlotte as if she is being abandoned once more.

Back at Hickman's, she finds Lia and distracts herself by thinking about Bruno. Lia and Charlotte loiter near the field where the boys are kicking a ball about. If the ball happens to come in their direction and one of the group has to come and retrieve it, they laugh loudly as if one or other of them has told a joke and they are having a marvellous time.

'I'm telling you, he fancies you,' Lia says, when it's Bruno's turn to come near. 'He's bloody gorgeous.'

Thinking about Bruno takes away some of the pain of losing Nanny. It's a welcome distraction to daydream about romance rather than death.

By Monday, Lia has found out Bruno's timetable.

'How on earth did you do that?'

'I saw a book with his name on it on the side in the science department, so I opened it. There was a copy of his timetable inside. I thought you needed cheering up, so I took a photo of it.'

Charlotte and Lia construct elaborate plans to make sure that they bump into Bruno and his two friends almost everywhere they go.

But now it seems that their behaviour has created the wrong sort of attention. On the field, one of the boys turns around to Charlotte and Lia and says, 'Why don't you two dopey slags just fuck off?'

Charlotte's bubble is immediately punctured. She goes bright red and charges off towards the school buildings, Lia trailing in her wake.

'I'm never bloody listening to you again!' Charlotte says, mortified.

But she can't help herself from wanting her path to cross with Bruno's again.

It becomes clear in the next few days that some older girls also like to hang out with Bruno and his friends. One of them is Avril, who looks very glam and cool. Perhaps if Charlotte could be like her, she'd have more chance with Bruno. Some of the girls are nastier and more spiteful than the boys, whispering as Charlotte and Lia pass and generally finding ways to make them feel uncomfortable.

'Kill yourself,' Charlotte hears as she scuttles through a corridor with Lia.

Worse, when Charlotte is on her own after a science lesson, waiting to meet Lia by the loos so that they can go to their art class together, one of the boys sneers in her face.

'You're a fat cunt and Broons thinks you're a dick, so do one.'

The words cut deep.

Only Avril has a kind word. 'They're just immature little boys. Ignore them.'

The boys are all in Year 11 or lower sixth and, although they are still a few years younger than her youngest brother, Oliver, they remind her of him. She wonders if he was this evil at school.

'How could I ever have thought that he liked me?' Charlotte asks Lia. She is so ashamed for thinking it. For believing Lia that Bruno liked her when all along they were mocking her.

As the week goes by, things only get worse. The boys crank up their humiliating bullying and no one seems to notice or care.

Charlotte confides in Kirst, who is sympathetic but powerless to do anything to really help.

'Just stay away from them.'

'It's not that easy. I pass them every day.'

'They're just dicks. Loads of boys are these days,' Kirst says airily. 'My mum says it's because of Donald Trump.'

'What on earth have Bruno and his mates got to do with Trump?'

'Oh, you know, *your body, my choice* and all that crap.'

The girls sit together on Charlotte's bed eating Skittles, cuddling their teddies, talking about patriarchy and how hard life has always been for girls.

The conversation leads, as it often does, to Charlotte and Kirsty talking about their mums and how it must have been so hard for them to get to where they are.

Charlotte decides that Kirst is right. She just needs to ignore the three arseholes and stay in her lane. How hard can it be?

V

By the weekend Charlotte has forgiven Lia for her role in Bruno-gate, and they decide to catch the local bus into town together to celebrate surviving their second week. They can do a bit of shopping and mill about in the mall. Better than hanging around school like a loser. They square it all with Sarah, assuring her that they will be very sensible about taking the bus into town, will be back in plenty of time, and their mobile phones are fully charged.

Sarah smiles and says, 'I wasn't quite born yesterday. Go and have some fun. You deserve it. It's been a stressful start to your term, especially for you, Charlotte.' She gives them some details about where to catch the bus and where to get off in town.

Charlotte asks Kirst if she'd like to come, but Kirst is excited to be meeting her mum.

'We're heading out somewhere for lunch today,' Kirst explains.

Charlotte is pleased for her friend but can't help the pang of envy she feels at the same time. She's hardly spoken to her mum, who was, according to the family WhatsApp group and her private Facebook page, having an 'amazing' time in her new role. Her new colleagues are 'wonderful' and she's having 'enormous fun' furnishing the apartment. Charlotte wouldn't dare to put anything even remotely negative on the Ashmans' social media; James has explained to them numerous times that all of these platforms are seen by people he needs to keep onside. Nothing must go up that could embarrass or jeopardise the family or their reputation. Charlotte just puts up a heart in reply to her mother's post, even though reading it is breaking hers.

Charlotte and Lia have picked their outfits carefully. They are in almost-but-not-quite-matching hoodies and jogging bottoms. They sport smart trainers that neither have ever done any actual 'training' in, and the look is completed with sporty rucksacks. Both girls have spent a considerable amount of time applying their make-up and straightening their hair.

'Because we're worth it,' Lia giggles.

They walk off the school grounds through a little side gate into the village, not really sure exactly where they need to go until they see a few other people standing in line waiting for the bus by the Co-op. They join the queue, standing with their hoodies up and long hair leaking out at the sides. Both are wearing Lia's perfume swiped from her mum's dressing room when she was last home. It is gorgeous and very expensive.

'Mum has it made in France, especially for her,' Lia explains. 'She went and had her Ph and all that stuff measured and her character examined to find exactly the right smell.'

'Wow.'

'It should have been cat wee if it was honest, but this is what she came home with.'

'Won't she mind you taking it?

'Naah. She can reorder it when she wants to 'cos they keep a record of it, so it doesn't matter. It costs, like, £1,000 a bottle.'

Charlotte knows that even though her own family is wealthy, her mum would not agree to something like this. 'It's because she's Scottish,' Charlotte says, echoing what Kirsty always says when she judges that any indulgence is about to become obscene.

It doesn't take long for the bus to arrive, and the girls head towards the back of the bus, their hoodies acting like a passport to the back seat.

A couple of stops later, three young lads jump on the bus and head towards them, but not quite. The boys sit down on the seats that are perpendicular to the back seat so that they are facing each other. They are all dressed identically in black hoodies and joggers with black bags strapped across their fronts.

They talk loudly and look in the direction of the girls.

Charlotte and Lia brace themselves for a verbal attack. Charlotte's late night chats with Kirst have led her to anticipate only misogyny and verbal abuse from teenage boys, particularly white, working-class teenage boys. It's also once bitten, twice shy after the whole Bruno thing, and, after the last week Kirst has encouraged her to shift her view to include all teenage boys as being nasty. Charlotte is a little resistant to this, as her brothers have always seemed okay, especially her big brother Henry, who is her favourite and the one who seems to care the most about her.

They get off the bus in town just where Sarah advised, outside Next, and head off towards the shop, aware that the boys seem to be following them. Charlotte doesn't want to make the same mistake twice in thinking that she's drawing male attention only to discover that she's the target of a joke. So she keeps an eye on them, using the reflections in shop windows to see how far behind they are.

As they turn down different streets, there can, this time, be no mistaking that they are being followed.

One of the boys calls out, 'Hey, you, the beautiful girl with the blonde hair.'

Charlotte can't help but turn around to look. Lia's hair is so dark as to be almost black, so it must be Charlotte they mean. It's the tallest one who has shouted. But she doesn't want to stop and talk. Instead, she shrugs as if she's got far better things to do than stand in the street and talk to boys, thank you very much and, heart beating a little faster, she carries on walking.

It doesn't put the boys off. In fact, if anything, they start to pay the girls a lot more attention. The shopping trip becomes a game of cat and mouse as everywhere the girls go the boys are always there. Charlotte overhears one of the other boys call the tall one 'Danny'. It's Danny who seems to have set Charlotte in his sights. He smiles at her every time he catches her eye and, when he walks past her, turns back to say, 'You're cute.'

Danny is definitely not as good-looking as Bruno, in Charlotte's opinion, but the fact that he has singled her out feels flattering.

When the girls go to get a bubble tea, the boys are waiting for them outside. Danny looks directly at Charlotte and they lock eyes.

Charlotte swallows.

This is such new territory for her. Lia, on the other hand, is uncomfortable with this level of attention and tries to pull Charlotte away. In New Look, as well as choosing a new top, on a sudden mad impulse she buys a black G-string. It is *totally* out of character and unlike anything else she owns. But meeting Danny has made her feel bold and sexy, as though something big could be about to happen.

Would it hurt to talk to him?

The group of three boys soon becomes seven as more join

them, the others arriving on bikes and electric scooters. They seem to be very cool and popular; loads of people are saying hello and going up to them as they stand next to the clock tower.

Lia encourages Charlotte back to the bus. They have their shopping and they promised Sarah they'd be back to school in good time. But when Danny calls Charlotte over, she goes, leaving Lia to stand by Boots with the bags.

Danny stands to one side, away from his friends and talks to Charlotte.

'What's your name? I can't just keep calling you Cute – even though you are.'

Charlotte tells him.

'Hey, you've got some hair in your eyes.' Danny reaches out and gently pushes a few strands of hair away from Charlotte's face. 'That's better. I can see more of your pretty face now.'

Charlotte basks in all his compliments.

He takes her phone from her hands.

'Hey, what are you doing?'

'Just adding my number,' Danny says, punching it in before returning it to her. He's so self-assured. Not good-looking in the showy kind of way that Bruno is, but there's definitely something about him.

When he takes off his necklace and takes a seductively long time to clip it around Charlotte's neck, her tummy does that fluttery thing that feels like it's going to flip over entirely.

He gently pulls Charlotte towards him and kisses her on her cheek, then strokes it.

Charlotte can see Lia fidgeting and signalling to her from across the road, and knows she's probably becoming bored – but Charlotte can't tear herself away.

'Lotts! Come on!' Lia calls, eventually.

As the girls walk back towards the bus stop to catch the bus back to school, Charlotte's phone pings continuously.

She smiles at each of Danny's silly messages, asking when he can see her again because he doesn't think he's going to be able to sleep until he does.

'I don't know what makes you so special,' Lia says, a note of resentment creeping into her voice. 'And it wasn't exactly friendly to leave me standing there like a lemon while you got all smoochy with a boy you've only just met.'

'You're just jealous,' Charlotte says, putting her hand up to feel the weight of Danny's necklace deliciously at her throat.

'I'm just telling you what I think. It's strange, that's all.'

'Strange that someone should like me, you mean?'

'I didn't mean that.'

They reach the bus stop and Lia stares at Charlotte.

'Why would he just give you his necklace like that?' Lia continues. 'That's just weird.'

'No it isn't. It's romantic.'

Charlotte continues to smile down at the pinging messages.

'I'm here, you know!' Lia shouts, frustrated at Charlotte's pre-occupation with her phone.

'Sorry. I don't want Danny to think I'm ignoring him.'

'Oh, but it's okay to ignore me?'

If Charlotte is honest with herself, she also wonders why Danny hasn't chosen Lia over her. Or why one of the other boys didn't try to hit on her. Lia is much more striking looking and has a far better figure than Charlotte. But love moves in mysterious ways, as they say.

Even dirty looks from Bruno and his cronies bounce off Charlotte today when they return to school.

Back in her room, Charlotte decides not to tell Kirst about

what happened today. Not yet, anyway. For now, she wants to keep Danny all to herself. Even so, it's hard not to give herself away. Charlotte twiddles with her hair as she scrolls back over the messages from earlier and can't help smiling once more.

'Don't you want to know how my lunch with Mum went?' Kirst says.

'Sure,' says Charlotte, though she isn't really listening.

'Who are you texting?' Kirst asks, suspicious.

'No one,' Charlotte says, but she's reluctant to give up her phone when Sarah comes in to collect it just before 10.30pm.

'No exceptions!' Sarah is firm.

VI

After breakfast the next morning, Charlotte tries on her new top from New Look. She's pleased with the choice, although it's a little lower-cut than she would normally choose. Even though it's a Sunday and she isn't going anywhere, she has spent some time putting on make-up and it is thick – she is wearing much more than she usually would, even if she was going out. Her hair has been freshly straightened.

'You've cheered up. What's got into you this morning? Don't tell me this is all for Bruno. I thought you were over him,' Kirst says, frowning when Charlotte comes back from the bathroom.

Charlotte responds by first taking a pouty picture of herself from up high.

'I am.'

'So who's that picture for? Who are you sending it to?'

'No one. Just a selfie.'

Kirst shakes her head. 'You don't seem like yourself.'

'How can you say that? You've only known me for a fortnight!'

'But I'm sharing a room with you. You get to know someone pretty quickly.'

'If you say so.'

'Is that necklace new?'

'Might be.'

Charlotte's phone pings. This time it isn't Danny, but Lia.

Do you want to walk into the village and get a Bad Boy from the Co-op? I'm fed up of all this healthy shit they keep feeding us!

Going against the healthy-food regime planned so carefully by the catering team at the school is actually quite a rebellious act, Charlotte thinks. Part of Mr Whitney's speech was all about how at Hickman's they believe that the brain works better when it receives the right nutrition at the right time. That's why, unless they had an allergy, every student had to eat a banana before lessons for the slow release of potassium. Charlotte was already sick of bloody bananas. But the healthy diet was part of the agreement signed by both child and parent on entry. The children and parents were all expected to be supportive of the rules for the greater good. So a Pot Noodle was pretty taboo. But 'Bombay Bad Boy' was the real trophy to aim for.

Bad Boys here we come! Ready in 5?

'And who keeps sending you messages? You haven't stopped looking at that phone!'

'It's Lia,' Charlotte says. 'We're going to go and get a Bad Boy from the shop. She's got a kettle in her room. D'you want to come?'

Kirst chuckles. 'Yeah, why not? I'm well up for that. Although I feel a bit underdressed compared to you. You look more like you're going out clubbing than to the shops.'

They sign themselves out, head down the gravel path and out the side gate.

Lia also frowns when she sees how 'done up' Charlotte is for a Sunday.

'I didn't realise it was a fashion parade.'

'I'm only trying out the new top I bought.'

'Yeah, well. I didn't get the make-up memo either.'

They walk along the road. Just before they reach the shop,

Charlotte's phone pings. She looks down at it. 'You go ahead and get me that Bad Boy.'

'Why? Where are you going?'

Charlotte is already on her way to a black car on the other side of the road along from the café and gift shop. She knows that Lia and Kirst will be watching her, so her walk is just as much a performance for them as well as for Danny. She leans in towards the driver's window.

'Hi, Danny,' she purrs.

In the reflection of the car mirror, Charlotte can still see Lia and Kirst watching her, standing behind the National Lottery sign. Danny, his arms trailing over the driver door, hands a small package to her then whips his head back inside the car, quickly looking from side to side as if checking to see if they have been seen.

Charlotte is thrilled to have been selected to look after the package. She's not stupid, she knows what's inside, but it shows that Danny trusts her and that makes her feel good.

Charlotte turns back to her friends.

'I told you, go on without me.'

Then, to Danny, 'Don't worry about them. They're sound. They won't say anything.'

Her friends disappear inside the shop, but Charlotte can see that they are still watching what's going on, peering over the top of the sweets and crisps in the window. Well, let them. She hopes they get a good eyeful when Danny leans over and kisses her full on the lips.

When she joins them again in the shop, beaming, she sees them try to pretend that they haven't just darted towards the other end of the aisle where the Pot Noodles are.

Who cares? Charlotte is floating on air.

When Sarah comes in to collect the phones in the evening, Charlotte happily hands hers over.

'Much better attitude, Charlotte – well done,' Sarah congratulates her.

'That's strange,' Kirst says, once Sarah has moved along the corridor to the next room. 'Yesterday you were surgically attached to it.'

During the night, Charlotte receives and sends lots of messages to Danny, making sure that the new phone he has given her is on silent and well hidden under her bedding. She waits until she is sure that Kirst is fast asleep and therefore cannot hear the soft buzzes of the alerts.

In the morning she is tired because she has been messaging Danny until the small hours. But she is far too happy and excited to let a bit of tiredness affect her. She can hardly concentrate on lessons, she is so besotted by her new boyfriend, as she has already begun to think of him.

When Bruno walks into the hall at lunchtime she doesn't even notice him until Lia gives her a sharp nudge in the ribs; she is too busy thinking about Danny. Bullies only bully because they get a reaction, so if Charlotte isn't even noticing them their efforts are futile.

Perhaps her nonchalance is noted by Bruno and the other boys who leave them alone for today.

'Maybe meeting Danny has its benefits after all,' Lia says.

After lessons, Kirst is keen to go for a walk in the grounds with Charlotte.

'I've got some tobacco,' Kirst says with a grin. 'We can make some roll-ups and go for a smoke.'

'Nah, you're alright,' Charlotte says. 'You go.'

'God, you're no fun,' Kirst says. 'You're so boring.'

Kirst hangs about in the room, much to Charlotte's annoyance; she wants to phone Danny.

'Aren't you going to go, then?' Charlotte says after a while.

'Not on my own I'm not, no.' Kirst's tone is sulky.

'Right. Well perhaps I do want a breath of fresh air. On my own. See you later,' Charlotte says.

By the end of the week the students are all once more making their various plans for the weekend. Lia is going home for her birthday, which is actually next Tuesday but her family are gathering together to help celebrate in advance of the big day. Kirst is getting the train to London to meet her mum and grandmother and is very excited about the plans: they are staying in a hotel near Victoria on Saturday night after going to see *Wicked* at the theatre. 'I've seen it before, but it's sooo good. And we're going to go out for dinner at The Ivy first.'

There are no such family treats in store for Charlotte. She's had a few texts from her mum, who is very busy with her life in Switzerland. This weekend James is flying out to stay with her in her new apartment. Normally this would make Charlotte unhappy, knowing that she is not included in family plans. Not this time. She has plans of her own. And, of course, they include Danny. She tells her parents that she is going to stay at a friend's house for the weekend, and has told Sarah that her parents are happy for her to stay away for both nights. It's surprisingly easy to get away with white lies when no one really cares what you are up to. No one will be any the wiser about where she's been.

It's all set.

At midday on Saturday, Charlotte throws her carefully-packed rucksack onto her shoulder and signs out from school. She skips down the path, out of the side gate and into the waiting little black Corsa.

'Hey, gorgeous!'

Before she can reach for her seatbelt, Danny pulls her in for a huge snog, strokes her face, tells her he's missed her and has never felt this way about anyone before. He starts the engine and says, 'You want to go to a party tonight?'

Charlotte beams back at him. 'Absolutely!' She imagines the thrill of walking into a party full of guests on Danny's arm. Girls looking at her with green-eyed envy because she has bagged the coolest of all the dudes. She is buzzing with the thought of it as Danny drives.

'Where are we going now?'

'My place.'

'Cool.' Charlotte is impressed by the fact that Danny has his own place.

'Well, not just mine. I share it with a few other people.'

Danny takes her to his house in town. Charlotte is a bit disappointed because, in her mind, this bit should be romantic. But the house is a dump, really. Music with a heavy bass is playing loudly out of an old buzzy speaker on the floor. The hallway smells of damp washing, cigarette smoke and burnt food. She quickly has a stern word with herself. She's well aware that her family is very privileged. Danny is young, of course he hasn't got much money, he's just starting out. She needs to lower her expectations a bit. She knows that not all families are like the ones who send their children to Hickman's.

On the way into the party, Danny greets a couple of boys with a knuckle punch.

'Alright, blud?'

'Yeah, man.'

They seem old to Charlotte. Older than Danny. Maybe 18 or

19? It's hard to tell. They are wearing big black puffer jackets, even though it's a warm day for late September.

The boys don't acknowledge Charlotte. It's as if she isn't there. They're too busy concentrating on rolling a joint. There's not much space left on the coffee table, which is covered in discarded Domino's pizza boxes. One has a handful of dry pizza crusts left on one half and cigarette butts squashed into the sour cream sauce pots. A can of Foster's lager also has ash around the top of it. Nearby, a half-empty bottle of Fanta lies on its side and there are a couple of bottles of water with their lids off. There's a pair of sunglasses and lots of ripped green Rizla packets. She notices some needles, too.

In the corner of the next, smaller room, sitting on the edge of a small single bed and looking totally out of place, is an old lady in a pale blue fleece dressing gown. Charlotte can't work out what she's doing at a house party. On the floor next to the bed is a tray of old food. Perhaps she's not very mobile and someone has brought it to her. Danny notices her looking through the open door. 'That's Nanna. Don't worry about her.'

But Charlotte can't help worrying about her. She looks scared and sad, wringing her hands. Charlotte notices what looks like bruising on her face, but then again, it might just be the poor light.

The whole set-up doesn't really make much sense. And even though Danny has told her it's a house share, the decor looks like a strange choice for teenagers or young guys. All the furniture looks quite old fashioned, more like what her own poor Nanny and Bob's house was filled with. It doesn't feel quite right. Maybe this is actually her house, not Danny's? There are some little ornaments on the shelves that look exactly the same style as the ones she remembers Nanny used to have. For a moment all the grief comes flooding back and washes over her in a giant wave of sadness. Nanny was probably a similar age to this Nanna. But then she pulls herself together. Danny won't want her feeling blue at a party and bringing everyone else down.

This place would shock her parents, there's no doubt about that. Charlotte is quietly amused by the idea of them seeing where she is right now; perhaps it would wake them up and make them take notice of her. Charlotte knows that if she is to keep hold of Danny and be a good girlfriend she can't allow herself to be all sensible and middle class about her judgements.

Danny leads her into his room. 'This is mine.'

It's okay, Charlotte thinks. A double bed, clothes on the floor and a black leather coat with a hood hanging from the dark, old-fashioned wooden wardrobe. The curtains are cornflower blue and lined, but hanging off the rail at each end. The net curtains behind them are grey. Danny closes the door and pulls Charlotte towards him. He holds her face and begins kissing her. Charlotte might be in heaven. Especially the way he keeps saying, 'God, you're so fucking gorgeous.'

He pulls her onto the bed and they sit down together. There is a little table next to the bed which he pulls closer to them. He tips some white powder onto the mirrored top and begins chopping it around with a credit card.

He looks towards Charlotte mischievously. 'You want some?'

Charlotte has older brothers. She knows all about cocaine. But she's never tried it herself. She doesn't really want to. Her legs start to shake and she feels completely out of her depth. Despite all Danny's attentions and her own desire to please him, she's totally terrified. She knows that this is all wrong.

Danny shapes two lines on the mirror, and uses a straw to snort the first before pushing the straw towards Charlotte.

'One line won't hurt you. Try it.'

His tone is casual, gentle. But 'try it' also sounds like a command.

Without really knowing what she's doing, or why, Charlotte follows suit. She doesn't get all the powder up in one go. It makes her eyes water and the back of her throat sting.

'Good, eh?' Danny laughs. 'Hits the spot, nah?'

Danny uses his finger on the mirror to dab at the remaining spots of powder, putting them to his mouth. Charlotte nods, eyes wide. Her head feels like it might explode, if that's what 'hitting the spot' means.

Next, Danny rolls a spliff and pours some lager into a glass for her to drink. When she's taken a few tokes on the joint, he says, 'You ready?'

Her head is spinning and for a minute Charlotte is a little relieved to think he must mean they're going somewhere else. Isn't this where the party is happening though? She's lost all track of time. But then he puts some music on: loud gangster-rap music that Charlotte has never heard before. It's not really her thing, but perhaps they're going to dance. Instead, Danny gently tips her back on the bed and begins to undress her.

'You're so beautiful,' he murmurs. 'God, you're making me hard.'

Charlotte giggles.

'So hard… I really want to fuck you.'

Charlotte is scared. This is not what she had in mind at all. She has talked about going 'all the way' with a boy, never thought of it as 'fucking'. That isn't what she wants. But the line of coke has done strange things to her head. She feels strangely relaxed and detached from what's going on. And Danny is so kind and has paid her so much attention. No one else does. She doesn't really know what she's doing, but she wants to please Danny and make him like her. It feels like she finally has some power and she wants *so* much to be loved. She is so tired of being overlooked and feeling invisible.

Danny runs his hands all over her body and pulls down the little black G-String that she bought in New Look the day she met him.

'Looks like you were ready for this,' Danny says. 'God, I love you.'

Nobody has said that to her before. So that means it's okay that he takes her virginity. And she doesn't want to let him down. She did wear the G-string, after all. At some level, she must have known things would lead this way. She believes him when he tells her again that he loves her. And, if it wasn't quite how she imagined it would be: more painful, with lots of grunting from Danny before he rolls off and turns away − at least she feels like she's living a bit.

'I gotta cut for a while,' Danny says. 'But hang out here, yeah? I just got some business I need to see to. I won't be long.'

Charlotte wants to fall asleep. It feels like it should be the middle of the night rather than the middle of the afternoon, but her heart and mind are racing with the combination of the drugs and the enormity of what has happened today. She retrieves the G-string, wipes away the mess that has been left, and dresses herself while he's gone.

When he comes back they go out again in the car. They park in the car park around the back of Poundland and Danny waits until some younger kids come up to the car. They are much younger than Charlotte, maybe 10 or 12 years old. Danny gives a package to each of them and they disappear off on their scooters. Very little is said. Everything seems to be done through nods and eye contact. The kids know exactly what they're doing.

Danny puts the engine into gear and parks in a little alley, away from a street of pubs and restaurants, but positioned so that they can see some of the action through some missing fencing in the alley. The pubs are busy with Saturday night crowds, people moving in and out of different venues, some stopping to buy stuff from the kids. Charlotte isn't stupid, she knows it's drugs they're dealing and it makes her feel scared. At the same time, she feels safe in the car with Danny. He seems so in control of everything. There's no danger of them being caught, and anyway, she hasn't done anything wrong.

'Nearly done.' He flashes his lights once, then the kids melt out of the darkness back to the car. They hand over a load of cash and disappear again, their work done. Danny starts the engine, smiles at Charlotte, and blows her a kiss, 'God, you're beautiful,' he says again. Charlotte thinks she'll never tire of hearing it.

They drive along another side street back into town. Danny slows down outside a barbershop that still seems to be open. A man in a hoodie comes out, leans through the window and performs the knuckle-punch greeting that Danny favours. The man looks at Charlotte and nods at her. That's more acknowledgement than she received from the men back at Danny's place and she's grateful for it. Danny passes him the bag of money and the man hands a similar bag back to him. Once again, Charlotte isn't sure exactly what's happening but realises that this is all still about drugs. There are a few more similar stops and exchanges through the window, before Danny drives back to his house.

Inside, Charlotte follows him into the kitchen where he opens a can of beans and pours them onto a plate which he sticks into the microwave. He pulls a fork out of the drawer and, when the microwave pings, he takes the plate and fork into Nanna. Charlotte hears him say, 'Nanna, you gotta eat, yeah?'

Charlotte peers around the door and watches as he takes a magazine off the chair next to her and puts it on her lap, then puts the plate on top.

Nanna doesn't say anything.

They return to Danny's room where they have sex once more. This time he uses a condom. She falls asleep with him whispering in her ear that she is the most beautiful girl in the world.

VII

Back at school on Sunday afternoon, Charlotte hugs her pillow close to her chest, feeling the thrill of being inside her own body for the first time, and smiling at all the new knowledge and power that the world has now given her. She basks in the realisation that she is no longer a girl, she is sexually active and she is in love. What a difference a few weeks makes. How nervous she was about coming to Hickman's. And now she has a boyfriend and has lost her virginity. All in the space of three weeks. It feels amazing. From now on she will be a different person. Things will be different. She is no longer little, insignificant Whoopsie. She is a woman.

'Well, he-*llo*. Somebody's had a good weekend,' Kirst says, when she returns from her London trip. 'You look like the cat that got the cream, as my mum would say. Care to share?'

It's an odd thing to say for a teenager. It strikes Charlotte that Kirst really is quite square. No wonder she was bullied at her previous school. *And it wouldn't have been just for her weight*, Charlotte thinks.

'Not really. You wouldn't understand,' Charlotte says, her new maturity giving her a level of superiority. Although part of her really wants to tell Kirst.

'Whatever.'

Kirst babbles on about the show and the swanky dinner and

the minibar at the hotel, but Charlotte isn't really listening to any of it.

'Here, try this.' Kirst is armed with chocolate from a smart new Belgian chocolatier on Regent Street where they went shopping before the theatre.

Charlotte refuses the chocolate. It is now her mission to lose a bit of weight. Danny had teased her gently about her little food-baby belly and her wobbly bottom. He had done so while kissing her lovingly in all those places, but the comments have cemented themselves deep into her soul. Everything about her life is going to change from now on. She's even going to embrace all the healthy-eating stuff at Hickman's.

All week long she glides around in a love trance, as if drunk on sex and attention. She no longer even notices Bruno and his little gang. They are children compared with Danny. She is with 'da man', hanging out with an actual man, a man who has important business to conduct in his little black Corsa on a Saturday night, a man who keeps knives in his bedside table drawer.

That had shocked her a little. It's such a different world to the safe, boring and cold one she has known until now.

He took a knife with him when they went out in the evening, fingering the blade when they sat in the car park. It gives her a little tickle of delight just thinking about how her parents would react to that little detail. Danny is definitely 'from the wrong side of the tracks' as her father would say, and Charlotte is drawn to him all the more as a result. The whole idea of Danny and his dark world creates a kind of joy and excitement within her. School is a blur. Lessons go above her head as she daydreams of being back at Danny's place, in his bed. Lia and Kirst are young, immature and irrelevant. She is waiting only for the weekend and the next opportunity to be with Danny.

Her parents call, separately, at different times during the week. Instead of being desperate to speak with them and then feeling desolate when the conversation is over, now she is polite but indifferent on each call. She has other things on her mind.

'It sounds as if you are all grown up in just a few weeks, Whoopsie. That school is doing you good,' James says.

If only they knew.

The weekend follows the pattern of the last one. She does a bit of coke and smokes weed and Danny has sex with her, and tells her a hundred times how beautiful she is. This time he can't drop her back to school on Sunday because he has 'business' to see to, but Charlotte understands that. After all, he's an important man.

There's a bit of a wait for the bus, being a Sunday, and she isn't really dressed for standing at a bus stop, given that the weather has suddenly turned more autumnal. Still, the glow from thoughts of their sex keeps her warm. It hurt less this time. Eventually a bus arrives and she catches it back to Hickman's. As long as she's back before the curfew, she won't draw any attention to herself.

Kirst is offish with her when she gets back. 'Something's different about you. What are you up to?'

'Nothing.'

'I'm worried about you. Who've you been hanging out with? Is it that boy again? Do you think he's a good influence?'

Charlotte almost laughs in her face. 'God, you sound like your mum sometimes, d'you know that?'

It has the desired effect and shuts Kirst up. She's becoming very irritating these days, Charlotte thinks. She's so immature.

'What's that?' Kirst confronts Charlotte when she notices the second phone after Sarah has done the rounds one night.

Charlotte smiles. 'What do you think?'

'Oh, that's clever!'

'Isn't it?'

'I might get one.'

'Yeah? And who would you call?' Charlotte asks, rather cruelly.

Kirst looks crestfallen for a moment. 'No one. But I could watch stuff on it.'

When Charlotte is getting changed for bed, Kirst spots something else. 'What the fuck? Lotts, have you been eaten by a monster?'

Charlotte blushes, but the words come out as a kind of boast. 'Love bites.'

'Oh my God! What's his name?'

Charlotte smiles again. 'Bad Boy.'

Kirst giggles. 'What, you mean he's a Pot Noodle?'

'He's *my* bad boy.'

Kirst shakes her head in mock disapproval, but the gesture is envious and admiring and respectful all at the same time and Charlotte glows in the attention.

The pattern repeats again at the weekend, although this time Charlotte returns to school with a little wrap of cocaine and some weed. Danny has taught her how to skin up. Lia isn't interested, but Kirst, with her little pouch of tobacco, is a little more into it. Charlotte takes great pride in showing her how to roll a spliff and on Thursday evening, when the weather is fine, she and Kirst go outside and walk to the back field near the sheep and woodland. They sit down and smoke the spliff together. It's Kirst's first time and she is overwhelmed by the whole thing. She has a bit of an out-of-body experience that terrifies her, turning her completely white.

'It's just a weed panic. Pull yourself together.' Charlotte is stern. And she's heard Danny talk about this sort of thing happening.

'I want my mum,' Kirst cries out. To Charlotte's horror, she takes out her phone and calls her mum who answers straight away. Kirst begins to sob down the phone.

'Don't you dare tell her what you've been smoking,' Charlotte hisses, trying to reach for the phone to snatch it out of her hands.

After the call, when Kirst has somehow managed not to spill the beans, Charlotte walks her at speed back to their room. She puts her in her bed, puts on some music and pretends to be relaxing when Sarah knocks on the door. It is Sarah's habit to give a quick knock and walk straight into the room, not allowing for time to hide the evidence should any of the students be up to no good. The rapid walk in the fresh air has helped to steady Kirst and it's no longer obvious that she is stoned.

'She's been saying she's tired all evening,' Charlotte explains. She's learning fast from Danny and his crew about how to be devious. 'Since dinner,' actually. Charlotte does her best but-ter-wouldn't-melt-in-her-mouth face and reassures Sarah that Kirst is fine, probably just ate something bad at dinner. 'I'll look after her and come straight to you if I think she's not okay.'

Charlotte guesses that Sarah will be nervous about the suggestion of anything to do with food poisoning, particularly given that so much of the school's reputation has been built on the idea of wholesome 'brain food'. Sarah stays for a few minutes longer than usual, to see if Kirst is alright and to make sure that she drinks some water. Kirst sits up in bed and smiles.

Good performance, Kirst, Charlotte thinks. But she knows that Kirst will also want to make sure that no one else knows about what's happened. Her wholesome mother would, no doubt, be very disappointed in her offspring if she knew what she'd been up to. Kirst won't tell.

Their ruse is successful.

'Make sure you do come straight to me if there's any change,' Sarah says.

Kirst flops back down onto her pillows the second the door closes behind Sarah.

'Just about got away with that,' Charlotte says.

VIII

Charlotte is exhausted after each weekend, and the fatigue translates into poor behaviour in lessons, especially on a Monday and Tuesday when she's still coming down from the excesses of whatever party she has been to with Danny until the early hours of Sunday morning.

And because she's never been particularly good at learning, Charlotte sees even less of a point in school and all things academic these days. Lessons are just something to get through before she can be back with Danny. Her mood is low and it makes her snappy with not just Kirst and Lia, teachers around the school are also on the receiving end of her change in attitude.

They are studying some stupid poem in English when Miss Sevini asks what a half-asleep Charlotte thinks of a particular image. Lia gives her a sharp dig in the ribs.

'What, what?'

The rest of the class laugh.

Sevini is well known for her sarcasm. 'I'm terribly sorry, Charlotte, are we keeping you up?'

Later, in French, she is caught looking at her phone, receiving one of the many texts sent by Danny every day, telling her that she is special, that she is his princess, that he loves her.

'You leave me no option but to report this,' the French teacher says.

'For fuck's sake,' Charlotte says, just low enough under her breath for the French teacher, Madame West, to be unsure of what she's heard.

But all the 'I love you' and 'you are so special' and 'my princess' texts, along with all the attention she's unused to, have made Charlotte more confident than she has ever been before. Who cares what Miss Sevini thinks?

When she is called to Sarah's office in the afternoon and Sarah asks her how she is and whether there is anything she needs to talk about, Charlotte taps the side of her nose.

'Nosy parker.'

'Charlotte, it's not being nosy, it's having your welfare and your best interests at heart. When a student's behaviour changes as dramatically as yours has, we wouldn't be doing our jobs properly if we didn't look into what was going on. There's usually an underlying cause. Now, I know that the beginning of term was difficult for you with all the upheaval, your mum's move abroad and the grief you suffered at the loss of a close family friend. That would be enough to upset anyone.'

'Yeah, I'm still sad about Nanny,' Charlotte admits, which is true, though she hasn't thought about her much in the last few weeks.

'And that's understandable. We can arrange for you to have some bereavement counselling if that would help?'

'No. I don't think that would help.'

'Is there anything else that you want to talk about?'

'I told you, no.'

Sarah sighs. 'Look, I'm here whenever you want to talk, okay? But we can't have any more of this kind of behaviour in lessons. It isn't fair on the members of staff to be spoken to the way you've done lately. And, of course, I'm going to have to let your parents know.'

The last thing Charlotte needs is her folks breathing down her neck. She is immediately defensive.

'Say what you like. They won't care anyway.'

'That's not true, Charlotte. Of course they care about you.'

'Whatever. If there's nothing else, I'd like to go back to my room,' Charlotte says, sulkily.

When she escapes from Sarah's office, she heads back to her room and is relieved to see that there is no sign of Kirst. Her hands are shaking. She's sailing too close to the wind now. Things feel out of control.

She takes a disposable razor from her washbag. She has kept a strict leg-shaving regime since she first started seeing Danny. She begins dismantling it to remove the blade. She feels as if she wants to cut the shame out of herself, or punish herself for the way she has behaved. Something. And it works. The pain is a kind of release.

'Shit! What the fuck are you doing?' Kirst shouts when she walks in and sees the blood.

'Uh, I'm… branding myself.'

'You're *what*? What does that even mean?'

Kirst drops onto her bed next to Charlotte and stares in silent disbelief at the roommate she is suddenly struggling to recognise.

More episodes of seeking relief through cutting result in another summons to Sarah's office.

'Charlotte, I know this is going to sound strange, but I only want to help you. I've had a report from another student and I have a duty of care. I'm going to ask you to take down your trousers and show me your legs.'

'Fuck off! You can't ask me to do that.' Charlotte lifts her hands to her head, partly in defence, partly in mortification.

'You're right, and I don't actually need to. I can see from your arms.'

The baggy white sleeve of Charlotte's sweatshirt has moved back up her arm. Charlotte tugs at it self-consciously, but the damage is done. Sarah has seen the fresh little cuts that she has made on her arm.

'Oh, Charlotte.'

A meeting is called immediately via video link, as neither of Charlotte's parents are available to attend in person. Kirsty is not due to return from Geneva until just before Christmas, while James is busy with parliamentary duties.

Martin and Sarah express their concern at what has been discovered and put it down to Charlotte feeling homesick.

'I don't imagine it's homesickness.' Kirsty seems surprised at the suggestion. 'Charlotte is perfectly used to being away at school for weeks at a time; she's been doing it since she was seven years old. She's never suffered with that before. She knows the drill. Perhaps there's a little unfamiliarity in a new place. It's still the first half-term. She's still settling in.'

'What I want to know,' James says dryly, sounding increasingly like a politician, is what exactly the school are going to do to help Charlotte?'

'Well, we were wondering,' Sarah clears her throat, 'whether there might be any possibility of Charlotte taking a bit of a break to recover and coming home for half-term a little early?'

'Don't be ridiculous. We're both up to our necks in crucial work commitments. We weren't planning on her coming home to us until the end of the Michaelmas term.'

'Given the seriousness of what's happened, is there no way that you could take a bit of time out?'

'Absolutely not!' James seems genuinely annoyed by this request.

Sarah looks apologetically towards Charlotte, who is sitting on the chair in the office waiting to be invited properly into the conversation.

Martin chips in, 'Look, we totally understand. Of course. But could you both do more Facetimes and Zooms with Charlotte as the next best thing, so that she's getting that regular contact?'

'I'm tied up with the legislature for this damned bill, and Kirsty's finding her feet with a new job in Switzerland! What do you expect us to do? We've got to pay the school's exorbitant fees somehow,' James quips.

Sarah is keen to pursue a kind, supportive approach to resolution. 'I really think that it would be in Charlotte's best interests…' she persists.

Martin cuts her off. 'I think it's up to the parents to decide.' He shoots his wife a look which silences Sarah. 'After all, as James has just reminded us, they're the ones who pay the fees.'

'This is about welfare,' Sarah says.

'Look, perhaps we could manage to schedule a weekly Zoom and at least one of us can try to be there,' James says.

'I'm not an expert, but it does sound to me as if Whoopsie is depressed,' Kirsty says, in an attempt to diffuse the situation. 'So many kids suffer from it these days, don't they? It seems to be the modern malaise.'

'Don't call me that!' Charlotte shouts from her off-screen position. 'I hate it!' Why is everyone talking about her as if she isn't there?

'Sorry, darling, it's only because I love you, you know that. I can't help it. Just trying to sort things for you. Look, do you think we could talk privately, without Charlotte, I mean?' Kirsty asks.

'Talk about me rather than to me, you mean,' Charlotte shouts. It's easy for her mother to say that she loves her. But Charlotte doesn't believe it. Why doesn't her mother ever *show* it?

Kirsty ignores her, but Sarah tries once more to diffuse the situation. 'Given that it's Charlotte's health and wellbeing that we're discussing, I really think it's important that she's part of the conversation.'

'Look, is the phone part of the problem? Is she getting enough sleep? Is Charlotte on the phone at night?'

'Absolutely not!' Sarah explains about how she begins collecting all phones at 9.30pm in accordance with the school agreement.

Charlotte doubts that her mother has stopped for long enough to read the school agreement, but where once all these words would have hurt her deeply, she now begins to feel strangely detached from it all. It feels strange to see adults laying into each other like this, trying to apportion blame.

'And another thing,' Kirsty says. 'Charlotte tells me that all the students buy food at the Co-op to supplement the healthy diet. Is poor food the issue here? How are you regulating that?'

Martin raises his eyes to heaven. 'Look, of course that kind of thing goes on. We know that it does. But we know teenagers and we also think it would do more harm than good to try to stop it, Kirsty. If we turn supplements from the village shop into contraband, it doesn't leave us much room when something serious happens.' Martin tries to appeal to his old friend on a personal level. 'You know what it's like at this age. Children can enjoy the feelings of illicitness and power without actually doing too much harm.'

'Yes, well, it's all very well as a philosophy but perhaps a little naive at best and misguided at worst.'

'Perhaps we could bring Charlotte fully into the conversation now,' Sarah says quickly, 'and take into account her perspective.'

Charlotte sits between Sarah and Martin as directed. It's a difficult and rather false conversation and Charlotte responds by rolling her eyes and fiddling with the elastic band that Sarah has given her to put on her wrist to use as a distraction and alternative to the need to cut. After 15 minutes of her parents asking her how she is and what has she been up to, she is asked to leave once again.

Charlotte can't get out of the room quick enough, but at the door she hears Kirsty say that she wants the contact details of the GP used by the school.

'I'm going to contact him, and our private family doctor, and suggest that Charlotte is given a prescription for fluoxetine.'

Out in the corridor, Charlotte Googles 'fluoxetine.'

'Prozac,' she mutters under her breath. 'She wants to put me on fucking Prozac.'

IX

Charlotte isn't the only student to stay behind in school over the half-term break. Lots of the international students also remain at Hickman's.

Each morning after breakfast Sarah administers the tablet to Charlotte. There are a few other students who are on various medications for anxiety and depression, all approved by their parents. They too stay behind in the dining room each day as instructed.

'Well, isn't this a sad little club,' Charlotte says, looking around her.

Worse than the tablet is the fact that she is no longer allowed to go away for nights until her behaviour improves.

That realisation means that her mood takes even more of a downward swing.

The half-term weeks are long and boring without Kirst and Lia around, and Danny says he's working during the week so can't see her. The week after, back in class, is even harder. Charlotte is 'on report' each lesson to try to get her 'challenging behaviour' under control.

She feels more anxious than ever before and reports headaches and dizziness. Alone in her room she imagines that Nanny is still alive, that she can just phone her up and talk to her. She dreams of being wrapped in Nanny's arms, of those innocent days of playing cards and games, of being safe with Nanny and Bob looking after her.

A couple of times a week Charlotte sits in a Zoom meeting with Martin, Sarah and her parents, or usually one of them at least, because often one of them can't make it for some or other reason. They aren't easy meetings and are entirely superficial. It is impossible to say anything she really wants to say to her mum or dad in the presence of the teachers – nice though they are. It makes the conversation false and superficial, full of bright, meaningless pleasantries that get them nowhere but out of the room as quickly as possible. She wouldn't dream of telling them about Danny.

A pattern soon establishes itself. Kirsty, if she is there, tends to take the lead, especially on matters medical.

When Charlotte, backed up by Sarah, tries to talk about the symptoms that she's experiencing: the dizziness, anxiety and loss of appetite, Kirsty has the answer.

'The transition onto Prozac isn't easy, but it will be worth it when you finally get there. I'm surprised, actually, Sarah, that you don't already know about the side-effects. I mean, Charlotte can't be the first child at the school on the stuff.'

Even Martin baulks at Kirsty's tone at times.

'How long do you think the adjustment to the medication will take?' Sarah asks. 'I mean, until Charlotte is likely to feel some benefit?'

'I think we need to be patient. Up to 12 weeks on new medication I should say. Again, something I'd expect you to be well aware of.'

'Quite. But I'm also asking because, as I'm sure you can understand, we have to take into account the learning environment for all of our students, not just Charlotte.

Charlotte's mood and behaviour are adversely affecting her fellow students as well as members of staff.'

Kirsty leans into her laptop so that her face is enlarged on screen. 'Whoopsie, darling, give it another month, then you will begin to feel much happier, I promise you.'

She leans back and directs her next question to Sarah. Her tone is belligerent, and it is always the school who is at fault. 'Meanwhile, what are you doing to remedy her lack of academic progress? The first half-term's grades were terrible. We're not paying money for her to go backwards.'

'Quite, but until we get her health sorted, the school work is secondary.'

James pipes up. 'Look, darling, I've had an idea. How do you fancy the Canaries this Christmas? We can stay in a lovely hotel and you can snooze by the pool and relax and get yourself on top of all this. How about that, Whoops? Doesn't that sound good?'

It does not sound good to Charlotte. What she really wants is to be cosy at home by the warmth of a fire rather than winter sun, helping in the kitchen and putting up the Christmas tree, like she did when Nanny was there.

Her father's suggestion makes Charlotte feel sad about the loss of Nanny all over again. She realises that she just wants to be at home with Nanny, not with her parents, and certainly not to be driven by taxi on her own to the airport to meet her family for two weeks of expensive fun, where she will constantly be introduced to more posh, sloshed adults as 'Whoopsie, our little mistake.'

'Marvellous idea, James,' Kirsty agrees.

It seems to be settled, even though it's the last thing Charlotte wants for Christmas. It will also take her away from Danny at a time of year when there will, no doubt, be plenty of partying. It's a hideous meeting, and she finds solace after it with her blade.

She knows now to choose the places that are most covered by clothing: her ankles, shoulders, tummy and thighs.

Charlotte feels even worse when she learns yet more depressing news: her roommate is leaving at Christmas. Kirst is vague about the details, just that her mum isn't sure that Hickman's is the right place for her after all. She'll be attending a boarding school in Wales that is en route to the airport for her mum's work and much closer to their home.

'I'll miss you, Kirst.'

She can be a pain at times, a bit of a 'neek', and she obviously grassed Charlotte about the cuts, but underneath all that she's the closest thing that Charlotte's had to a friend.

Now she'll have to wait for someone else to move into her room and start all over again. It had been surprisingly easy to make friends with Kirst; she was comforting and straightforward, even if Charlotte hasn't exactly made the most of the friendship that was offered to her. She might not get on so well with someone else.

Years of private education and being in social situations with successful adults from a young age have made Charlotte very good at saying the things that adults in authority want to hear. Just a few weeks of being with Danny, however, has made her devious and honed her budding skills of deception. On a Saturday, even though she isn't able to organise a 'sleepover' – how innocent that word seems to her now – she can manage to wangle a pass out of school for a while.

'It's not like I've done anything wrong,' she pleads with Sarah. 'I'm being penalised because I'm displaying symptoms that are associated with starting my meds. There's no reason to keep me here like a prisoner.'

Her performance is convincing, and Charlotte is given permission to leave as long as Kirst is with her.

Kirst, being the nice, accommodating person that she is, obliges by going with her into town, but doesn't hide how fed-up she gets when Charlotte goes off with the 'Bombay Bad Boys' at the earliest opportunity.

'I thought you actually wanted to go into town with me, Lotts.'

'I do – but I also need to see Danny. You get that, don't you?'

The following week, Kirst makes excuses. 'I'm going away.'

'You're leaving at the end of term; why do you have to go away this weekend?'

'Look, I didn't want to have to tell you this, okay, but all this,' she waves her hands around to indicate Charlotte herself, 'is part of the reason that I'm leaving the school.'

'All what? What do you mean?'

'You know what I mean. The cutting, the secrecy, the general weird behaviour. You're not the easiest person to share a room with, you know.'

'I thought you were a friend.'

'I am. But I know you're taking drugs and drinking, and you're just so different to when you first got here.'

'God, you're such a neek, aren't you?'

'Charlotte, don't do this. You're not this mean girl that you pretend to be.'

'How do you know what I am? Why does everyone think they know what I am?'

What's worse is when she overhears people talking about her. She is coming back from the toilet later when she overhears Kirst talking to Sarah.

'I'm concerned about her. I think she's making some bad choices.'

'I really appreciate you coming to me, Kirsty, and I know that it's coming from a good place, but another student's health issues are confidential. Rest assured that it's all in hand. Charlotte will start to feel much better soon.'

'How dare you!' Charlotte shouts when Kirst returns to their room. 'Who do you think you are, you little snitch?'

'I was looking out for you.'

'Bollocks.'

There is a pause. Charlotte is furious. 'I don't know how you expect me to carry on sharing a room with you for even the last couple of weeks of term. Seriously, how dare you go to a teacher and talk about me!'

'Mum was right,' Kirst says, shaking her head.

'What?'

'My mum doesn't want me hanging round with you anymore. I told her she was wrong when she said that you use me.'

'What are you talking about?' Charlotte is really confused.

'But she's got a point, hasn't she? You *are* just using me to get you out of school, not because you actually want to spend time with me.'

'So you're changing schools because of me?'

Kirst doesn't hold back now. 'Your mum's a user too. She tried to create a friendship with my mum so that you would have somewhere to go during the holidays. She actually asked if you could stay with us for half-term, did you know that?'

Charlotte feels sick at Kirst's words, but she isn't surprised.

'She wouldn't stop texting my mum,' Kirst continues. 'But mum says she's met women like your mum before. And you're just like her.'

It's about the worst thing that Kirst could say to her.

'Fuck off back to Wales then,' Charlotte says, with a sneer. It's the only defence she has left.

X

Charlotte has more luck with Lia, though Lia, perhaps having a little more self-esteem than Charlotte's roommate, is not as easy to manipulate as Kirst. Lia is still up for Saturdays in town but, though a bit more of a thrillseeker than Kirst, she knows her limits.

'I'll come with you, but so we're clear, I'm not doing anything dodgy, Lotts.'

'Thanks, I owe you.'

On Saturday they get ready together, Charlotte straightening Lia's hair and helping her with her make-up.

When they're ready, Lia seems surprised that they aren't walking to the bus stop.

'Nah, don't worry. Danny's going to pick us up.'

The meeting point is a little way up the road from the school, in a lay-by close to a gate that leads to farmland.

Charlotte has been told by Danny to make sure that she brings a friend with her. *The one that was in town with you that day*, his message said. Danny has another boy, Biff, with him in the car, and they're already waiting when the girls arrive just before 11am.

Biff gives out a low whistle of appreciation when he sees Lia.

Lia frowns and Charlotte ignores her look of concern.

'Let's go and get you two a drink,' Danny says.

The girls get in the back of the car. Instead of driving into town, Danny takes them further, into the next city. They park in a side street by a pub. Danny puts his arm around Charlotte as they walk into the pub, but Lia removes Biff's arm when he tries to do the same. The place Danny has taken them to is actually a sports bar which is mostly full of white, balding men in hoodies, holding pints and watching football. There are a couple of women there, 'Rough old birds,' as Charlotte's father might describe them.

'I didn't realise pubs were even open at this time of day,' Lia says. 'I thought we were going for a milkshake.'

'A milkshake! Good one. Your mate cracks me up,' Danny says.

Danny walks the girls through to an area behind the circular bar where there are some men playing pool. No one seems to bat an eyelid at the fact that they're underage.

'What do you girls want to drink?' Danny asks.

'Half a lager,' Charlotte says, and Lia shrugs then nods for the same.

Biff heads off to the bar to get the drinks while Danny chooses a table for them to sit at. Lia whispers to Charlotte, 'I don't like this one little bit. I don't like Biff. I'm not into him. He's just a creep.'

'Relax,' Charlotte says, quietly. 'Don't ruin it for me.'

Not long after, they're joined at the table by a couple of older men. Both are wearing leather jackets. Danny introduces the girls to his 'good friends', Afrim and Dardan.

'Lotts, I mean it, I really don't like this,' Lia whispers. 'I don't like the way those two are looking at us.'

'We're having fun, aren't we?' Charlotte whispers back. 'Just go with it.'

Afrim moves round so that he's sitting next to Lia. He puts

a hand out to stroke her face and puts his other hand on her thigh.

Lia says to Charlotte, 'Let's go to the loo.'

Charlotte sees Danny shoot Biff a look.

Biff stands up. 'Girls, I'll walk you to the ladies. It's a bit lively in here today and we don't want anything bad happening to you.'

He leads them through the bar and down some stairs to the toilets and says, 'I'll wait here for you,' putting his foot in the door.

'Sorry, this is the ladies,' Lia says, firmly. 'Can you remove your foot? It's intimidating.'

Inside, Lia pulls Charlotte into a cubicle. 'What are you doing, you nutter? Have you got some kind of death wish? We have to go. Straight away. I've got no idea what's going on here, but we're not safe.'

Charlotte, who is beginning to feel a little drunk even though she's only had half a lager, wants to stay.

'Look, I know Danny, alright? Of course we're safe.'

'You don't know the others,' Lia hisses. 'And they're all way too old.'

'Well, fuck off if you don't want to be here, just go!' Charlotte's words come out more loudly than she intended.

From inside the cubicle, it's clear that the door to the toilets is open again. Biff calls out, 'Ladies, are you alright in there? Hurry up and come on out. You're missing the fun.'

As they walk back up the stairs, a large huddle of men are standing near the top.

Lia turns to Charlotte and raises her eyebrows. 'Last chance,' she says. With no response she quickly walks around the group and out of the door. Charlotte feels a flutter of nerves, then shrugs and walks back to the table with Biff.

'Where's your mate going?' Danny says, clearly unhappy.

'Oh, she's stropped off, the little madam.'

Biff goes back to the bar for another round of drinks. Afrim and Dardan sit either side of Charlotte and smile as they watch her drink the lager that Danny passes towards her; this time it's a pint.

It's late afternoon when Charlotte begins to come round. The curtains are open but it looks as if it's already starting to get dark. She's lying on a sofa in a strange house. Her trousers are on a chair. Her mouth feels dry and her body feels like she's been hit by a train.

'Ow,' she says, rubbing her temples. She has a cracking headache.

Danny sits down next to her. 'Baby girl, it's time to go back to school.'

Everything feels a little off-kilter. Dardan and Afrim are sitting at a table counting cash. There's a strange smell in the room, and a bottle of baby oil on the floor. As Charlotte becomes more aware of her surroundings, she senses that there are other people in the house, too. In an armchair in the corner a girl seems to be sleeping. Her legs look very scratched up, as bad as Charlotte's own. Another girl passes by the door to the room. Her mascara is smudged all down her face as if she's been crying.

'There you are, princess,' Danny passes Charlotte her trousers.

'Why are my trousers on a chair?' Charlotte asks, confused.

Danny, as always, has an answer. 'I took 'em off you, baby girl, to make you comfortable.'

Charlotte shivers.

'Danny, where are we?'

'It's a party house, babe. We came back here to party, don't you remember?' He smiles, reassuringly. 'You had a little bit too much to drink in the pub, I reckon.'

'Did we, er, have sex?'

Charlotte genuinely can't remember.

Danny shakes his head and laughs. 'Don't worry about it, babe.'

He walks her to the car which is parked just along from the house. Four girls who seem to be wearing only their underwear with hoodies over the top climb into the back of a grey van parked behind the Corsa.

'Let's get you back to that school of yours if you're not feeling so good.'

Charlotte nods. Her head is banging. The last thing she can remember is being cross with Lia for bailing out on her. She wonders if Lia got back okay and begins to wonder if she should have left with her.

Charlotte still feels unwell in the evening. Sarah takes her temperature and puts her to bed. Kirst is away all weekend with her mother, and Lia is not answering her phone or messages. She texts Danny; he doesn't get back to her either. Charlotte is too sick to do anything else but lie in bed with her phones. She reaches for Teddy Gertie and cries herself to sleep. She feels utterly alone.

Later, when she wakes up needing to go to the loo, it feels as if she's on fire and it's difficult to wee. When she wipes herself, there's blood on the tissue. She stands in front of the mirror in her knickers and sees multiple bruises coming up all around her thighs. Did Danny do this to her? Or someone else? He told her they didn't have sex, didn't he? She bursts into tears again. There is no way she can tell Sarah this. Or anyone. Though Charlotte is no stranger to feeling lonely, and has felt abandoned at several times in her life, nothing compares to the feeling of misery that washes over her now. What has she done?

XI

'Are you okay?'

'No thanks to you.'

Charlotte and Lia are sitting on the wall near the football pitches. Once, this would have been a spot from which to try and catch a glimpse of Bruno. Charlotte barely even recognises that child version of herself from the start of term.

'Do you want to talk about it?'

'Not really,' Charlotte takes a puff of her vape.

'Well, I was properly worried about you.'

'Not enough to stay, obviously.' Although, if Charlotte is honest with herself, she knows that she wouldn't want her friend to have gone through what she did. She shivers, still not entirely sure what it is she has been through. She's got a pretty good idea, though.

'I phoned my mum and told her she had to come and get me. And I went home for the rest of the weekend.'

'So she knows that you went into the city?'

'*God, no.* I'm not that stupid. I got a bus back to town and phoned her from there. I didn't want her to know how far we'd gone.'

'Nice that you can phone and say that to your mum, though. I couldn't. Well, I could, but she wouldn't listen and she wouldn't do anything about it.'

'I didn't tell her all of it. I didn't tell her that I'd gone with you and I didn't tell her that I'd felt in danger.'

'Thanks. But what did you tell her?'

Lia looks directly at her. 'I told her I was worried about you.'

'Thanks, but I don't need you to worry about me.'

'Are you sure? I don't know what you've got yourself mixed up in, but I think they're bad men, Charlotte.'

Charlotte laughs, bitterly. 'Grow up, Lia. Did you tell your darling mum about the *bad men* in the pub? I bloody hope not. I don't need you interfering.'

Lia bites her lip.

'You bloody well did, didn't you!'

'I had to tell her something. She wanted to know why I was so upset. Why I wanted to come home.' Lia pauses. 'They're going to stop me from boarding.'

'Christ. Not you as well.'

'At least they're going to keep me here at Hickman's though. They actually looked at other schools. They wanted to send me somewhere that was a bit closer to home. There is another one in the area but it's much more expensive, and most of the kids who go there end up going on to military careers, which isn't really up their street.'

'God, don't tell my parents, they'd probably love that.'

'They're advertising for a childminder to supervise my travel to and from school. How embarrassing is that? Like I'm a little kid. The money they save on boarding fees will cover the cost of the nanny.'

'That's shithouse.'

'Yeah, well, better than leaving and starting somewhere new all over again. At least we'll still have lessons together. I just won't be able to see you at the weekends.'

So Charlotte's second out-of-hours buddy is taken away, too. Kirst, or 'the bitch' as Charlotte now thinks of her, is due to leave soon and, as far as Charlotte is concerned, that departure can't come soon enough. Their relationship has become very tense. Charlotte sees Kirst as having betrayed her. But now it seems that Lia has too. She must have mentioned drugs to her mum, because now there is a focus on this. Charlotte denies all accusations and it's hushed up pretty quickly. No doubt Martin prefers to hear the 'medication' description of Charlotte's behaviour rather than the 'is she taking drugs?' version.

Her parents, too, are keen to shut down any mention of drugs when it's raised with them. At one point her father even says, 'We pay *you* to deal with our daughter, so I don't want to hear it mentioned again.'

James' other helpful intervention is to cut her allowance.

'Your mother and I have discussed it. It's a temporary measure. If we don't give you money, you can't buy drugs – if indeed that's what's happening. Simple as.'

Charlotte dutifully attends the scheduled video meetings which take place in Martin's office. From a couple of times a week at first, they seem to have dropped down now to only once a week, which fits in better with her parents' working schedules. They are dull and repetitive and the conversation quickly runs dry.

'You're looking a little thinner, I have to say,' Kirsty observes.

'If you say so,' Charlotte brushes past the comment, as if her weight isn't and has never been an issue. But she takes it as a compliment, especially coming from her judgemental mother, and is quietly pleased. Danny has been encouraging her to lose weight. He says things like, 'God you're hot, you're beautiful' when he touches her.

She's conscious that her appearance *is* changing. Not only is she thinner, she's also going blonder, trying to cover up the mousiness. She likes the way she looks now. It's older and edgier than the pudgy kid who arrived at Hickman's knowing nothing about anything. But part of the control over her appearance is connected to the cutting, which she is somehow managing to keep hidden from Sarah and everyone else at school. She cuts where she can reach on her torso and upper arms. She smuggles in rolls of kitchen towel to mop up the blood, then packs the soiled paper into a carrier bag in her rucksack and disposes of them while she's in town. Because things have escalated quickly since the sports bar day.

Danny has drummed into her that she needs to be clever and cover her tracks so that she can keep getting out of school. The idea now is that Charlotte goes out on a Saturday by herself and Danny makes sure that she is back at school by 7pm. Her drinks are no longer spiked as they were on the day of the sports bar. Now she is learning to do what the other girls do: have a few drinks and a line of coke or two so that she's relaxed. The set-up at the house has gradually become clear to her, and her role within it. She is to make herself available to men. Other men, not just Danny. Men that are chosen by Dardan and Afrim.

'You'd do it if you loved me.'

Which she does, even though she doesn't want to do it with the other men. But it's okay, because Danny has assured her that he likes her better for it. At first she tried to refuse, but he told her that he didn't expect her to cry like a little girl. She's a woman now, and this is how modern women behave.

'Perhaps you're just a kid after all. I thought you were like me, but maybe I made a mistake. Go back to school, little girl. Go and play with your teddy bear.'

It was humiliating. When she does what she's told, he is much nicer.

The cocaine makes it easier. It makes her feel detached when it comes to the sex part, almost as if she's outside of her own body, but it also makes her chatty and amusing and confident and marvellous, and she even makes people laugh; it's a magic potion that makes the reality of what she has to do go away.

Afrim and Dardan are in charge, and they are clear that they like gamine, skinny girls. The cocaine helps with that, too, because it takes away her appetite. Her new body works better in the outfit they make her wear: a black leather bikini with chains attached to a high collar. It's very sexy. She couldn't have imagined herself wearing anything like that even a few weeks ago, but Danny has helped her choose it. He told her she looked gorgeous in it.

There's one man in particular who liked her cuts. He spent a long time running his fingers over every cut and scar on her body. He called her The Cutting Girl and asked for her specially the next weekend. Danny said that was a really good sign.

The Cutting Girl has stuck now, as a kind of nickname. It's become part of who she is.

Dardan gives her one of his special lessons to help her learn more about pleasing men. In a way, it's like doing drama at school. Playing a part. They like it when she screams out theatrically in pain. He has also trained her in how to give excellent oral sex and he's filmed her doing it. She didn't want to, but when she tried to refuse, Afrim held up his phone with a picture of her dad's face, and then a picture of him inside and outside Parliament. Whatever else has gone on in her family, Charlotte was raised to be loyal. She knows exactly how much the family's reputation means to her parents. She has to do this for her dad, now, as well as for Danny.

In school, she really needs a friend. The friendship gap left by Lia and Kirst is filled by Avril, the cool girl who was nice to her when Bruno and his mates were mean. She's in the upper sixth, and she tells Charlotte that she 'likes her look' one day, then asks if Charlotte wants to go with her after classes to 'grab a coffee'.

Charlotte would once have found it weird that a sixth former wanted to talk to her, and might have worried about how to hold her own in a conversation, would actually have found it intimidating, but now that she spends so much of her time in adult company and is a lot more streetwise than she was a few months ago it doesn't phase her in the slightest.

She soon finds herself telling Avril more than she ever told Lia or Kirst about what has been going on with Danny and Biff, Dardan and Afrim, and the other men. What she has been up to for the last four weekends. Words that she never thought she'd be able to say out loud. Avril isn't shocked. In fact, she seems to be quite in-the-know about the whole thing.

'Girl, you know what you need to do, don't you? You need to drop Danny.'

'But I love Danny.'

'Don't be ridiculous. When was the last time you spent any time with him?'

It's true. For the last month, or so, he has only picked her up and dropped her back at school.

'When you go with these men, he's taking the money that they pay. Your money.'

'What are you talking about?'

'You really are naive, aren't you? Those men are paying him, and you aren't seeing a penny of it. You need to smarten up, my friend.'

Somewhere deep down, Charlotte knows that what Avril says

is true. She remembers Dardan and Afrim counting money at the table that first day.

'But Danny loves me.'

Avril smiles, kindly. 'Think that if you want to.'

'He gives me cocaine.'

'But look what he's done to you. I bet you didn't even realise it was happening the first time, did you?'

Charlotte shakes her head. 'I think they spiked my drink.'

'Course they did. It's what they do.'

It is such a relief to unburden her dark secrets to Avril. It's like a weight being lifted from her just to know that someone else knows. And understands. Charlotte has been existing in a world that is completely alien to her. It's only been a short time, just days, weeks – but it feels like forever. Now here is someone who actually seems to get it, really get it, and not be shocked.

'How do you know so much about this? Has it happened to you, too?'

Avril shrugs, but in a way that seems to suggest it's just one of those things.

Over the next few days, Charlotte gets to know Avril much better. She learns that Avril joined Hickman's late, part way through Year 10, when her parents, both in business, came over here for work. 'My mother's Italian,' Avril explains, which makes her sound exotic to Charlotte.

'And your dad? Is he Italian, too.'

'Oh, no, he's English. That's how come we ended up here.'

'Are they wealthy?' asks Charlotte, sensing a kindred, abandoned spirit, a story a little like her own.

'Well, my father drove me here in a Tesla,' Avril says. Somehow it sounds matter-of-fact and not as if she's trying to show off. 'But enough about me. Let's talk about you.'

Avril has a way of making her talk. Charlotte pours her heart out to Avril about her fucked up family. 'The only one who really loves me is Henry.'

'He sounds quite a guy.'

'He is.'

'But don't do yourself down. There's something really special about you, Charlotte.'

'Is there?' Charlotte feels singled out and flattered by Avril's attention. Talking to her *does* make her feel special.

'You could be great without Danny, you know. Think Girl Power. You don't need him tagging along.'

'I don't think there's any way out of it,' Charlotte says, remembering the photographs of her father in Afrim's phone.

'It's easier than you think. I can help you to ditch him,' Avril whispers.

'Thanks, but I very much doubt that.'

Avril seems so much older, cooler and wiser than her years.

'Look at me, Charlotte. I promise you that I can.'

Charlotte wants so much to believe her. There is something knowing about Avril that makes her feel safe.

'Do you trust me?'

Charlotte nods.

So, when Avril offers to become her handler and to make sure she gets paid every Saturday, it sounds like a solution.

'How much?'

'I'll square things with Danny, and with Afrim and Dardan.'

'You know Afrim and Dardan?'

'I do. And I know how to handle them. So let me sort it. I do the business, you do the sex. Men like you – that's a good thing. I'll make sure you get £200 for your little Saturday job, instead of doing it for nothing.'

The idea is appealing. Now that her allowance has been cut, and her taste for cocaine has grown, finding a way to make it through the week is difficult, it helps her forget how miserable she is, too. £200 will more than cover the weed and coke – and anything else she wants.

'You'd really do that for me?'

It sounds like the answer to her prayers.

It's actually an invitation to hell.

XII

Charlotte looks up to Avril. With her olive skin and dark eyes she looks beautiful, but in an effortless way. She looks tanned, even though it's November. It must be her Italian heritage. She doesn't wear all the make-up that Charlotte is growing used to caking on. She just looks cool. And she has managed to achieve what Charlotte has not: maintaining a low profile at school. Avril works hard, keeps her head down, and is of no concern to the teachers or anyone.

'How do you manage it?'

'It takes *a lot* of work,' she laughs, 'but I've cultivated the art of being beige. It's not an insult. It's the way to be if you want to get anywhere in this world.'

She even seems to have Bruno eating out of her hand.

'You know Bruno?' Charlotte asks, when Avril stops to talk to him one day.

'I know everyone.'

Charlotte hasn't really paid much attention to Bruno because she's had her own thing going on, but now that she thinks about it, Bruno and his friends have been far quieter around her. She thought it was because she'd grown up enough to no longer seem vulnerable, but Avril shatters that illusion.

'Oh, don't worry, I didn't do much. I just told him to lay off you.'

'Uh, thanks. I think,' Charlotte says. 'So, how come he listens to you?'

'Charlotte, my lovely, you'll learn that everyone listens to me.'

Charlotte opens her eyes very wide. Avril is astonishing.

After that, Bruno and his sidekicks seem to look at Charlotte around school with new recognition. Bruno even takes her to one side to apologise one day.

'I was a dickhead. And I'm sorry. But you're one of us, now.'

That doesn't make any sense to Charlotte. Rufus and Felix are equally contrite.

'Whatever.' Charlotte really isn't very interested in them anymore. Up close, Bruno isn't nearly as attractive as she once thought he was. Besides which, her senses in that department have been somewhat dulled. She no longer feels as if she has a choice. Dardan and Afrim choose men for her, and she does what she's told. And in that world of men that she now inhabits at the weekend, Bruno's just a child in comparison.

Under Avril's 'business plan', Charlotte is no longer collected by Danny. Instead Rufus takes her out and she spends the next two Saturdays at the house which she comes to know as the chicken farm. It's no longer an *actual* chicken farm, but that's what it was, apparently, until a few years ago, when the farmer sold up to the gang. It's another location run by Afrim and Dardan.

'That farmer thought he was selling it to some dumb Londoner who wanted to turn it into a cheese farm,' Afrim laughs.

It's a secluded location, surrounded by barns. It's been left to look like a working farm, despite there only being a few cows in a barn who act, Charlotte learns, as cover. They are poorly looked after, but not so poorly as to draw attention from the RSPCA. The girls, like Charlotte, and the paying guests, are brought in in vans and minibuses, picked up by drivers. Business is brisk in the run-up to Christmas. All the passengers are asked to wear blindfolds so that they don't know exactly where they are.

'Adds to the thrill,' Afrim adds.

Her new chicken-farm name, aside from The Cutting Girl, is Sally-Anne.

'To protect your identity,' Avril explains.

Charlotte is shocked and embarrassed to discover that Bruno and Felix, as well as Rufus, are all part of the driving team. She wonders how someone like Bruno, who seems to have everything going for him – rich, confident, good-looking – could ever have been drawn into something like this. She barely understands how it has happened to her.

Avril, who continues to treat Charlotte as if they're best friends, explains it to her.

'Girl, they're the easiest of the lot. I mean, if they were that bright, they wouldn't be at Hickman's in the first place, would they?'

It stings, but it's another home truth. Charlotte has always felt behind at school, her whole life, or at least back when she cared about things like that, but before the drugs, she didn't feel out of her depth in the classroom at Hickman's. Perhaps there was a reason for that.

'Don't be so naive. It was easy to turn Bruno and his friends. They were perfect. They were perfect because they were nice boys, who speak well and do as they're told, but who wanted so desperately to be seen as rebellious. They were thirsting to show the world just what rebels they were! I didn't have to do very much more than show an interest in them; pretend to like their music.'

Charlotte thinks back, ruefully, to how besotted she'd been by Bruno at the start of last term. Was it only a term ago? How was it possible for so much in her life to have changed so dramatically in that time? She realises, suddenly, how fragile everything is.

'I mean, I did my homework,' Avril continues, enjoying the powerful role in which she casts herself in her story. 'I made sure I bumped into them out and about in town, made sure they saw me with the right people.'

'The right people?'

'Clothes, money, swagger. It's easily done.'

As Avril talks, Charlotte realises that she may as well be telling the same story about her. She was hooked in, first by Danny, in exactly the same way that they have been.

'It was perfectly obvious that they were virgins,' she laughs, 'so I sorted that out straight away by arranging for them to come to one of my brother's parties.'

'Your brother?'

'Tut, tut. Always so slow on the uptake, aren't you? Yes, my brother. Dardan is my brother.'

'What? But you're not even the same nationality! Isn't he, like, Albanian or something?' Charlotte has heard him talking to Afrim in a different language. 'I thought you were Italian, not Albanian.'

'Well, that's what I tell everyone. It's what the school thinks, too. It makes life easier. Not everything is what it seems.'

Charlotte tries to process this. No wonder Avril is able to 'do business' if she's related to Dardan.

'So – a few parties for Bruno and his little friends, a few drugs, then a few jobs for good money. It doesn't take much. Then they were owned by the gang. Like you are.'

Charlotte can see it all. She is sickened by it. It would have been 'perfectly obvious' that she was a virgin, too. Is that what Danny saw? It's all so fucked up. And by the fact that none of the adults around her have any inkling that any of this is going on here. How would Sarah and Martin feel if they knew what was happening in their little school? It seems hilarious that they're worried about 'diet' and learning, when they should have been worried about drugs, gangs and prostitution.

As if reading her mind, Avril says, 'It's the dream when a gang can infiltrate a private school with boarders. Most of the staff are clueless, the pupils are unchaperoned and the schools are terrified of reputational damage.'

In all the conversations that Martin has had with her mother and father, Charlotte knows that protecting Hickman's has been the priority for her headmaster.

'Those boys all have their own cars, and parents who are… elsewhere. So they drive up and down the country for my brother. All through the night. Hundreds of miles, doing deliveries. They *totally* know they're owned.'

'I don't understand why they don't do anything. Tell someone,' Charlotte says miserably. But even as she says the words, she knows the answer.

'They started out thinking that they were special,' Avril smiles, sweetly. 'That's how grooming works. Now they know they're owned. They're too scared to make a false move and they could never say anything because they couldn't bear the shame – and they all love their families.' Avril pauses. 'Just as you do.'

Charlotte is struggling to process the scale of the whole enterprise. But instead of understanding that she has been groomed in exactly the same way, Charlotte thinks that all

Avril's confidences and revelations mean that their friendship has grown even closer.

'There are plenty of people out there – men – with money, who want to pay for a good time. Girls, drink, drugs. An afternoon at the chicken farm can cost the right person a whole lot of money. The illicit nature of it all just adds to the thrill for the punters.'

With Avril's explanation, lots more falls into place. But Charlotte is in too deep now for it to stop her turning up on a Saturday for work at her new job. Anyway, she owes too much money after one of the packages she was entrusted with went missing. Dardan is turning a blind eye as long as she continues to work, which is really generous of him, because it was a lot of money.

Danny and his little crew are history. In fact, it turns out that Danny has been arrested.

'Part of his deal,' Avril says. 'To do time. Oh, don't worry. He'll be paid for his stint. That's how it works.'

Bruno stays away from Charlotte; Rufus has been allocated as her new driver. At school they pretend to be in the early stages of a relationship and are allowed to go out together on a Saturday. Rufus drives her to the car park where she gets out, buys something in the shop, then leaves and gets into the van. All the 'work clothes' are kept at the chicken farm. After the girls shower, put their clothes back on and drink water, they are bundled back into the van and dropped off at various spots. Avril often waits with Rufus and always has a frappuccino waiting for Charlotte. Like a good friend.

Around school, Charlotte's behaviour is ever more volatile and unpredictable.

More meetings.

'We need to get this sorted before the end of term. I've spoken to the GP. I've told him that Charlotte needs to increase her dose,' Kirsty says. 'To help her regulate better in the classroom.'

So typical of her mother. Throw money at a problem or medicate it.

But the increased dose, combined with the increased amount of cocaine she has consumed for the last couple of weeks at the chicken farm, is having a strange effect. The cutting is increasing. The more she cuts, the more in demand with the men at the chicken farm she seems to be.

'Don't ask me why, but they like it. They like you,' Avril says.

During a video meeting with her parents in the final week of term, Charlotte sits, spaced out with a bland smile plastered onto her face. She no longer feels anything. She can't remember a time when she did feel. It's like a part of her has been completely shut down. She is numb, anaesthetised. She can see her mother's lips moving on the screen, but isn't registering the words.

'Whoopsie? Are you listening? I said that the family holiday has already been booked, darling. We're all going to the Canary Islands for Christmas. It will make up for not seeing you at half-term. Mummy and Daddy are so looking forward to seeing our little Whoopsie Daisy Doo.'

Charlotte can't even remember who that person was.

But her father looks excited about the trip.

'We'll all be back together,' James says.

'With the three bears!' finishes Kirsty.

Her brothers. Charlotte has barely thought about them. But the holiday itself is a big problem. Not only does Charlotte not want to go, but Avril and Dardan want Charlotte to work a New Year's Eve party. She won't be able to get out of it.

'I want to be back home for New Year,' Charlotte declares to her parents. 'I'm only going if I can be back for New Year. There's a party.'

'No problem, darling. We all want to be back in the UK for the New Year. Your brothers all have parties to go to, as do we. I love that you have made friends that you want to be with over the holiday,' Kirsty gushes. 'That's wonderful.'

On the last weekend of term, Charlotte has a break from the chicken house. Instead, Avril takes Charlotte shopping and helps her choose some beach and pool wear that doesn't reveal her cuts too much. She has left the cuts on her arms alone for a while so they look more like old scars.

'But definitely no bikinis for you with that tummy!'

Charlotte's torso is covered in cuts and scars. They manage to find all-in-one swimsuits that cover the tops of Charlotte's thighs and the deep cuts she has made around her crotch. Avril pays for all the clothing.

The end of term is a flurry of packing and excitement, and plans and goodbyes.

'I guess it's time to say goodbye,' Kirst says on the final day.

Charlotte nods curtly, but doesn't offer anything more. Sharing a room has been awkward since their row after half-term. They've barely acknowledged one another.

'Right then, I'll make tracks.'

'Yep, you do that.'

'I got you something,' Kirst says, placing a small gift bag near Charlotte's pillow. 'As a farewell gift.'

Charlotte nods once more.

Kirst looks back one last time from the door. 'Look after yourself, Lotts.'

Once she's gone, Charlotte reaches for the bag. Inside is a

teddy, just like Kirst's teddy bear, Mushroom. The little card with it says, *Something to remember me by* and Kirst has signed it off with a kiss. Charlotte wishes suddenly that she had been nicer to Kirst. That she had listened to her warnings. That she had been a better friend.

Charlotte reaches for Gertie and the new teddy and sits on top of her bed, crying silent tears. She holds on tightly to both toys, remembering the two little girls who arrived here at the end of the summer and introduced their teddies to one another. How did everything go so wrong?

XIII

'Well, isn't that my little sister all grown up,' Henry says when he sees Charlotte at the airport. They've all travelled from different locations to converge at London Gatwick for the flight to Tenerife.

Charlotte has already had enough of being 'Whoopsie' and 'Daddy's little flower.' If only Daddy knew what his daughter had really been up to for the last couple of months.

'You look… good, I think,' her older brother says, but he hesitates and frowns.

'You *think*? Charming! You really know how to make a girl feel special.'

'Oh and sass, too. Where's that come from?'

'I think Whoopsie is finally embracing teenage life,' Kirsty laughs. 'I think that school's been good for you,' she says. 'I agree with Henry. You have grown up. You're definitely losing some of that puppy fat too.'

On the plane he tells her that she seems different. 'But I can't quite put my finger on why.'

'It's the hair,' Charlotte assures him. 'I've gone blonder.'

'Ye-es,' says Henry, but he doesn't seem convinced. His brothers soon distract him with a round of drinks, 'because the sun is over the yardarm somewhere,' Edward says, as though it's an original observation.

The hotel is exclusive and has its own private beachfront area, though most of the time the family converges around the pool, eschewing the black sand for poolside sun-loungers and cocktails on tap. Charlotte arranges her outfits carefully, wearing a sarong over her new swimwear, avoiding getting in the pool and covering her shredded ankles with a towel, 'so I don't get sunburn.'

It's Henry who notices her clothing, too. 'Why are you so covered up?'

'Why do you care?'

'I just think it's weird that my sister is the only teenage girl in the area not in a bikini apart from the two gender fluid girls over there.'

'And I think it's weird that you want to see your sister in a bikini,' Charlotte says, attempting to fob him off.

'You just don't belong to that brigade. You're not one of those with cropped hair wearing denim shorts and T-shirts.'

'How do you know what brigade I belong to? And why does everything always have to have a military flavour. What is it with this family?'

'Alright, keep your hair on.'

'Anyway, you know how much I burn. I'm not blessed with your dark skin. I got mother's Scottish version, remember?'

Her mother has always been so perfect and untouchable that Charlotte delights in seizing on the one thing she can have a dig at her about.

'Well, you can blame our mother for lots of things, but that's hardly her fault.'

'I blame her for everything.'

'Ouch. Look, forget all that. Just come and play with us in the pool.'

'Sod off.'

'Come on, Charlotte,' Edward echoes.

Charlotte only turns over on her sunlounger. It's easy to resist the calls to join her brothers in the pool for water polo. Their invitations are only half-hearted anyway; they're used to her not joining in.

Later, when he's had a couple of drinks, Henry tries to talk to his sister again.

'Look, Whoops, what's going on?'

'Don't call me that.' Charlotte's tone is sharp.

'Don't get mad, but I saw some of your cuts when you were by the pool. I know you're trying to hide them. You won't talk to me so I asked Mum what was going on. She told me that you're now on Prozac because you're struggling at school.'

Kirsty walks past at that moment, her expensive scent filling the night air. 'Whoopsie's always struggled with being the baby in the family, haven't you, darling?'

'So let's all stop calling her Whoopsie, or our little mistake. Her name is Charlotte.'

It's the first time her brother has defended her so vehemently. Six months ago she'd have been delighted. Perhaps now it's too little too late.

A wave of guilt appears to wash over her mother's face. Hearing those words from Henry actually seems to have hit her like a hammer. Charlotte watches as she orders a double gin and tonic and sits in silence for a moment.

Good, thinks Charlotte. *Chew on that for a while, why don't you?*

In the morning, she overhears Kirsty talking to James. What Henry said really does seem to have hit home.

'I think Henry's right. Our use of Whoopsie and referring to her as a *mistake* is stopping right now. We've all been guilty of it.'

Kirsty, who has always liked to fiddle and fix Charlotte's hair, now tries to cuddle her and be as physically close as she can be.

Charlotte pushes her away.

Again, Henry intervenes. 'You're freaking her out! Just act normally and use her actual name. Respect her space. She's not a little girl anymore. How hard is it?'

If only they knew what was really going on.

Charlotte's new predilection for coke and weed scratches away at her on holiday. Because it's an all-inclusive resort, when her parents aren't looking she is at the free bar ordering drinks for herself, and survives by keeping her alcohol levels topped up.

She doesn't know what to think or how to feel. On the one hand, she wants to be enjoying this time with her family – included for once, and almost the centre of attention. She likes her brother's protection and the elevated status it seems to have brought within the family dynamic for the first time. On the other hand, it's boring. There are moments when she very much wants to be back with Avril and all the 'excitement' of her role at the chicken farm. Her need for a hit of some kind is huge. Tenerife is hot. There is nothing to do. Her family are no fun. She is grumpy.

'She's touchy,' Edward says, of his sister.

'She's itching for a party,' Oliver decides. 'Teenage boredom.'

'And you'd know,' Henry jokes, 'being a teenager yourself.'

The banter carries on as Henry and Oliver now start sparring. But Charlotte knows that Henry isn't entirely convinced. At times he becomes her shadow, appearing beside her when she least expects it and sometimes making her jump. Once she drops a drink because he appears suddenly beside her lounger when she is distracted and thinking about Avril.

'Butterfingers,' he says, but there is no mistaking the frown of concern on his face.

The week passes. At the airport he watches his sister when they are all seated in the departure lounge.

'Keep your leg still,' he says. 'I can't concentrate on reading my book with your incessant twitching. What's the matter?'

'Sorry.'

Her leg stills, but only for a minute, then the twitching starts up again.

She puts her phone in her bag and reaches for the other one she keeps in the side pocket. It's a quick manoeuvre, just to see if there is a message from Avril about New Year's Eve, but perhaps she isn't quick enough. She worries that Henry has spotted it. Her big brother isn't daft. If he knows she's got two phones he'll definitely suspect that something's up.

She smiles at him and firmly zips up her bag, nestling back into her chair as if she's perfectly relaxed and carefree at the end of a week of summer sun. She fiddles with her fingers, spinning them round and round each other on her lap, before realising that, too, probably gives her away.

Her pale skin is a tiny bit more tanned after the week of sunshine, but it's still the same skin, and still the same wreck inside.

XIV

Back at home, Henry is staying around for a few days and offers to take Charlotte to the New Year party.

'That's really sweet of you Henry, but honestly there's no need to take me all the way. A lift to the station would be great though.'

Henry becomes the teasing big brother once more. 'Does your friend live in a tent? Is that why you don't want me to meet her?'

'Of course not.'

'What's her name?'

'Avril.'

'I see. In that case, she must be a princess – Princess Avril – and you're so ashamed of me and you don't want your princess friend to see us?'

'Nope, nothing like that.' Here she manages to pull a blinder. 'I'm just so pleased that I'm finally being called Charlotte and not Whoopsie – so I want to sit quietly on the train and read my book.' She holds up a copy of *Rock Paper Scissors* by Alice Feeney.

'Since when did you become a reader?'

'I took a leaf out of your book on holiday.'

While she is packing to go, her mum comes into her bedroom and goes straight for the hair-stroke move. 'Darling, bleaching hair can make it so dry, and that bit of sun causes havoc, so why don't I give you this?'

Kirsty hands her an incredibly expensive hair serum from Switzerland. Alongside it are a bag of other products. 'The very best on the market, worth a small fortune!'

Charlotte, who still firmly believes that Avril is her friend, decides that these items will make a great present for Avril, and that makes her feel happy inside.

Kirsty gives her a hug and James comes in to kiss the top of her head.

'Well done, darling. Happy New Year. This one's going to be better, yes?'

On the way to the station, Charlotte confides to Henry that she's stolen a bottle of vodka from their parents' drinks cabinet.

'Well, who hasn't done that?' Henry says, conspiratorially. 'Though I'm not sure about the vaping, Sis. I don't want to get all parenty about it, but it's not very good for you. Lay off it a bit, yeah?'

'Like you never!'

'I never! Wouldn't want anything to interfere with my sport.'

'No, of course not. Thanks for the lift.'

'Stay safe, Kiddo. Don't do anything I wouldn't do.'

Yet again, Charlotte thinks, if only you knew the half of it. She is nothing like the 'kiddo' that her brother believes her to be.

Avril meets Charlotte at the station. 'Looking good, girl.'

They are heading to a different location, not the chicken farm but another property, to get ready first. 'One of Dardan's properties. Just a place we use for business,' Avril says. 'Because this party is a really special occasion.'

When they reach the house, Avril has already prepared a healthy meal for Charlotte to eat on arrival.

'I'm not hungry,' Charlotte says.

'Eat,' Avril insists. 'This is going to be different from the Saturdays you've done before, although you may recognise some of the men. It's going to be a long night, and you're going to need to keep your strength up. You're going to be on duty, working until 3am, which is when the guests will leave.'

Though Charlotte has little appetite for food these days, she does as she is asked and eats as much of the plate of chicken and vegetables as she can force down.

Avril has also prepared the outfit that Charlotte is to wear: a very glamorous red evening dress which is all laid out waiting for her. Charlotte fingers the expensive fabric. 'This is different.'

'Like I said, this is a special occasion. And this is just the first of your outfits for this evening. Only the top quality for you, Charlotte. And we want you to be looking your best. We know that you are very much sought after by some of the men.'

Yes, the sickos who have a particular taste for young, scared girls, thinks Charlotte. But she knows that she has no choice.

'You have two appointments this evening, very well paid. Clients who have asked for you, specially. There is a bonus for the New Year. Each session will earn you £500. That's a grand in a single night.'

Still without a full allowance, Charlotte is excited by the idea of beginning her new year with £1,000 in her pocket. And even if she wasn't, there is no longer any choice. She showers and puts on a bathrobe, and Avril helps her to prepare.

'So, you'll begin the evening in this red dress. I think I've got the sizing just right. Your hair with a little wave in it, and some bright red lipstick. Here,' Avril says and hands her a brand new lipstick in gold packaging to try. As if they are ordinary teenagers getting ready for a night out, when the reality is they are anything but.

'It's a big party this evening. A very special event. There are 20 girls on tonight and you will all start in evening wear. There is a grand feast to start: Lola is on the menu. I don't know if you've met Lola?'

Charlotte shakes her head. The name isn't familiar.

'She's the starter. The men will help themselves to food from her body.'

The shock Charlotte feels must show on her face, because Avril shrugs, 'Well, like I keep telling you, it's a special occasion. What's the matter? Are you sad that you haven't been chosen?'

Charlotte isn't sad, just uneasy, and a little bit creeped out by visualising what Avril has just described. This feels like a sick step up from the chicken farm.

'Never mind. I don't think it would be terribly hygienic if it was The Cutting Girl they were eating from, do you? They are allowed to touch her but no funny business. It does get them nice and aroused though. A couple of lines of coke, and then it's time for the parade, which is you! That's what the evening wear is for. You all walk in – nice and seductive, like Dardan has shown you. It's all for show, though; they've already selected which girls they want.'

'Okay.'

'And then the *piece de resistance*. Later there is an auction for mystery girls. Five girls will be in full black bondage, faces and heads covered so that there's the allure of the unknown. They bid blind for a girl. Lucky you. You will be one of the girls because, if they are still able to see after the drink and coke, they will be able to detect it's you. The bumps from the lovely scars across your torso are like braille; they'll want to touch you and you will be their prize.'

Charlotte shivers.

'Oh yes, The Cutting Girl is very much sought after!'

'Avril, I'm not sure about – all this.'

'Don't be ridiculous. It's all planned. You will go upstairs with the first man at 9pm for one hour. He wants a schoolgirl.'

'Right, so that's me then?'

'That's right. So, after the parade is complete, you will change into this.' She holds up a red tartan skirt and tight white top that wouldn't look out of place in a Britney Spears video. 'And don't forget the socks.' She holds up a pair of long white socks.

'So, is this outfit chosen for me because I'm the youngest here tonight?' Charlotte asks, doubtfully.

'You are one of the young ones, but no, you're not the youngest tonight.'

'Don't tell me. I don't want to know.'

It's just not possible that someone even younger than her should be subjected to all this. For the first time in a long time Charlotte feels sick and more than a little bit scared. There is no fun here. What was she thinking when she told her parents she needed to be back in time for this? It's not just perverse, it's depraved. It's fucked up. She no longer feels cool and worldly-wise. She feels 'owned'. Charlotte can't believe that there was any part of her that felt bored by the pool in Tenerife. Now that she's here she feels the contrast of being safe with her family acutely. Why didn't she listen to Henry? She'd love to be back there right now. Why did she ever want to come back to this?

'I don't want to. It doesn't feel right.'

Avril gives her a look.

'Girl, you know feelings don't come into this. And you know

better than me how much you have to protect your family's name.'

When Avril first started calling her 'girl' it sounded empowering. Now it just feels belittling. Charlotte feels trapped and afraid. This has gone too far. She wants out.

But Avril is too clever and too experienced to let her escape. She looks at Charlotte and says, 'You *will* do this, and you will do it well, you understand?' Avril grips her wrist and hurts her. 'And you know what will happen if you don't.'

There is no more argument.

The third outfit Avril holds up is red leather. 'Red evening dress, then schoolgirl outfit, then red leather. Three costumes altogether. Someone will be there to help you dress.' Avril packs the outfits into a black, zipped sports backpack, showing Charlotte that there are also stockings and a dressing gown. 'Each girl is supplied with a gown that they can move about in after the first appointment,' Avril explains.

Before they leave, Charlotte snorts a very long, thick line of cocaine. It feels good. And necessary. It's raw and energising. She's missed that while she's been away. She has another wrap of coke in the backpack for later. In the car it's dark, and the police are not patrolling the country lanes on New Year's Eve.

After that, the evening is a blur. Charlotte looks out for younger girls but doesn't see them. There are helpers to get Charlotte changed into other clothes at the right time. Some of the men are violent and rough with the girls as their bruises attest, but that's all part of the deal.

She recognises Afrim's voice during the auction, by which time she and the others are off their faces with drugs. The men are rowdy and wild.

'Oh yes, they're in high spirits tonight,' Avril says, pushing

Charlotte forward at the right moment as Afrim performs his auctioneer role.

Standing on a makeshift stage, Charlotte can't even see the four other girls with her because her head is covered, but she can hear the whimpering of the girl to her right. She sounds young. Charlotte knows she is number four in the line. When Afrim begins his patter, one man, whose voice sounds remarkably like Dardan's, calls out, 'Is that The Cutting Girl?'

The auctioneer says, 'You know the rules. I can't say.'

There is lewd laughter. Charlotte blocks out the numbers and the noise around her until she is led off by the highest bidder.

XV

On New Year's Day, Charlotte wakes up in a strange bed. It takes her a moment to realise where she is: it's the big house where Avril took her to get ready before the party. She hurts, inside and out, and can smell her own stale sweat. She remembers very little. She is just glad that it's all over. There is no fresh start for the new year, just more pain.

Avril bustles in and passes her the dressing gown from the night before. 'Put this on and get up. Time for breakfast.'

There are other girls sleeping in the house and Avril wakes them up, too. Charlotte feels hungover and exhausted. And… just empty. She is a shell.

When she drags herself down to the breakfast table, six or seven other girls are sitting around, wearing the same satin dressing gowns. They look like a strange, sad little club. Charlotte doesn't know where the rest of them are − if there were indeed 20 here last night − and she doesn't recognise any of the faces. They acknowledge each other, but not all of them are English. There are a mix of accents and languages at the table.

There is a buffet to choose from, as if they are in a smart hotel, but no one seems to have much of an appetite. Charlotte tries to ask one of the girls if she has seen a younger child. The girl holds her finger up to her lips in warning, waits until Avril has turned her back and mouths, 'Children's Home.' Charlotte isn't sure she's heard correctly, or what that might mean, but there is no opportunity to find out more. Avril makes sure that they all keep firmly off the subject of last night.

After breakfast they are directed to shower and then to dress back in their own clothes, returning the outfits and evening dresses to the lounge.

Avril sorts out the pile.

'What happens to that lot?' Charlotte asks her.

'I'll launder what I can and send the rest to the dry cleaners. This Cinderella doesn't go to the ball!'

But Charlotte is not in the mood for jokes or levity. The other girls leave during the morning.

'We'll stay here in the house for a few days,' Avril explains. 'Until term starts again. Much nicer here than at Hickman's, hey? More freedom!'

The irony is that Charlotte has never felt less free. Avril makes sure that Charlotte contacts her parents and her brothers, but is always in the room when she Facetimes or calls.

'How was the party, darling?'

'Eye-opening,' Charlotte says, which is the truth.

Charlotte's regular phone is held by Avril in between the contacts, and Charlotte knows better than to question the arrangement. It seems perfectly normal just to hand it over. She has plenty of time to herself: to think, to heal.

In the evenings she stays in her room, or takes a long bath. Sometimes she creeps out to the landing where she hears fragments of conversations, but they're meaningless. Sometimes there's no English spoken at all. Just husky voices and the smell of weed wafting up the stairs.

Charlotte is booked in for a health check-up. 'Well, we've got to make sure that we're looking after you, haven't we?'

On Saturday, The Cutting Girl, or Sally-Anne, is required for work at the chicken farm as usual. Working back at the chicken farm again seems like no big deal after New Year's Eve. It's routine, just work. She manages to sober up and be back with Avril for dinner and then, the following week, they are back at school ready for the start of the new term. Or at least as ready as Charlotte can be under the circumstances.

Avril continues to be brilliant at keeping her school profile discreet. She has mock exams in January and performs well. She is clever. She is even presented with some sort of history award in assembly and has to go up and collect a shield from Martin while everyone in the hall applauds. She hangs out with 'safe' girls during the day but always makes sure that she has time for Charlotte. It used to feel friendly. Now it feels threatening, as if Avril is ever-present.

Charlotte herself just about manages not to cause too much concern to her teachers. The laptop calls from Switzerland continue, and are stepped up when Sarah reports to Kirsty that she believes Charlotte's cutting has increased and she has a tendency towards volatile mood swings. She has thrown a book at a teacher and upturned a desk on separate occasions. It's not the sort of behaviour they are used to seeing at Hickman's.

Kirsty and James are disappointed.

'What a shame after our lovely holiday!'

They discuss the possibility that Charlotte may have some sort of personality disorder.

'That would account for the strange or unpredictable behaviour. Can we get her a referral for that?'

Kirsty has done some Googling: 'Suspicion and distrust, taking risks, extreme mood swings or emotional outbursts, the need for instant gratification, difficulty with relationships, problems at school or work. I mean, it's classic, isn't it? We need some specialist intervention here.'

But, even with all the money that they have, there are still waiting lists.

On weekends, when Charlotte isn't at the chicken farm, there are other gang duties to perform. She is often out with Rufus, checking up on their little recruits from the lower years at school. One Friday, they sit in Rufus' car, parked on the High Street in town, watching one of their boys, Drake, a little lad from France. He hangs around by the post office door as instructed, until a shiny new black Porsche drives up. The window on the driver's side is wound down and Drake leans in to hand over his package. A hand comes back out and Drake pockets the cash. For a second, she catches a glimpse of the driver. It looks remarkably like Lia's father, though she's only met him a couple of times, very briefly.

When the Porsche drives off, Drake scoots over and hands the cash straight to Rufus who hands it to Charlotte. She puts it in a blue cloth bag and shoves it under her seat. She remembers the first time she was out with Danny and all this was going on but she didn't realise the details of what was actually happening. Now it's all become second nature. Everyone knows exactly where they are in the chain of command and what it is they have to do.

Drake is not the only little runner from the school. Avril is a master at running her operations and does her research meticulously. What she is after is kids with families that are dysfunctional or absent. Ideally abroad. The psychology is simple but so effective: find a vulnerable child, circle around them, separate them from the pack and start the grooming work to turn them against the people who care about them. It all happens under the nose of Martin and Sarah. Sarah seems to know that something is up, but can never quite put her finger on it. How could she? Avril covers her tracks perfectly.

Charlotte's behaviour continues to be erratic. She swears at teachers who are trying to be nice to her and smashes a test tube in a science lesson. Kirsty's persistence results in the dose of her meds being increased – again.

Charlotte feels nothing. She uses words like 'empty', 'numb' and 'zombie' to describe her emotions when Sarah tries to ask her how she is.

Saturdays are spent working at the chicken farm. There are different men. She loses count. Some she recognises. The other girls working there change frequently; they come and go and are never there long enough to become friends.

One of Charlotte's 'usuals' is Peter. He comes most weeks and pays for the privilege of spending two uninterrupted hours with Charlotte, The Cutting Girl. He's kind of a weird one, but Charlotte doesn't mind. He likes her to sit on his lap while he runs his fingers over her scars. Sometimes he wants to rock her like a baby, or hold her face and stroke her hair while asking, 'What's wrong, Sally-Anne?' Charlotte doesn't mind her chicken farm name. At least it helps her to feel that everything that is happening is happening to someone else, not her. Sometimes Peter cries real tears. But it's all sexual, because he gets off on it and after he has come he likes to rock her some more.

Charlotte no longer questions what is asked of her. She is beyond finding anything weird. She just gets on with it, thinks of the money and tries not to do anything to upset Avril. Because, as caring as Avril seems, you don't want to get on the wrong side of her. Charlotte hears her speak to one of the eastern European girls one day. Well, not just speak, she shouts at her and then, from out of nowhere, whacks her hard across the face.

'You never, ever try anything like that again. Do you hear me?'

Charlotte doesn't know what the 'anything like that' is and doesn't want to. She understands a lot of what goes on, but so much is also hidden – like the younger girl at the New Year's Eve auction.

The pincer-cold of January and February starts to release its grip and sun appears in the sky some days as the year edges towards spring. There might be more light, but the nights still feel long, dark and heavy, an invitation to hibernate. Charlotte is due to sit a round of mock exams and veers between feeling insanely anxious about them, and then completely numb and empty. She knows she'll fail the exams. She doesn't have the capacity to think. It could be due to her work, the drugs, the meds, or just being Charlotte. Who knows?

The Peter thing has grown. He seems to have developed quite an attachment to Charlotte, but it isn't the worst thing in the world. He's one of the nicer ones. He's clean and doesn't smell bad, and there's a lot to be said for that. He's always kind. His sexual behaviour is soft and gentle and it's all over quite quickly. She needs to 'perform' a bit, but it's all straightforward. He just likes her to lean into him when he is coming and do a little bit of whimpering.

Until one Saturday that changes.

Charlotte must have said something that upset him. Although it also seems to coincide with finding out that she is really called Charlotte. He has always called her 'Sally-Anne', but it's Avril who slips and refers to her as Charlotte within his earshot.

'Charlotte?' He frowns.

Charlotte freezes. Perhaps he knows her father. He looks the type. Has Charlotte ever seen him before? It's impossible to tell. Hundreds of faceless suits have appeared at her parents' parties and gatherings. Charlotte never even listens to the names. Although it's highly likely that his name isn't 'Peter' anyway. After that Saturday, he doesn't return. Somehow, that is Charlotte's fault.

'You must have upset him,' Avril accuses. 'Be more careful in future!'

Charlotte spends the evenings in her room at the school. Following Kirst's departure, she is yet to be assigned another roommate. Perhaps Hickman's admissions are down. Or perhaps they don't want anyone to share with her. There is just the empty bed as a constant reminder of how empty she feels. It's dark and lonely at night with just Gertie and Fred as her only friends.

It has taken a little while to realise it, but Charlotte is finally coming to terms with the realisation that Avril is not her friend. That she is, actually, scared of Avril. More scared of Avril than of Dardan or Afrim. She does exactly what Avril says. As do Bruno and Rufus. And, unlike Charlotte, they have perfected the art of behaving normally at school.

Alone, Charlotte is like a ghost. She feels invisible, and as if she doesn't belong to the 'real' world of Hickman's. She is a shell with nothing inside. She spends hours cutting her stomach and groin to see if there are any feelings anywhere in her body. It is harder and harder to find them.

Sometimes she sits on the floor with her knees pulled up, shivering, unable to understand what has happened to her. She has no one to talk to. She can't talk to Avril anymore. Instead, she fears her. Who knows who else is under Avril's control?

Charlotte is paranoid and it wouldn't surprise her to learn that even the teachers are working for Avril. Everyone else seems to be. Unlike Charlotte, Avril can get out of the school whenever she wants. How is she able to do that? She is even reported to be a good mentor for the younger students, befriending some and taking them under her wing. It's beyond belief. The powers that be in the school see Avril as a good student and a decent person. She seems to be able to play everyone, deceive everyone. How can no one see what she is?

It seems monstrous, but Charlotte is too tired and depressed to fight it. Sometimes, when she cries, she can't make any tears because she is all dried up inside and there is nothing left to feel, not a thing. She thinks of her family and wonders again why they never really wanted her. The only one that is the tiniest bit interested in her is Henry, and he is busy with his life.

Night after night, day after day, there is only sadness.

XVI

Sarah continues to express her concerns about Charlotte's wellbeing at every opportunity. Charlotte's replies, as always, are non-committal. Sarah appeals to Kirsty and James in their online meeting.

'Things are going downhill. But I'm convinced that increasing her meds again isn't the answer. In fact, I think it might be a big part of the problem.'

Of course, Charlotte is a 'problem'. As she has always been. What else would she be?

She suggests to Kirsty and James that they push again for Charlotte to see a counsellor or therapist.

'We're doing everything we can here, and nothing is working. She's losing too much weight. Her hair is lank and dry. I know that she's cutting, although she won't let me see and she won't let me help. I'm walking on eggshells around her. All the staff are. I don't think she's coping and it's very distressing to witness. She is a shadow of what she was. It's as if she's disappearing into herself.'

'So what do we do about it?'

As ever, they are talking about her as if she isn't there. And really, in some ways, she isn't. The words wash over her.

'Are you sure there's nothing else going on?' Sarah asks Kirsty.

'I should ask the same question of you, since you are responsible for her during term time,' Kirsty snaps.

What would happen now, if she told them? What if she explained what went on at the chicken farm every weekend, or what happens on the evenings that she drives around with Rufus?

But she can't.

Because that would only get other people into trouble. Rufus' parents are architects and run a small but award-winning practice. They wouldn't cope with knowing what their darling son is up to. Avril knows what she's doing, alright. This is what she and her gang look for: kids from busy successful backgrounds.

The ones who will be given material love but not time. The ones who already have the flash clothes and cars. The ones who've probably gone through life having everything they ever wanted or needed – apart from their parents' attention. No one should underestimate the lengths that a teenager who has suffered from middle class neglect will go to. We are the clean skins, Charlotte thinks, the kids who crave to be rebels, piss off their parents and get their attention. Loneliness and the need to belong are a powerful double-act.

When she is alone in her room there is some respite from Avril. Although she is always on the end of the second phone, there is relief for Charlotte in being out of her physical presence. Until Sarah has a bright idea about trying to help.

'I know that you've had some contact with Avril in the upper sixth. I'd like to build on that and formalise it. Avril is a good student, who has an extremely good track record of working with the lower years. How would you feel if she became your mentor?'

As if there is no escape, are the words that Charlotte is unable to say.

Avril smiles politely when Sarah asks her. 'Oh, I would love to support Charlotte; she is such a nice girl.'

Charlotte sees that this is actually fun for Avril. Avril loves how stupid people are.

It's even worse that James and Kirsty are pleased that she has the support of an older girl. They don't seem to join up the dots and realise that this is the same Avril with whom she was 'partying' on New Year's Eve. Perhaps they are too busy to question it, or perhaps they simply don't think. This is how easy it is for a person to disappear, Charlotte thinks.

'I'm sure she will be a wonderful role model and influence for Charlotte,' Kirsty says.

A wonderful role model who is taking her to work at a sex factory every Saturday.

In one fell swoop, Avril has total power over Charlotte. Now Avril doesn't even have to hide their connection. But actually, Charlotte couldn't care less. She has begun to let go and give up.

Avril's tone is cutting when they're alone in their first mentoring session.

'You're going to have to try harder, Charlotte. At school and at the farm. You are drawing attention to yourself in all the wrong ways. You are no longer a star attraction at the chicken farm.'

'Tastes change. The clientele move on,' Charlotte says, parroting something she has heard the other girls say.

'Indeed. There are some new girls there with different attractions to The Cutting Girl.'

Charlotte knows exactly who Avril is referring to. Hasina is another student at Hickman's, younger than Charlotte, only 12 or 13 years old and from Mombasa. Avril polishes her black skin with baby oil and the bruises barely show. She only goes once a month, a strategy for not raising alarm. Avril gives her ketamine and Hasina says she doesn't remember what happens. The withdrawal takes a few days and just looks like a cold.

'You're going to have to sort yourself out, girl. You don't want to become a liability to the operation. Look at you! You're like a zombie. We've had complaints.'

'My whole life is a complaint,' Charlotte says, miserably.

'Don't answer me back! You can't just lie back and do nothing! The men at the chicken farm expect a performance. They want you to engage and play their games.'

Charlotte's meds, the drugs, the numbness, the lack of feeling anything has made her absolutely distant from what happens. She no longer feels scared or revolted by the men or the gang. She wonders if this is the kind of mentoring her headmaster and Sarah had in mind for her. But Avril does turn the conversation to school.

'It's also part of the deal that you do well at school. We can't attract this level of scrutiny. You have got to make an effort in class. Stay awake, at least. Pay attention. Look alert, even if you don't feel it. I'm warning you, girl.'

During maths on Monday morning, Charlotte feels herself beginning to drift off as the teacher, Mr Chandlers – also known as 'Charlie Macfarlie' – spouts meaningless words about something called matrices that have no place in her warped world. She is powerless to resist the pull of sleep, even though she wills her eyes to remain open. Perhaps if she just lays her head down on top of the desk for a moment it will go unnoticed.

It does not go unnoticed. Macfarlie walks towards Charlotte and puts a gentle hand on her shoulder to wake her. Having been unaware of his approach, her reaction is instinctive and instantaneous.

She jumps up, screaming, 'Get off me, get off me!'

It is out of all proportion to what has just happened and the lesson descends into an ugly scene. 'Fuck off, Charlie,' she yells as she leaves the classroom yet again.

But all this does is create even more of a spotlight on her, becoming the start of a school-wide information-gathering cycle.

Martin explains that he is going to email each of Charlotte's teachers to ask for reports on their thoughts about her wellbeing and behaviour.

Less than 24 hours later she is back in his office.

'I'm going to share the results with you, Charlotte. Every single one of your teachers reports that you seem distracted at best. Some teachers have described you as being bored or out of sorts. In the core subjects there are accounts of rudeness, of not doing homework and prep, and often falling asleep. That wasn't a one-off in maths on Monday. Miss Sevini, in English, says that you sometimes play the class clown. Charlotte, that doesn't sound like you. Something more is going on here. What can you tell me?'

Charlotte is unable to tell her headmaster anything.

There are yet more discussions planned. Martin and Sarah meet with the two deputies who are also safeguarding leads at the school. Charlotte is called in for part of the meeting and asked to wait outside for part of it.

They decide that if she requires this high dosage level of meds that results in such drowsiness and unpredictable behaviour in lessons, then perhaps she should not be attending school at all.

'We think that perhaps being at home with your family, or even at another school that is better able to meet your needs, would be the best thing right now.'

Charlotte, usually impervious to everything around her, almost laughs out loud, knowing full well that there is no such school and that her family's busy careers are hardly going to allow for a little bout of home-schooling.

Martin calls Kirsty first, but does not get a reply. When he calls James there is also no answer straight away, but James sends a message a few minutes later requesting that Martin try again in an hour when he will have finished doing a spot on the 6 O'Clock News.

Martin, Sarah and Charlotte sit in Martin's office drinking tea and watch the interview on Martin's computer.

'He's an impressive man, your father,' Martin comments, biting his lip.

While they wait for James to call them back, they make small talk about their own children.

'Teenage life is difficult, we know that,' Sarah sighs. 'One of our own children is beginning to show signs of behaviour issues. It's a time of change, and it's not always easy to navigate.'

No it isn't, thinks Charlotte, *because nothing changes. Nothing ever changes.*

When James calls, Martin explains that he is putting the call onto speaker so that Sarah can join in the conversation.

'Hi, Martin, hi, Sarah.' James' tone is bright and breezy and he's clearly buzzing after his television appearance. 'What's young Charlotte done? Is she behaving herself?'

Martin begins to tell James the story of the last few days, detailing the ways in which Charlotte's behaviour has declined dramatically since the start of the new term. How she has become unpredictable and irrational and that has made teaching her very difficult.

Sarah talks about how she seems more depressed and vacant. She is not complying with the school rules. 'She won't tell us what's wrong,' Sarah looks directly at Charlotte as she says the words, 'but I'm certain that there's something more to this. Something that we can't yet pinpoint.' She shakes her head. 'Some of the contradictions in her behaviour don't seem to make sense.'

James is quiet on the other end of the phone. Probably

thinking about his diary and how he doesn't have time for this right now, thinks Charlotte.

What comes out is, 'Okay, thanks for calling me and I am so sorry to hear this. What can I do, right now, Martin, to help?'

Sarah pipes up, 'You could come and get her. She clearly wants her family. She has always struggled a little bit with homesickness. I don't think that's ever gone away.'

'Oh, my poor little girl. This is terrible to hear, Charlotte. I'm so sorry that you're feeling this way, but, you know, it's just not possible for me to drop everything right now. I'm just about to push a new bill through on housing and I can't leave London for a few weeks.'

The words wash over Charlotte. It is nothing less than she expected.

Sarah is agitated, though. She gets up from her seat and paces around the desk, around Martin and Charlotte, in circles. Her arms are folded and her face is red. Charlotte sees her mouth to Martin, 'She needs to go home!'

There is an awkward silence. Charlotte has the same feeling of helplessness she had on New Year's Eve, the night of the auction, when strangers were bidding over her. Now it is her family and people she should be able to trust. At least at the auction the men *wanted* her. Here she is just an unwanted burden: for the school and for her family.

James says, 'Um, look, I've got to go back to the House for a vote this evening. Can I call you later tonight, Martin, or perhaps tomorrow after I've had a chance to speak to Kirsty?'

Martin sighs. 'Yes, okay, James. Let's talk then.'

'And Whoops… *Charlotte*, darling, I'll give you another ring later, too, if you've still got your phone when I come out of this damned thing tonight. Bad timing, my darling.'

'Right.' As ever, she is an afterthought. The timing is always bad.

'I'm sorry, Charlotte. I wish we could do more,' Sarah says, with a sad smile.

As they send Charlotte back to her room, Charlotte lingers in the corridor and overhears a little of the conversation that takes place between Sarah and Martin.

Sarah is very cross and wants Charlotte to go home, to be with her family. Martin reminds her that her family are not there, they are not available, 'And, no matter what the website says about academia, we are an expensive 24/7 babysitting service. And, since we're trying to recruit more students while our buildings crumble, we suck it up. It's as simple as that.'

'This is about people: children, not bloody buildings, Martin.'

'But we've got a school to run. The art block is about the only part of the school that's actually up to spec, but that refurbishment wasn't cheap and was a couple of years ago. Hickman's has been boasting about it for two years now with nothing more to add. All our marketing and publicity is based around it, and people will start to see through that. Especially when they see the crumbling shower block and gym.'

'Right now I don't care about the gym. I care about a child.' Sarah's voice has risen.

It takes Charlotte a moment to realise that Sarah is still talking about her. It's a while since Charlotte has thought of herself as a child.

'And I care about our business. We need to invest more money and, after the last trustees meeting and the significant resignation of one of our directors who happens to own a massive construction company, we have to think realistically! Charlotte has problems, yes, of course she does. I'm not denying that. But we can't afford for her to go. And we're doing everything we can for her, aren't we? And, let's face it, Sarah, she's not killing anyone, is she? She's not an absconder, and she's not taking smack.'

Charlotte edges along the corridor, but Sarah has raised her voice so the words keep on coming loud and clear. So, she is less important than a shower block. It's good to know.

'I think putting children on opioids and Prozac is the same as taking heroin, don't you?'

The caretaker comes along the corridor, keys jangling, clearly intent on locking up, so Charlotte remembers to smile at him in a simulation of normal human contact, and scurries back to the dormitory quarters and the solitude of her room.

The last thing she hears is Sarah, screaming, 'I hate this place!'

Me too, thinks Charlotte, *me too.*

At 10pm Charlotte is back in her room when Sarah does her night rounds. There is a knock at the door. Charlotte is standing at the window and turns around when Sarah pushes the door open.

'Time for bed, Charlotte. Come on, you need your sleep.'

Charlotte is cold. She doesn't know how long she has been standing by the window in her sleep shorts and little top.

Despite the dim lighting, fresh cuts are visible at the top of Charlotte's arms. Sarah makes a wincing sound, but doesn't berate Charlotte.

Instead, she says, 'Do you want a hug?'

Charlotte nods slowly, and leans in.

Sarah puts her arms around her and just holds her close in front of the window.

They stand there, moonlight falling into the room, for a long time. Neither speaks.

Charlotte isn't entirely sure who needs the hug more.

XVII

At the end of period six, a dull history lesson on the Cold War that might as well be in a different language for all Charlotte understands of it, she's called to Martin's office once more.

There was a time when Charlotte might have felt nervous and intimidated by a summons to the headmaster, and in terms of days, weeks and months it wasn't that long ago; but her visits have become so routine that she no longer cares. Besides which, at the chicken farm she has encountered a whole different scale of intimidation at the hands of men. Very little that happens at school could faze her now.

'Ah, Charlotte. Thank you for coming to see me. I have some good news,' Martin says.

For a moment, Charlotte registers some tiny flicker of hope. She wonders what 'good news' might actually look like. Whether such a thing actually exists. Perhaps the miracle of miracles is happening and her mother is returning from Switzerland to look after her, or her father is retiring from politics so he can homeschool her.

She looks up at her headmaster expectantly.

'Your father phoned earlier,' he says, and clears his throat.

'Yes?' Charlotte says, eagerly.

'And he wanted to find a way to thank the school. I'll play you his message.'

Why is Martin doing this to her? Her headmaster has the emotional intelligence of a sock! What did she expect? He's a friend of her father. The sinking feeling she knows so well immediately returns.

Martin finds the right voice note on his phone and turns the speaker on. Her father's voice comes through loud and clear.

'Hi Martin, I'm sorry I haven't been able to return your calls today. Choc-a-bloc with constituency business from the word go, I'm afraid. Now, about Charlotte. I'm afraid there is no way that we can drop work to have her back here. You know how it is. But we both recognise that you are all working hard to support our girl, and we're very grateful. A little bird tells me that you are considering plans to improve your gym facilities. You know that we are huge fans of sport and all the good it can do, so would you accept a cheque for £300k to go towards the works? No need to do anything flashy like name the gym after us, but thought you could use the donation in these difficult times. Got to dash, old boy. Keep up the good work.'

Martin ends the recording and looks at Charlotte. Martin is certainly a massive dick but surely even he must realise that she doesn't give a shit about £300k for the stupid school gym.

'That's great,' Charlotte says. 'Just great.' She smiles. It doesn't reach her eyes. She knows exactly what's just happened here: her father effectively just bought her headmaster. Terrific.

The familiar objects in Martin's office: the framed certificate on the wall behind his head, the trophies in the cabinet, the long thin picture of all the pupils in the school from a few years ago, the funny cactus plant on top of the bookcase, all disappear in a wet blur. They might be tears forming. It's hard to tell. It's been a long time since Charlotte has cried.

In the evening, Charlotte sits at the same table as Avril, but they are at opposite ends. Avril is the table steward this evening, which means that her role is to ensure that 'manners are adhered to' and conversation is 'appropriate'. The noise of chatter and knives and forks against plates echoes loudly around the large dining hall, but to her sounds far away. Charlotte finds that she is able to tune it out, like turning down the dial on an old radio. Avril walks around the students carrying a large metal water jug to fill their glasses. When she reaches Charlotte she leans into her. The whisper is loud and clear, 'Check your phone after dinner, and do what I say.'

Charlotte nods. It's a tiny movement that would be barely perceptible to anyone watching. It's as if the exchange hasn't even taken place.

Charlotte has no appetite, but that's nothing new; she rarely does. Dinner is cleared away and students disperse to lounges and bedrooms. Charlotte goes up to her room. She takes a deep breath before she pulls her burner phone from underneath her mattress and reads the short message: *Pack your rucksack. We're going out tonight. Be at the side gate by 8pm.*

A few minutes before the appointed time, Charlotte is in position as directed. There is no part of her that would question a command from Avril these days.

No alarm bells ring when the driver is not Rufus or Bruno. Instead, in the car are two men she has never met before. That seems normal. She is always with strange men. Who cares? It seems to Charlotte as if she doesn't even know who she is. The Cutting Girl no longer feels anything when she cuts herself, so there's no point in doing it anymore. The reason was to *feel*. Even pain was better than nothing. But that no longer works.

She sits in the back of the car, next to one of the men, who introduces himself as Luan. The driver is Kristo. They are both Albanian, like Dardan. She has learned their look, their particular style of black clothing. She doesn't understand a word of Albanian, but she has absorbed its sound patterns and can recognise it. The car smells of cigarettes and weed; again that's nothing new. The car seats are stained and dirty. Like her. The car itself is old, so when she doesn't put her seat belt on there's no warning beep, no reminder to be safe.

She fantasises about dying. She could open the door of this car just as they are on the motorway bridge and jump. She could throw herself in front of a train. The only thing that stops her is that she doesn't even have the energy to do it. And there is one person in her life that she doesn't want to hurt, who always comes into her head whenever she has thoughts like that: Henry, her oldest brother. Over the years he has always been the one to really 'see' her, to take an interest, to care about what she feels. It is his face that is imprinted on her eyelids when she closes her eyes. He is the only bit of good left in her life since Nanny died.

The driver puts on some music and plays it loud, his hands dancing on the wheel as they drive into the night. The man sitting next to Charlotte checks his phone every couple of minutes. He talks to the driver intermittently, occasionally looking across at Charlotte. She has forgotten both of their names. She doesn't understand a word they are saying.

The journey is long. Very long. Too long for a trip to the chicken farm, and too long for a party.

By the time she realises, it's too late.

PART TWO

Hickman's School

I

'I don't like it one bit,' Sarah says.

Already tired, and weighed down by the pressure of the whole Charlotte situation, Sarah argues that they've now effectively been manoeuvred into a corner by James and his 'generous and timely' donation to the upkeep of the school.

'He's done it very cleverly. He knows that we need the money – that *Hickman's* needs the money. But it now means that Charlotte has become entirely *our* problem. Not theirs.'

'I think you're being a bit harsh. James is an old friend. We take his donation in the manner it has been offered; as a thank you for all the work we've put into looking after her.'

Sarah shakes her head. 'Tell yourself that if you want to. If it makes you feel better. If it makes it easier for you to live with yourself. But I'm telling you, I don't like it.'

The conversation, which has been going round in circles, switches to what their next move should be. If they now have even greater responsibility for Charlotte's wellbeing, then they need to get her behaviour under control. At the moment, she's impossible to deal with on a day-to-day basis. They never know quite how she's going to present next; which version of Charlotte is going to turn up in the classroom or around the school site. One minute she's like a zombie, walking the corridors blindly, impervious to everything around her, the next she is manic and abusive, lashing out at teachers and other students over the tiniest thing.

'We've got to do something for her, beyond trying to medicate the problem. Because it can't just carry on,' Sarah says. 'Each day feels like we're fighting just to keep our heads – and hers – above water.'

The 'handover' from James – or what amounts to a relinquishing of parental responsibility according to Sarah – has already translated into putting a huge amount of time and energy into dealing with Charlotte. Perhaps it has also come at the expense of looking after their own family because, to their horror, they suddenly find that they also have their own little domestic crisis going on. They discover that their youngest child, Thomas, has sent a dick pic to an older boy in the school.

'Jesus, Sarah. What do we do about it? An inappropriate picture to an older boy? It's a bloody mess. What do we do? Do we report it?'

'Martin, we can't report our own child. And who are you suggesting that we report him to? The police? Thomas is only 11!'

'I know that. But I need to think about it. I need to work out how to manage this for the best.'

'Thinking isn't going to make it go away,' Sarah snaps, mortified that her own family is involved in something sexually explicit.

'No, but thinking about it will allow me to explore all the options.'

'Well, you sit there and think about it. I'll go and do the nightly rounds.'

Because Charlotte's room is in the boarding house closest to the Whitneys' domestic quarters, it's very close to the end of Sarah's route. When she knocks and there is no answer, she waits a moment before entering. At first, Sarah assumes that Charlotte has just gone to sleep early. It would hardly be surprising given the level of meds she's on, but she goes through the motions of double-checking. She's not falling for it if it's a ruse and it wouldn't be the first time. It's a ploy sometimes used by students who want to hang onto their phones overnight, pretending that they're already asleep when Sarah turns up. It's unlike Charlotte though, because she always relinquishes hers easily. She tiptoes towards the bed, anxious not to wake Charlotte if she has indeed fallen asleep. She knows how badly she has been sleeping lately. But as she nears the bed, there's no rise and fall of breathing. The hump of 'sleeping teenager' is actually made of the pillows from Kirsty's bed.

'Fuck.' Sarah doesn't swear often, but something inside her tells her this is serious. It's not some sort of harmless attempt to have a midnight feast with mates, because Charlotte has no friends to speak of.

Sarah puts down the box of phones she's already collected and uses the torch on her own phone to take a quick look around the other buildings. Perhaps she's wandering the grounds, taking a night-time walk to clear her troubled head.

But deep down, Sarah knows that she won't find her.

After a quick recce, she rushes back into their quarters to let Martin know. 'Charlotte's gone.'

Martin goes white.

'I think we need to call the police,' she stammers.

'Right.' He puts his hand out towards his phone, then hesitates before picking it up. There's so much at stake. 'You've checked everywhere?'

Sarah nods.

'But the police? I don't know. Is that the right call?' He sits down. 'I need to think.'

'You always need to bloody think! Why can't you just act?'

Martin shrugs helplessly.

'I'm sorry. I didn't mean that. I'm just worried. I don't know what to do. Martin, this is bad. She could have done anything. You know how she self-harms.'

'I know. I know. Let's not panic. Let's think this through logically. How long do you think she's been gone for?'

'No idea. She was at dinner. Or at least I think she was. I'm pretty sure I saw her. So, it could have been anytime between the end of dinner and now. That's at least a three-hour window. Maybe a little longer.' Sarah looks at her watch.

'She was, she was at dinner, you're right.' Martin speaks slowly as he mentally recalls the scene. 'She sat on the end of the table nearest to the door and barely spoke to anyone; I watched her sitting in her own little world. Oh, Sarah, this is bad.'

'We know that she leaves Hickman's regularly at weekends. Let's not assume the worst. Let's assume she's headed to wherever she usually goes. Where does she go?'

'Into town?' Martin thinks out loud. 'But there aren't any buses at this time of night. How would she have got there?'

'Could she have started walking? If we assume she left immediately after dinner, even if she was on foot, she could have covered a good few miles in that time. Unless someone picked her up. She had a boyfriend at one stage, didn't she? What if she's gone with him? If she was in a car, she could be anywhere by now.'

Martin runs his fingers through his hair. 'Where do we even begin?'

'If it was planned, rather than spur of the moment, then someone must know. We know that she doesn't seem to have many friends these days. She hangs out with Rufus occasionally, and Avril is her mentor.'

They try Rufus first, running to his dorm where they discover him fast asleep.

Next they dash to Avril's dorm. She is also asleep, but they decide to wake her up.

'If she's confided in anyone, it will be Avril.'

Sarah turns on the light and gently wakes her. She is bleary-eyed and blinks uncomfortably in the light.

'Avril, we're so sorry for disturbing you like this, but I hope you'll forgive me when you understand why. This is an emergency. We need to talk to you about Charlotte. Did you see her at dinner this evening?'

Avril frowns and makes a show of thinking back over the evening. 'Ye-es,' she says uncertainly, then nods with greater conviction. 'Yes, she was definitely there at dinner. I remember I poured some water for her. She sat at the opposite end of the table from me,' she says. 'Why? What's happened? Is she okay?'

'We're not sure. How did she seem to you at dinner?' Martin asks.

'She seemed okay. A bit quiet, maybe, but then she has been quiet lately. I think it's because of her meds. She often talks about how much they seem to affect her.'

'But nothing out of the ordinary?' Sarah asks. 'She didn't say anything about how she was feeling?'

Avril shakes her head. 'Why? What is all this? What's happened?'

'I'm sorry to say that Charlotte has disappeared,' Martin explains.

'What do you mean, *disappeared*? She's not in her room?'

Martin and Sarah shake their heads.

Avril jumps out of bed and grabs her dressing gown and slippers. 'Well, let me help you look for her.'

'Thanks, Avril. That's very kind of you, but there's no need for you to-'

'I must. She's my friend. There's no way I can go back to sleep wondering where she is. You have to let me help find her.'

Avril's commitment is admirable…

Thus Sarah and Martin unwittingly allow her to be privy to what happens in the search for Charlotte.

'Perhaps you could let me have my phone to check if I've had a message from her?' Avril says. 'We text sometimes when we're going to meet for a mentoring session.'

'Good idea, I'll fetch it,' Sarah says.

The trio make their way to the building housing Martin's office. Martin puts the kettle on while Sarah runs back to Charlotte's room to retrieve the box of phones.

Avril shakes her head sadly when the phone is given to her. 'Nothing.'

Sarah notices that Avril seems to be fidgeting with something in her dressing-gown pocket. The poor child must be very anxious.

'I'll message her now and ask her to ring me.' She looks across to Sarah and Martin, eyes wide. 'Have you called the police?'

139

'Not yet. We wanted to make sure that she wasn't somewhere on site first, but we're just about to.'

'What about her parents? She might have spoken to them. Maybe she's even trying to go and visit them, especially if she was feeling down.'

'Yes, she might have. That's another great idea, Avril. I'll do that first.'

Avril sits quietly with her hands folded on her lap. Sarah rubs her arm and praises her for being so mature.

Martin stands and paces behind his desk as he phones James. 'Uh, James, it's Martin here, at Hickman's. So sorry to phone so late. We were just wondering if you happen to have heard from Charlotte this evening?'

'No, Martin. I haven't spoken with Charlotte. Is everything alright? What's going on? Is my daughter alright?'

'Look, I'm so sorry to have to tell you this, but we've discovered that Charlotte is missing. We don't know exactly what time she left, but anyone we thought she could be with is here.'

'How long has she been gone?'

Martin tells him what they know: that she had dinner then went to her room. Then, when Sarah did her rounds at 10pm she noticed that she wasn't in her bed.

James' voice is controlled as he asks if Martin has called the police.

'I'm just about to. Just wanted to check in with you first.'

'I'm glad you did. But don't call the local police just yet. Let's hold off and wait for a while to see what happens. Look, Martin, I'm heading to Hickman's right now. I'll be with you in a few hours. Let's keep calm. She might walk back in any minute.'

'Rrright, if you say so.' Martin is unable to keep the note of questioning surprise from his voice. James has taken the news that his daughter is missing surprisingly calmly.

'Her father is on his way,' Martin says.

'Just messaging Charlotte again,' Avril explains to Sarah when Sarah raises a questioning eyebrow at more phone use. 'I've tried ringing, but it goes straight to voicemail.'

Sarah suddenly realises how much they've been treating Avril like one of the adults here, when she's not, she's a student that they're responsible for. 'You've been a brilliant help, Avril, but I think it's time that you went to bed. I'm not sure how much more we can usefully achieve tonight. I promise we'll let you know if there's any news.'

Avril bites her lip and nods. 'But, I don't want to-'

'I know, I feel the same. But there's really nothing more we can do now. I'm going to go to bed myself, Avril. We all need to get some rest. It will be a good couple of hours before Charlotte's father gets here and it's very late. I'll walk you back over to your room. Do you want me to stay with you?'

'No Miss, don't worry, I'm fine.'

'You can help us again in the morning. Keep your phone for tonight, in case she gets in touch.'

Avril nods solemnly. 'I'll let you know straight away if I hear anything. I promise.'

When Sarah returns, Martin is still pacing.

'I don't like it, Sarah. I don't like it all. I feel like we should call the police, but I can't go against James' wishes. I'll stay up and wait for him, but you should definitely get some sleep.'

'What are you going to do for three hours while you wait?' Sarah asks.

Martin gives her a grim smile. 'Oh, don't worry, I have plenty to do.'

On the way back to her room, Avril reflects on how stupid Sarah is. She never noticed the switch in phones, or that Avril was using a second, burner phone in her dressing-gown pocket to send a message to her associates with news of the imminent arrival of Charlotte's father to Hickman's; that will play nicely into their hands.

II

Hickman's School

By the time James reaches Hickman's in the early hours of the morning, Martin is showered, dressed and back in control on headteacher mode. From his office window he sees the headlights that announce the arrival of James' car through the trees and walks outside to meet him. James isn't alone; there are two other men in the car with him. The slamming of doors sounds absurdly loud in the small, still hours of the morning.

'Martin, this is Adam,' James begins the introductions. 'A family friend.' It transpires that he's not just a family friend, though. More importantly, Adam is a police commissioner for another region of the country. He nods impressively and shakes hands firmly with Martin.

The other man, who is tall and bony, stands almost a foot taller than Martin, and is introduced as Derek, one of James' members of staff.

'Derek manages damage,' is all James says about his role.

Martin and Derek shake hands too. It's as if Derek's height has depleted his mass. He is unnaturally skinny, all elbows and knees. Martin thinks of a giant stick insect. Derek, like the police commissioner, wears a dark suit. There is an air of forced formality about the whole situation that makes it feel quite surreal, at odds with the emotional reality of a missing girl. Martin leads them towards his office and offers to make coffee.

'Is Kirsty aware of the situation?' Martin asks while he waits for it to brew.

'Not yet. I'll contact her after this meeting.'

It quickly becomes clear that under no circumstances must news of Charlotte's disappearance be leaked. James is adamant that not a word of it should get out. 'There's a lot going on in terms of this new terrorism bill that's going through Parliament. And it's not beyond the realms of possibility that Charlotte's disappearance may be connected to that in some way. We'd like to rule out that line of enquiry first.'

Adam then explains that he will work directly with the police commissioner responsible for Hickman's region to seek information. Given his seniority, confidentiality will not be a problem.

Despite being headteacher of his school, it quickly becomes clear that Martin is nothing more than a puppet in this machine now. Decisions are no longer his to make; he is simply to do whatever these people say.

'It's obviously your call, James, but I find it more than a little concerning that no police are being brought in.'

'What do you think Adam is?' James' tone is dismissive.

'I just feel that we should be *actively* looking for her.'

'And we will be. We'll do all the searches we can, including tracing her phone. But if this is connected to the terrorism bill, then we're expecting to receive a ransom demand before too long.'

Martin swallows. 'You think this is a *kidnapping*? Jesus.'

Derek ignores the question and proposes absolute silence around all information about Charlotte. 'A lockdown of information, if you will.'

'I understand. I'll explain to the students in assembly tomorrow morning and let them know not to discuss it under any circumstances.'

'You will say *nothing whatsoever* in the assembly tomorrow morning,' Derek says, sharply. 'The fewer people who know, the better.'

'I see.'

'Now, who does Charlotte associate with? Who are her friends?' Adam asks. 'We need to run some checks, and we may need to speak to one or two of them, being careful not to cause any ripples of alarm.'

Martin shoots a look at James. 'Well, since Kirsty left, she's actually roomed on her own. She sometimes hangs about with a lad called Rufus, but we don't think he's a boyfriend, and she's mentored by a girl in the upper sixth called Avril.' Martin draws in a breath. 'But Avril knows she's missing. We spoke to her as soon as we discovered she was gone. And we checked Rufus; he was asleep.'

'So, we need to create a plausible narrative to explain Charlotte's disappearance for these two. We tell this Avril girl that Charlotte has been sighted, and the police are doing all they can to locate her to bring her home.'

'But that's not true,' Martin points out.

'But we need them to think that it is.'

Martin shakes his head. This is all a little bit bewildering. 'Whatever you say.'

When Sarah gets up just before 7am she's weary from a restless night, during which she managed to quieten down the flames about the photos sent on their son's phone. Overnight, she has ensured that all images on both phones have been removed – since the other boy's phone is also in her possession.

She messages the older boy's parents to say that there has been a minor issue and that their son has displayed incredible maturity and should be rewarded for the way he's handled the situation. That should put the situation to bed. At least something is within her realm of control.

When she is introduced to Adam and the skinny man, she's quickly brought up to speed and tasked with sharing the false information with Avril.

Avril nods and offers a smile when she hears that Charlotte has been seen. 'Oh, that's good news, I'm so pleased. I've hardly slept for thinking about her.'

'You're a good friend to her, Avril.'

'But do let me know if there's anything more I can do to help,' Avril says. 'You promised to include me, and I'm here, whatever you need.'

Sarah nods, but Avril doesn't seem to want to move. Sarah can't read her expression.

'I'm beside myself with worry,' Avril persists. 'Is that the right expression in English?'

'It is the right expression, Avril, and I am still worried, too. But it's in the hands of the authorities now and they seem confident that things are under control. We just need to sit tight and wait.'

'Yes, Miss,' Avril says, meekly.

Something about Avril's response feels a little bit off, but Sarah isn't quite sure why. If she was pushed to articulate what was wrong, she wouldn't be able to explain it. There's an almost fanatical willingness to help, but it doesn't feel entirely born of concern. Is it a sense that Avril knows something more? But that would be impossible, wouldn't it? Avril would have told them if she knew.

Sarah shakes the feeling off and plasters on a smile while she tries to get on with the business of running a school, managing her own son's inappropriate use of images, and pretending that nothing is wrong, all while covering up the fact that there is a vulnerable girl missing.

Avril, a master at concealing the truth herself, knows that Sarah is lying when she says that Charlotte has been seen. She needs to be closer to what's really going on here. Damn it. She's going to have to try a bit harder to win Sarah's confidence.

She has her instructions, and being excluded from the investigation will not be acceptable.

III

Redlands

Kirsty has dropped everything at the hospital in order to catch the next flight out of Switzerland. It's mid-morning by the time she touches down in London, to be met by James, fresh from Hickman's and waiting in arrivals at Gatwick, his phone buzzing with the latest updates and information.

James takes her bag and they march with purpose across the airport concourse, heading straight for the black 4x4 parked outside the entrance of the airport.

'Here's the plan.' Inside the vehicle, on the way to Redlands, the family home in Surrey, James quickly brings her up to speed. To the best of his team's knowledge, Charlotte has likely been targeted by an organisation seeking to put pressure on the government. Given Kirsty's military training, she, like James, switches straight into process mode.

'And we're absolutely sure that she hasn't just run away?'

'Why would she need to run away from school? And where would she go? Surely she'd come straight here? No, Derek's right on this. She's been kidnapped. But they won't want to hurt her. They want to score their political point. They, whoever they might be, have no reason to hurt her.'

'In which case, you're absolutely right to keep it all hush-hush,' she agrees. 'Given the political background, this can't get out, under any circumstances. There are too many reputations on the line, too much at stake. Does Martin agree?'

'Martin will do as he's asked. He'll be keen to keep things quiet. Hickman's doesn't need any more negative publicity.'

They go through all the details that Derek has outlined, even listing what things to pack in a suitcase for when they find Charlotte. Kirsty is, understandably, anxious as to the whereabouts of her daughter, but being active helps. Moreover, she has been persuaded by both Derek and her husband that this will be over quickly, and any ransom demand will be handled from the very top. This will be over fast.

As they turn into the gravel drive towards Redlands, it starts to really hit her that Charlotte isn't there. Kirsty bursts into tears.

'Our baby, our beautiful little girl. Taken by God knows who. James, what have we done? How did we let her get dragged into this?'

James turns off the engine and pulls up the brake lever. He reaches out and holds Kirsty's hand. They press their heads together and squeeze each other's hands. James sobs too, which sets Kirsty off even more.

'We've got to keep it together. Charlotte will be safe soon enough. I'm sure of it. We've got the best people in the country investigating what's happened to her.'

But this situation is not just about their daughter, or even just them and their careers. Given James' political circumstances, and the timing of the terrorism bill, this is now a situation for national security. All around them believe that she has been kidnapped by terrorists, by people who want to control the direction of the decision-making going on at the top of government. Charlotte is mere collateral. It is unfortunate and upsetting, but it will be swiftly dealt with. He has the best people on the job, and access to the highest levels of intelligence. They will, no doubt, have word soon enough.

Henry is in the hallway to greet them; he must have appeared on the stairs almost as soon as their key turned in the door. He knows exactly what's happening, having already been briefed by 'the Skinny Man'.

'Yes, that's Derek to you,' James tells him. 'And he knows what he's talking about. You need to listen to and do whatever he says. For Charlotte's sake.'

Nobody is calling her Whoopsie now.

Kirsty cries again on the shoulder of her oldest child and drops her handbag to the ground; the sound of the heavy chain-strap clattering onto the tiled floor is loud and harsh.

Henry leads his mother gently into the large, open-plan kitchen. Sunlight pours from tall windows onto all the surfaces, and the fresh flowers, placed on the central island by their housekeeper, Violet, are incongruous with the general mood in the camp. Kirsty moves them to the side of the room with a tut.

The three of them pull out stools from underneath the island and James and Kirsty immediately set up laptops and phones.

'What can I do?' Henry asks.

'It's all in hand. We'll hear something soon.'

'You mean you know who's done this? You know who's taken my sister?'

'Not exactly, but we're confident that we'll hear soon.'

While her laptop is booting up, Kirsty gets up and goes to the fridge to see if there is any milk.

'I think we all need coffee.'

The maternal instinct to nurture and care comes to the fore. Perhaps inside the marrow of her bones are layers of guilt for all the days, weeks and months she put herself and her career before Charlotte.

Within the next hour more cars turn up at the house. Ed and Oliver are brought home to join Henry, for their 'protection'.

'What do you mean, *protection*?' Oliver says.

'We don't know if you are a target as well as Charlotte,' Derek explains to the white-faced brothers.

By late afternoon it feels as if their home has been completely taken over by officials. There is security around the house and surrounding area. Adam, the police commissioner, and Derek are both ensconced in the kitchen, which has been set up like some sort of war room. They are accompanied by a lawyer.

'Another member of our legal team has been dispatched to Hickman's to work with Martin Whitney, the headteacher,' the lawyer explains. 'To ensure that he doesn't do anything stupid.'

'Can that be kept undercover, too?' James asks.

'Don't worry. Everything has been considered. Our lawyers leave no trace,' he smiles. 'The next few days in Government are too critical for any hiccups. This situation is extremely serious.'

'Of course it's serious. Our sister is missing. Why does this feel more like a cabinet meeting than a search for a missing girl?' Henry asks.

Nobody answers.

IV

Hickman's School

Avril is still hanging around in the corridor near Martin's office when Sarah returns from lunch duty.

'Go back to lessons now, Avril. I promise you, everything's in hand. There's nothing more you can do here. Charlotte has been sent home because of her, er, medical condition,' she pauses. 'But look, I'm worried about you. You seem to have taken it all pretty badly. Do you think you want to meet with one of the school counsellors for a bit of a chat?'

'No, Miss, don't worry. I'm okay.'

But Avril is not okay. Under pressure from her boss to report back on the inside story of the investigation, she's failing in her job because she's being excluded.

And Avril never fails.

All morning she has found excuses to lurk near Martin's office, which is the natural epicentre of anything that happens. She's going to have to be more careful, especially around Sarah, because she needs to be able to stay around here where she can at least overhear snatches of conversation. From what she has gleaned so far, Sarah was definitely lying. If all has gone as planned with Kristo and Luan, then the school cannot have had any word from Charlotte. But why are they covering it up?

Avril watches the car pull up outside and, when the man in a suit gets out with his briefcase, alarm bells ring. He doesn't look like police.

She seizes an opportune moment when the school secretary disappears from behind her desk to fetch coffee. Martin's calendar is open on a tab on the computer which she has left unlocked. Avril quickly scans his appointments but there is no mention of this meeting. That's a concern. Who is the man in the headteacher's office? Do they need to be worried about him?

She manages to hang around in the corridor with the intention of surreptitiously taking a photograph of him. If she can send the pic to her associates, she will have contributed something to her assignment this morning.

Eventually, the man comes out with Martin. She can't get a good picture because Martin is talking animatedly to him, right until he gets in his car. She photographs the number plate. She sends off the pictures to her brother using her second phone.

Kush eshte ky. Who is this?

Dardan sends the image off to his network, but they return with nothing. That is even more of a concern. Dardan's bosses have their fingers in every imaginable pie.

'Shit!' Avril smacks her hand against the window frame in frustration. This is all a giant headache. This isn't how things were meant to pan out with Charlotte. She doesn't understand what's going on, why the school are covering up Charlotte's disappearance, but whatever it is, something has gone very wrong. Charlotte was taken because she was becoming a liability at the school and because the gang wanted some money from her family.

A ransom demand should have been made by now, and they should all be lining their pockets.

153

But it hasn't. Why not?

What Avril needs is to be closer to what's really going on here.

Another message pings in from her brother on the second phone.

Ka një problem. There is a problem.

Charlotte never arrived.

Luan and Kristo have gone awol and haven't carried out their instructions.

'Shit!' Avril hits the window once more. This is a major fuck-up.

'Sort it,' her brother texts.

Avril shivers. The two men who took Charlotte, as arranged by Dardan and his associates, have evidently not carried out their orders – or been prevented from carrying them out somehow. She has no idea how to sort it.

If everything had gone according to plan, then Charlotte's parents would be doing everything they could right now to engage with her gang, pay a ransom and get their kid back. But no ransom demand has been sent. Nothing. Because those two men did not do what they were supposed to.

And they have disappeared off the radar.

Avril is managing to 'play' concerned so convincingly every time she encounters Sarah or Martin because she *is* concerned. Not for Charlotte's wellbeing as she claims, but for herself, for the money she will lose and more importantly the trouble this situation could cause her. This supposed great plan of theirs seems to be unravelling. Maybe they've bitten off a little more than they could chew.

She finds Martin again as he walks around the dinner hall, doing everything he can to present to everyone at the school that there is not a problem. It's business as usual.

'Mr Whitney, I'm ever so sorry to bother you again, but I'm very worried about Charlotte. Have you heard anything more?' Avril asks.

'Hi, Avril, I'm glad I've seen you. Good news. There's absolutely no need to worry about Charlotte anymore. I was going to come and find you to tell you that Charlotte is with her family. She is well and resting, thank goodness. Sorry to have raised the alarm. I know that must have been upsetting. But I'll let her know how concerned you've been.'

He is so convincing that Avril almost believes him. Could it really be that Charlotte is at home? That's impossible. Unless she escaped her captors somehow. Surely not. Luan and Kristo are experienced gang members who wouldn't let a teenage girl get the better of them. What the hell has happened? If she escaped, then how? But a part of her knows that can't be the case. Luan and Kristo would have sent word. Instead, Avril and her brothers have heard nothing. And Charlotte, if she was really 'well and resting', would have got in touch with Avril, surely? So, Martin must be lying.

Everything feels off. Whoever the man in the Jaguar was, Martin has been well-briefed. He's giving a good performance, but Avril, herself an accomplished performer, recognises it as exactly that – a performance. Charlotte is not at home.

The realisation is defeating. Avril really doesn't know what's going on. All she knows is that she is under increasing pressure to find out where Charlotte is and who the school have called in to help. The whole thing is a mess. The only conclusion she can draw that makes any sense is that another rival gang are involved. Avril has no idea where Charlotte is. Nor does she have any clue about the whereabouts of her own gang. The men have disappeared, and Charlotte with them.

If Luan and Kristo have gone missing too, have they double-crossed her brother? She shivers. They are fools if they think they'll get away with it. She needs answers. What have Luan and Kristo done? Where are they? She doesn't seem to have any way of finding out.

And, more importantly, where the hell *is* Charlotte?

V

Redlands

The 'suits', including Derek, the Skinny Man, are still in the kitchen when the boys come down to breakfast in the morning. It isn't clear whether they've been up all night working on the case, or have returned early to begin all over again.

Either way, it's unnerving.

Henry and his brothers are invited to attend the morning meeting, led by Derek, explaining how they will manage the publicity around Charlotte's disappearance.

'Of course, what we need to do is ensure that we are in total control of what is released to the papers and broadcast media,' Skinny Man explains.

'What we need to do is find my sister!' Henry interrupts.

'Henry, just listen to what Derek has to say,' James says, a warning in his tone.

'And to make sure that we dial down our response as much as possible,' Skinny Man continues.

'What do you mean *dial down* our response?' Henry is incredulous. 'We need this on every news programme in the country. We need her picture going viral on social media.'

'We all know that Charlotte has had a *difficult* time of late. The police and schools often put kids disappearing down to difficult children "running away". But, we cannot have any suggestion that Charlotte has run away. We need everyone to think that Charlotte Ashman is safe and well, and at home, to avoid any scandal for the Ashman family.'

Henry starts to interrupt again, but his father raises a silencing hand and nods to Derek to continue.

'Of course, we want to do everything we can to find Charlotte. As you know, we suspect that she may have been abducted. In fact, we think that is far more likely than her having run away. We will launch a police hunt, but we will do so via local teams without drawing attention to the Ashman name, given the delicacy of this particular stage of the terrorism bill and James' role within that. Charlotte's name will not be directly released to any media outlets. I need to guarantee that the Ashman name will not make it into the press in relation to this incident. Is that clear?'

He looks around the room.

'The news of a missing teenager must not be connected to Charlotte or this family. We use an old photograph of her and we go via regional, rather than national, channels.'

'Why are we doing it this way?' Kirsty asks. 'I don't understand. Surely we just need to find her the quickest way we possibly can?' Her face is paler than ever and her usually immaculately-styled red hair is piled up in a loose bun on top of her head.

'And we will. Our intel suggests that she was picked up outside the school and got into a car, which we're currently trying to trace. If this is a kidnap, we'd expect the terrorists to make their demands shortly. If her name isn't out there it creates a safer space for negotiations to take place. Behind the scenes, we're approaching organisations that we suspect may be involved in order to open the channels of communication.'

Kirsty nods, satisfied with Derek's answer. James puts his arms around her shoulders. 'We'll circulate the old photo of Charlotte first using local and regional Facebook groups and local radio and newspapers. That way we test the waters to see if anyone has seen her, or if this is a terrorism group. So, we're agreed, then.'

It isn't a question.

'We'll find her,' James whispers to his wife and son. 'We have the best team here. This is the right way.'

Kirsty moves to a shelf that doesn't need tidying and begins rearranging things on it.

'Meanwhile, no one is to leave the house. We'll have word from the kidnappers soon,' Derek says confidently.

As well as having to manage his family crisis, there is pressure from James' party to continue to lead the bill on terrorism. He divides his time between political and personal calls.

Kirsty copes by tidying up and making lunches for everyone. Because they can't leave the house and they can't draw attention to the house as a focus of activity, food is delivered to the constituency office and then transported to their home by staff.

The wait begins for the terrorists to state their demands.

By mid-afternoon, James is beginning to lose his cool.

'Where are the demands, Derek? We've done exactly what you've said. We've had absolutely nothing. No one has got in touch. No terrorists, no demands, no request for ransom money. What the hell is going on?'

Nobody, it seems, can answer that question.

There is a siege mentality at Redlands as the first 24 hours pass since Charlotte's disappearance, and then the second 24 hours. Kirsty busies herself preparing lunches and suppers and regular rounds of teas and coffees for her remaining family and the core team managing the situation. There is nothing left to clean, or sort, or organise.

But her patience is wearing thin, and the feeling of helplessness threatens to overcome her. She has postponed further work in Switzerland with the now-familiar excuse that she has to deal with 'an urgent family matter of a confidential nature.'

She was initially persuaded that this would all be sorted swiftly and her daughter would be found, but that hasn't happened. Charlotte is still missing, and with every hour that passes, everything feels worse.

Nothing makes sense.

They have access to the best intelligence personnel that their wealth and privilege can buy and yet, still, nothing is happening. Their plan has yielded nothing. The 'test' has been given, the Government has sent out its smoke signals to whichever terrorist organisation they believe to be behind the kidnapping of Charlotte, the local media has played its part. But there has been no response.

Everyone is stymied. This wasn't how it was supposed to go. Even Skinny Man, usually in control and unruffled, walks around with a worried frown.

By day four, the unnamed missing girl story falls away from local pages. Other things find their way to the top of the bulletins. On the fifth day after the first reports of Charlotte's disappearance, Derek once again briefs James and his lawyers, and other members of this confidential group. But this time he does so in a manner that sends Kirsty and the other family members into another downward spiral of speculation.

'Given the circumstances, specifically the lack of any ransom demand, I'm afraid we no longer think it's likely that Charlotte was kidnapped. Our investigations have drawn a dead end. We're at a loss to know where she might be.'

VI

Suffolk

On the other side of the country, far away from the corridors of power, a delivery driver is finishing delivering packages in one of the villages. Marcus is new to this particular route and is running a bit behind schedule today. Some of the addresses are hard to find because the postcodes are so vast and house names rather than numbers don't help. But the sun is shining and he likes the job because of the freedom it offers. He enjoys having his music turned up loud and seeing parts of the city, towns and rural areas that he would never know existed. He feels the tell-tale rumble of his stomach.

He can hear the words of his mother ringing in his ears, 'Make sure you stop and eat, or you'll fall asleep at the wheel!'

But he doesn't want to stop, because that might mean missing his delivery target. He pictures his mother running after him waving a Tupperware container in the air and his stomach gurgles again when he makes his next drop. He tells himself that a 15-minute break is better than an accident and drives a little further along unfamiliar country roads, looking for a suitable place to stop. He turns off into a lane where there are a few old fingerposts. One points towards an animal sanctuary two miles away. He follows the lane for a few hundred yards until he reaches a gateway to a field which seems like a good place to pull over.

He parks up and reaches for his phone before his sandwich. He wants to check to see if Tilly, the new girl in his life, has sent him a message. There are no notifications, but he decides that he's cool about that. He munches on the sandwiches his mum has made him and knocks back a bottle of Diet Pepsi. He checks the clock and jumps out of the van to have a pee. A few cars have driven by intermittently, so he's not quite as off the beaten track as he thought he was. He decides to walk a little further from the road, being too shy to wee where other drivers or a dog walker might see him.

So, with his hands in his pockets he walks along a path near a disused farm. He stands peeing, thinking about the colour of Tilly's hair, when he hears an unexpected sound. He finishes his business and pulls up his zip. The sound comes again. He listens, trying to decide whether he's imagining female voices. It sounds like cries and whimpers. He stands still for a while, wondering if it could be cats, or some other sort of animal.

He looks at his watch; still another couple of minutes to go of the break he's allotted himself. He walks close to the brambles lining the fence. There it is again, definitely female voices, he's sure of it. He darts to the floor when he sees two men walk towards the large outhouse that the voices seem to be coming from. One of the men has a baseball bat. As they walk around the exterior of the building, he drags the baseball bat along the outside walls, saying something in another language. Marcus has no idea what he's just stumbled upon, but the rumbling in his stomach has given way to a sick feeling.

He creeps back on all fours for a few feet until he reaches a tree which gives him the opportunity to stand up without being seen. He stays crouched over behind the hedge, walking quickly towards his van and pulling the keys out of his pocket as he goes. He climbs into the cab and locks the door. The sun has disappeared behind thick clouds and the day is much greyer than it seemed before. He makes a note of the features on his satnav but starts the engine and keeps going until he finds an A-road and then a slip road onto the dual carriageway. He keeps driving, anxious to put distance between himself and whatever monstrous thing it is that he's just encountered. He puts his phone on speaker and calls the police.

A couple of local police officers are sent to the area to take a look. They park some way back and manage to get close enough to take photos using a zoom lens. Marcus' instinct was right, and it doesn't take them long to ascertain that something is wrong. At least two men are clearly patrolling a large shed. The two officers head round to the other side, which means crawling on all fours through two fields to get to the boundary wall without being seen. On the other side of the shed, some distance away, is a dilapidated house and a caravan. Outside the caravan are two mean-looking dogs, XL bullies, attached to heavy chains. The chains are long enough to enable the dogs to get to the shed. The police officers manage to get some clear pictures of a few teenagers inside the old house. They're sitting around smoking and listening to music. There is someone inside the caravan, too, an older man drinking from a mug.

Parked nearby are three cars: a silver blue Ford Focus that has seen better days and two small black cars, one an Audi, the other a BMW. The officers look at each other. These don't look like the sort of vehicles that might belong to farm workers.

'Let's just run those number plates through ANPR, shall we..?'

163

While they wait for the number plate checks to be completed, they begin their retreat. This is not a job for two officers. There are at least eight people on this site, plus the dogs.

Their decision is backed up, when the response comes through a few minutes later. 'Whatever you do, do not approach that house.'

It takes several hours for the raid to be planned and approved. The operation is conducted undercover. The lead officer explains that no press is to be notified. 'If this comes off, it will be a big coup. We'll be bringing in, we think, at least two of the UK's most wanted criminals.'

At 6am the police move in, armed, and approaching the location from all angles. They target the house and caravan first. The men are brought from inside into the early morning light, handcuffed. Police vans with human-sized cages have been backed up around the perimeter. While the gang members are being locked inside the cages and the vehicle doors are slammed shut, the next phase of the operation begins: the door of the locked outhouse is broken down.

The smell inside the shed is pungent: the stench of human misery and neglect. Inside are a dozen naked and semi-naked girls, sitting or lying on mattresses on the floor. They are being kept in conditions that would be unacceptable for animals.

One of the younger officers goes back outside to be sick.

The female police officers wrap towels and blankets around the girls, and more ambulances are called for. They are weak, malnourished and in various states of need and sickness. One is dead.

The scale of this abuse is horrific. Some of the girls are from different countries and speak little English, some are from the UK. A few appear on the NRM framework. The National

Referral Mechanism is a register for identifying and referring potential victims of the complex crime of modern slavery. Some have been trafficked from eastern Europe on their way to be sold and sent across the Atlantic. There is a route by boat from Devon and Cornwall.

One girl, a blonde, is covered in cuts and scars.

Before she has given her name, Jess, one of the senior women officers who has been liaising with Adam, the police commissioner working on the Ashman case, has a hunch that she might know who this is. She wraps a blanket around the stupefied girl. Misery oozes from every cut and pore of her body.

'Can you stand up?'

The girl nods.

Jess leads her out to her car and helps her to sit down on the back seat.

'Are you Charlotte Ashman?'

The girl nods.

VII

Redlands and Suffolk

James and Kirsty are notified of the discovery immediately.

'Thank God. They've found her,' Kirsty says, coming off the phone and bursting into tears. 'She's alive.'

Skinny Man briefs them on the strange circumstances of how she was found, suggesting that it looks to be a highly-organised human trafficking ring. He prepares them for what to expect when they see her.

'A week is a long time. And modern slavery is a brutal business. We don't know exactly how she has been treated, but it won't have been five-star luxury,' he says, drily. 'Nor do we know how she got herself mixed up in this.'

Kirsty, James and Henry jump into the 4x4 and head straight to the hospital where Charlotte has been taken. James drives.

On the journey, Kirsty wrings her hands repeatedly, while Henry spends the time in the car trying to find out as much as he can about the heinous crime of modern slavery.

'I literally didn't know this kind of thing went on in the 21st century,' Henry exclaims as he reads.

'I'm just glad she's safe,' Kirsty says, over and over again.

'Yes, but don't you care about what she's been through?' He's far more shocked than his parents seem to be. 'I mean, how can human beings do this to one another?'

He's certainly more disturbed by the very existence of a slavery ring than his father, whose political work and connections to the Home Office has given him a bit more of an awareness of the scale of this kind of issue. Nevertheless, James is equally clueless as to how on earth his own daughter, supposedly safe in a private school, could have become a victim of this kind of exploitation.

'Of course I care. But I just don't understand how it can have happened.'

'I mean, there's actually a fucking register for this.' Henry shouts. He reads directly from the Government website. 'The National Referral Mechanism (NRM), is a framework for identifying and referring potential victims of modern slavery and ensuring they receive the appropriate support.' He looks up from the screen. 'Jesus Christ. I thought we abolished slavery in 1833.' He looks back down and continues, 'Modern slavery encompasses human trafficking, slavery, servitude and forced or compulsory labour. Victims may not be aware that they are being trafficked or exploited, and may have consented to elements of their exploitation, or accepted their situation.' He shakes his head, disgusted. 'Jesus, there's a referral form to complete if you think someone's a victim.'

It seems beyond comprehension.

When they arrive at the hospital, they pass one of the shared wards where some of the other girls who were found alongside Charlotte are recovering. Through the ward doors they catch a glimpse of them, all in a sorry state, some attached to drips and bleeping machines, malnourished and dehydrated. But far luckier than the one who has been taken to the mortuary.

They brace themselves for what condition they will find Charlotte in. Surely not like this. She's been gone for less than a fortnight.

At the door to Charlotte's private room, two police officers stand guard.

Kirsty is first into the room, desperate to hold her daughter. But Charlotte doesn't want her mum anywhere near her. She shakes her head and pushes her away. The only person she allows to come close to her is Henry. He sits down in the chair next to her bed and holds her hand.

Charlotte's blonde hair is lank, and she has dropped even more weight since a fortnight ago when they last saw her on Zoom. She is covered in cuts and scars.

James, not one for displaying emotion ordinarily, lets out a sob and steps outside the room for a moment to pull himself together. 'Let the doctor know we're here,' he says to one of the passing nurses.

The doctor treating Charlotte arrives at her room 10 minutes later. He has Charlotte's notes in his hands and signals to James and Kirsty to come outside the room so that he can talk to them.

He pulls no punches. 'As well as the malnutrition and dehydration, some of her self-injury cuts have become infected, so we have put her on antibiotics. The infection has made her quite ill. She's also experiencing withdrawal symptoms. We note that up until relatively recently, presumably the time of her disappearance, she was on a dose of 80 milligrams of fluoxetine. That is,' he pauses, selecting the right word, 'unusual.'

James breathes in heavily.

'If not dangerous,' the doctor continues. 'She'll be experiencing some pretty horrendous side-effects from the withdrawal. Let alone everything else that has happened to her.'

'What else has happened?' Kirsty whispers.

'We can see that Charlotte has multiple vaginal injuries. That would suggest that she has been raped, perhaps repeatedly, and for some time. There is some old scarring.'

This is unbearable news for a parent to hear about their child. James puts his arms around Kirsty.

'So, we're treating several things. Not only is she quite ill from the infected cuts, but we're also waiting to hear back on results for STDs. We're working with the police directly, and we suspect that, from what they've told us, she has sustained huge trauma. She is, understandably, experiencing high levels of anxiety and depression. She has had quite severe muscle spasms.' He looks up from his clipboard of medical notes and his tone is severe. 'God knows what this child has been through, but she will need time and good support to recover.'

Although they are in the corridor, Henry can hear some of what is being relayed to his parents. He looks at Charlotte, lying listless and broken in the bed and squeezes her hand. He is not a young man used to allowing his emotions to get the better of him, but he can't stop the tears that are springing from his eyes.

'How can anyone have done this to you, my sweet little baby sister?'

Martin receives a call from Derek to tell him that Charlotte has been found.

'Which is obviously excellent news, but you are still not to say a word to anyone. There are aspects of the criminal investigation at stake here. Charlotte is to be taken off the school roll with immediate effect. If you are contacted by any media outlets whatsoever then you direct them straight to me. Do you understand?'

Martin understands.

There is no mention of Charlotte on the news, but that is hardly surprising, since there has never, in reality, been any mention of Charlotte on the news. The discovery of a shed full of girls is not mentioned either.

Martin watches the bulletins that reveal the discovery of a drug house in a remote corner of the country. *A number of arrests have been made following the successful dawn raid. Two of the men were on the UK's most wanted list.* Martin joins up the dots for himself and keeps silent as requested, telling only Sarah of his suspicions.

Sarah goes to Charlotte's room and gathers up all her remaining possessions into a box. The last items to go in are Gertie and Fred, Charlotte's teddy bears. They look so innocent lying on top of the pile of clothes, as if they belong to a much younger child.

It was less than six months ago that they were all at a party in Cornwall, and the slightly awkward, pudgy girl was doing her best to mingle with guests. What happened in that intervening time? How much of a part has the school played, inadvertently, in what has happened? Sarah is wracked with worry and guilt. She sends an email to Kirsty to ask if she'd like the items sent to them, and while she's waiting for a response, she packs a pretty card underneath the teddies, signing it from 'all your friends at school'. She wraps the box in brown paper and drives it to the village Co-op which has a Post Office counter. When there is still no reply from Kirsty, she mails the package to the Surrey address that they have for correspondence on their records for Charlotte.

At the hospital, the family members stay with Charlotte all evening. Charlotte turns away from her parents and rejects all the attempts they make to communicate with her. It is easier to look at a wall than the people who should be closest to her. Henry sits by her bedside for a long time without speaking, and she tolerates this.

'What can we do to make this better?' he whispers eventually. She shakes her head.

He asks practical questions, like what things Charlotte needs with her while she's in hospital.

'Pyjamas, underwear, deodorant, toothbrush, toothpaste, shower gel, soap, shampoo, conditioner. What else?'

He prompts her to think of things that she wants and things that would be useful. He adds things himself. He compiles a list of items that includes clothes, pyjamas and toiletries, plus a set of good headphones and a new phone. By the time he has finished, the list is long. When he is satisfied that it's complete, he hands the sheet of paper to his mother. 'Here you go!'

'We should all get some sleep,' Kirsty says. 'It's getting late and we need to get ourselves into the hotel.'

James' assistant has found them a small hotel, a 10-mile drive away from the hospital.

By breakfast time the following morning, Adam, the police commissioner, and Derek, or 'Skinny Man' as Henry has taken to calling him overtly now, are at the hotel, along with the lawyer. They are concerned about security, and about political backlash. Charlotte's disappearance has stirred up ill feeling among the terrorist organisations whom the British Government have essentially accused of kidnapping Charlotte.

Every decision has a consequence, every move that the government makes risks upsetting someone. The mood is one of hyper-caution.

'So we tread carefully. Very carefully indeed.'

But Henry is reaching breaking point. He's had enough of the subterfuge and is more openly critical of his parents than he's ever had the courage to be before.

'Seriously, why are they here? The only thing that needs to be "managed" here is Charlotte's health. Not your bloody careers or any kind of damage limitation. The damage is done. The world should bloody well know about it.'

He needs someone to blame and is furious with them for putting their careers before Charlotte. 'Honestly, you're my parents and I love you and support you. But right now, I don't like you very much. I have a million questions. But my first priority is Charlotte – and it should be yours, too.'

James is patient with his oldest son. 'These people are here to help with all of it.'

Henry sits with his sister each day, taking the 4x4 in the morning before breakfast. 'You can get a lift yourselves,' he tells his parents.

James and Kirsty don't need Henry's criticism to tell them that they have failed Charlotte. But James makes it clear to Henry at dinner, after consuming a lot of wine, that he is too far in.

'There are matters of state at hand and, despite what has happened to our family, I cannot be seen to be weak.'

'And there we are,' Henry accuses, bitterly. 'You're still putting your own interests above my sister's.'

Adam and Derek are keen to be the first to interview Charlotte. They still need to understand how and why Charlotte was taken. Is it, as it appears to be, simply an accident of circumstance, or is there an underlying political reason that Charlotte was involved? They need to be sure.

'That's what we need to get to the bottom of, James,' Derek explains. 'You do see that, don't you?' he says, when James protests that Charlotte needs more time to recover.

Charlotte tells them what she knows about her abduction. Two men in a car. She remembers their names: Kristo and Luan. She thought they were taking her to a party. Her friend arranged it for her. She only began getting concerned after an hour or so in the car, which seemed a long distance to travel for a party. When they arrived at the shed, it was dark and late, nearly midnight. She saw signs on the road for Colchester and Ipswich, but not knowing that part of the country, she didn't know exactly where she was. She doesn't know how long she was inside the shed.

Eventually she gives the name of her friend, Avril. She doesn't mention Dardan and Afrim, or what has gone on before. It's too humiliating. She can't speak about any of that yet. Maybe not ever.

Somehow, in spite of the tight control on the release of information, there has been an unexpected leak to the media. A grainy video shows footage of the police moving girls out of the shed, and is shared all over social media. It has already been viewed thousands of times. This is not in the plan. Derek is agitated. He has a window of opportunity to control aspects of broadcast media, but once it reaches the socials, their influence is limited.

He conducts his own investigation into how the leak has happened and who is responsible. His first thought is that one of the police officers has done it and, if that's the case, they'll pay for their indiscretion that has upset his operation.

Unlike Charlotte, the other girls don't have wealthy and influential parents who can intervene. But they are all victims of human trafficking. Except that Charlotte's presence, given who her father is, changes things. It makes them all higher priority than they would otherwise have been.

The footage itself is deeply problematic.

'You can see it's her,' James bites his lip. 'If you know what you're looking at then you can see it's her.'

The footage shows Charlotte getting into a police car. Her face is mostly concealed, but not entirely.

'Which is why that puts her at further risk. We still don't know quite what's at stake here.'

'Her at risk, or us?' James asks.

'Potentially both. We need to think about damage limitation for your family and the Government. And we need to ratchet up security even more.'

Security at the hospital is already high, but Derek is taking no risks, and Charlotte is swiftly transferred to a secure private facility.

Meanwhile, a package arrives for Charlotte in Surrey. Since all parcels and mail are being carefully checked – for explosives or anything else – given the sensitivities around the Government negotiations relating to the bill on terrorism, the large box comes under scrutiny. One of the security staff takes the wrapped parcel out to one of the garages which has been temporarily transformed into a screening unit with X-ray equipment. When the package passes through, something unexpected appears to be inside. 'There, inside the teddy bear.'

Fred is cut open, to reveal over £1,000 in cash which has been stuffed inside his fur.

'Well, this complicates things,' says Derek.

Now there are more questions for Charlotte. Where has this money come from? What has she got herself mixed up in? Somehow, Charlotte's listless evasion is a match for Derek and the police commissioner's interrogations.

'The two Albanian men who took Charlotte evidently did so without realising who she was,' is the only conclusion they can draw. 'It was a mistake. We've been barking up the wrong tree. This is all about money and has nothing to do with politics.'

The Skinny Man pauses. 'In which case, why was the bloody footage released?' he says, perplexed.

'A message to the rival gang? That they should expect consequences, perhaps?' the police commissioner suggests.

Derek nods. 'Right, well let's get on with pushing through the terrorism bill. We've wasted enough of our time on this distraction.'

VIII

Hickman's School

The other person who sees the news item about the Suffolk raid is Avril. Like Martin, she too makes the connection between the drug bust and Charlotte when it's clear that *their* Albanians, Kristo and Luan, who were on Dardan's payroll, and should have been loyal to the gang, have been arrested. What the fuck were they playing at? They have evidently been acting independently, or working for a rival gang. There are just a handful of people in the world who know the truth: that they took Charlotte with the intention of trafficking her, disobeying the specific brief they were given to bring her to Dardan. More fool them.

Avril's associates will make sure that the two men are punished in prison. There are ways to sort these things. They have double-crossed Dardan's gang and for that they will pay. Nobody gets away with betraying Dardan. Their days are numbered.

Avril's 'parents' apply to Martin to remove their child from the school with immediate effect. They are returning unexpectedly to Italy due to 'family circumstances'. The request is not questioned, despite the decision that the move takes place with only six weeks to go before Avril's study leave for A-levels should have begun. Martin has never actually met Avril's parents, when he thinks about it, but she would have left in the summer anyway, and they have agreed to pay the full year's fees which is generous of them.

One by one, over the days that follow, Martin is approached by the parents of Rufus, Drake and Felix – and then by the police. With the gang broken by the raid, they are now free. Free from the debt bondage that kept them involved in something way out of their depth, but not free from the knowledge of what happened to them and what they've done. Each set of parents, having finally been confided in, removes their child from the school. Martin can see income draining away from all corners.

Life at Hickman's is once again in flux. This time it is Martin who is struggling to hold it together.

'I've had enough of the whole damn thing. We're working under impossible circumstances.'

Sarah is more positive.

'No, things are better. Since Charlotte left, I feel as if a whole weight has been lifted. And it's more than just workload and the demands that were being made on us. The whole atmosphere among the students has changed. I can't explain it, but it seems lighter, kinder and more fun.'

'Things have been grim for months. I just don't know if I can carry on.'

'We got used to the pressure and the heavier mood. Do you know,' Sarah says, 'I find it interesting that this has coincided with Avril leaving, too. She seemed like a good kid, but there was something about her that I never really liked. There was something not quite right there.'

'But we'll miss the income. Her parents were generous during her short time here. We'd never have been able to complete the improvements to the library if it hadn't been for them.'

'And that's the problem, isn't it? This seems to be the way. A handful of parents control the school. Most of the students are from wealthy families, of course they are. But a few are from *incredibly* wealthy families. Why would these people send their children to a school like Hickman's if they didn't have a story, maybe something to hide?' Sarah says miserably.

Martin is visited by more police officers. He is horrified at the news that Charlotte has over £1,000 stitched into her teddy bear.

'So we are fairly certain this means that there is gang involvement,' he is told. 'We think that something bigger is going on here and, unfortunately, it also means that the school is implicated – at the very least as a target for a County Lines gang.'

The revelation prompts Sarah to inform the police of her own observations and conclusions. 'I've noticed that a number of the children's behaviour and wellbeing has improved since Avril left. Dramatically, in some cases. I now think that she was part of it. Whatever it is that has been going on here.'

Martin is initially cross with his wife for speaking up.

'You have no evidence of that.'

'Call it women's intuition. Call it years of experience in schools. Call it whatever you bloody like. I know what I feel. Something was up with Avril.'

'Well, I think she was a good student, and her parents were very generous to the school.'

'Generous?' the police officer seizes on the word. 'In what way?'

When Martin explains, the police are keen to know what 'due diligence' Hickman's followed in order to accept the generous gifts.

Now it's Martin's turn to find himself under scrutiny. When the police begin to examine the school accounts more closely, the fact that the Ashmans have also made a very generous gift to the school generates even more questions.

In the light of Sarah's comments, and because Charlotte has also given Avril's name in connection with events leading to her abduction, Avril becomes central to the investigation. Martin passes on all the documents he has had from her parents, and investigations are done into Avril's Italian mother and English father.

'Guess what?' Derek tells James. 'They can't be found. It's as if they don't exist. The money they gave to the school for the library has no trail. The trustees approved *cash*. This is not a good look for anyone.'

Martin scrambles about trying to work out what to do and how to keep this quiet. Luckily for him, Derek and James want this to go away too.

So, when the press start sniffing about, there is simply no trail to find... Everything has been shut down and covered up.

IX

Surrey

Derek's further investigation draws some interesting results when he is briefed by his team. The video footage leak of the girls being rescued doesn't originate from police officers, but is actually traced back to one of the girls in the shed, Girl F.

'So what was she doing with a phone inside that shed? How the fuck does that work? Was she a plant?' he wants to know.

Girl F is indeed discovered to have been working *for* the Albanians directly.

'She was an insider. Kristo and Luan placed her in the shed to observe the other girls and make sure they didn't plan an escape. But the gang were smart. She's also already on the NRM Register. We can't touch her.'

The trafficking ring is sophisticated. To distract attention away from them, the gang use this mechanism to hide behind, claiming protection against slavery by placing their own members on the register as soon as they are arrested. This means that, ironically, gang members from other countries, particularly ones with a history of slavery, can go on this register alongside their victims. They are then identified as potential *victims* rather than perpetrators of modern slavery. This allows them to receive a kind of immunity from prosecution, and support from lawyers who are already on their payroll.

'It's a very handy register and, because the UK is not, historically, a country connected to slavery of its own people, charges are being made against the English girls who were found in the shed because they're not on the register yet. Even though they are the ones who were enslaved in the shed waiting to be transported for money, they themselves will be under investigation.'

'Right. Let's get Charlotte Ashman on that bloody register, quick smart.'

'The cash found in her teddy bear is enough evidence to suggest that she was already involved in some way prior to the abduction.'

Derek and his legal team immediately use their connections to put Charlotte on the register, which will prevent any chance of her being linked with prostitution as an abused minor. But it transpires that Kristo and Luan have also used the register. They claim that they have been slaves themselves, working for *British* gangs.

'So, you're telling me that the men who abducted my daughter are claiming immunity from prosecution?' Even James is struggling to keep up. Everyone is blaming everyone else and using all the laws they can to their advantage. It's hard to tell the difference between the government and the gangs given the subterfuge. They all operate with lawyers and fake names.

'So what you're, in effect, saying is that the two men who kidnapped Charlotte and kept her in those appalling conditions get to walk away from their crime.'

'That's the long and the short of it, yes.'

Derek pauses. 'The other discussion to be had is exactly what the next steps are for Charlotte. She can't stay in the private secure provision for much longer. Too many questions will be asked, mostly about the funding. Unless you can fund it yourself.'

'We've thrown a great deal of money at this already, as you know, and we don't have endless pots.'

Derek has already been in touch with a government financial adviser and is now overseeing what has become a tricky domestic problem; still, better that than a tricky terrorist-related one.

'Think about it, James,' Derek says, drily, steepling his long fingers together. 'It isn't a good look for your daughter to be staying in a private facility that might cost the taxpayer £50k a week. How would that look if it got out? It simply wouldn't do. So, the best solution, in order to keep her safe and secure, is to find a temporary foster home placement for her. That way, there's no further connection to you and the gangs won't be able to find her.'

'Foster care? Don't be ridiculous. I'm not having a daughter of mine going into care.'

'Think about it. Given the money that was found in her teddy bear, she's almost certainly mixed up in it all herself. That means that at least one gang could still be after her. If she comes back home, without full-time parental supervision, she's at risk. Can you afford thousands of pounds a week to keep her in the private facility? I suspect not. So it's unsustainable cost, or foster care. Your choice.'

'We can't afford £50k a week!' James says, shaking his head.

'Right, well, as soon as we can get her into foster care, that will cost a far more acceptable £500 per week.'

There are other factors which make the decision more palatable. Charlotte being in the secure provision has meant that they had to take time to go and visit her. It's been inconvenient for James and Kirsty, as it has been for Henry, Ed and Oliver. They have to get back to their lives, to their training, and to their studies. Kirsty signed a contract that requires her to be in Switzerland. She can't remain in the UK indefinitely without contravening the terms of her contract. Now that the situation has settled and is being managed, she has to go back.

'Frankly, it will be a relief,' she confesses to James.

They have spent a lot of time in close proximity with family under trying circumstances and each of them has found it suffocating.

'But what's the long-term solution for Charlotte? There is no question that she can ever return to Hickman's,' James asks.

'No. We keep her well away from there,' Kirsty says. 'It's absolutely clear that she needs a more sustained level of care than a boarding school can provide.'

'So, a foster family will meet that need, then. It's the only way,' Derek urges.

Charlotte has already been assigned a social worker, though she has yet to meet her.

'I've taken the liberty of getting in contact with the social workers,' Derek explains. 'And I think that the best way to take care of her is to place her within the care system. Putting her into foster care is the best outcome for her. It will efficiently move her out of harm's way for the time being. There are still investigations going on into exactly who was leaking information. We know that Charlotte has been caught up in gang activity. And, of course, it's only a temporary measure. But if you want what's best for your daughter then you'll follow my advice.'

James is thoughtful. 'We need to get this bill through Parliament. We have no way of guaranteeing that there won't be reprisals at a later date. Perhaps you're right. Perhaps it is the safest option.'

Dinner at the family home is a Thai take-away.

'Roughing it,' James makes the stale joke he's made for years, always bringing it out on the odd occasion when they have been 'reduced' to eating take-away food. Tonight there is news to discuss and important decisions to be made. All the boys are there.

'We think that Charlotte should go into foster care,' James explains.

The boys are initially horrified.

'What do you mean, go into foster care?' Oliver is outraged. 'She's got parents! It's chavs who go into care, not the daughters of MPs and surgeons.'

'We haven't come to this decision lightly, and we've looked at it from every angle, I promise you. But it's in her best interests. And it's not forever. It's just a temporary measure to keep her safe.'

There is quite a heated conversation. Kirsty is tight-lipped.

'Mum? You can't be going along with this, surely?' Henry says.

'As your father says, it's to keep her safe. She's been through an extremely difficult time, and we have to put her first. It's not as simple as just bringing her back here.'

Henry, as always, is the most level-headed of the three. He also had an inkling something like this was going to happen, having spent so much time at the hospital and having been involved in some of the conversations that his younger brothers haven't been party to. But none of it sits comfortably with him. It seems impossible to think that his parents could have let things get to the stage where his little sister needs to be *in care* because that's the safest place for her. Always practically minded, he's also been thinking about the logistics of what will have to happen next.

'It's hard to imagine where she will go, and part of my worry is that once she's in the system, then we have very little control over who she will go to for foster care.'

'In some ways, Henry's right,' James says. 'She's now in the process of something called Section 20 of the Children Act.'

Henry has been doing his homework. 'So because a Section 20 is granted as a voluntary arrangement, Charlotte has to agree. In order to do that, she'll have to go to a family court to formally agree the terms. We'll have to go, too.'

Edward is astonished. 'We'll have to appear in court? You're joking?'

'That's not how it will happen,' James explains. 'None of us will actually have to go in person, not Charlotte, not any of us. Our lawyer will handle everything. This family has to keep our name away from public attention, so we will all need to be careful. The best thing for Charlotte is to merge into the crowd and disappear for a few months while the police complete their investigation. Charlotte was a victim, yes, but she was also complicit in something at Hickman's. Much better for her to be taken away from all that.'

'So what do we say when anyone asks us where she is, or how she is?' Oliver asks.

'If anyone asks after her, we just explain that she's at an international school overseas. That will do. There's no need to expand any further on that.'

The boys all nod. Deep down, they know that this is a much easier way to manage the mess that they find themselves in.

But Henry is not in the least bit impressed and will not let his parents forget the betrayal, a situation which quietly amuses Violet, the housekeeper, and the security detail who are still working close to the house. One of the guards tells Henry that he grew up in foster care, which sparks a new level of respect from Henry.

'I'm still not sure about this,' Kirsty says. 'It seems like it's the last resort-cheapest option. Haven't there been all sorts of cuts in social care?' She almost visibly shudders as she utters the words. 'Is this really the best thing we can do for our daughter?'

James denies the cuts. 'There's plenty of money. They just need to spend it better. They should stop wasting it on daft "Cinderella projects".'

Once the decision has been made, things move fast.

'This is going to be interesting,' Henry says under his breath when they meet Kate, the social worker who is assigned to Charlotte's case, for the first time, although not quite loud enough that his father will hear.

Kirsty can't hide her dismay when she sees her. The red and white scarf that she associates with Palestine looks like some sort of statement and the old CND badge she simply finds offensive.

'Yes, I was at Greenham in the 80s,' Kate smiles when she sees Kirsty looking at the badge, as she marches ahead of them through to the kitchen. Kirsty's military background is at ideological odds with someone who spent years living as part of a peace camp in the 1980s. Kirsty finds people like Kate almost unbearable under the best of circumstances, and these are far from the best of circumstances.

'Tone it down,' James reminds her. 'Kate will write everything down, every comment, every bit of body language. That's her job. Be nice, for Charlotte's sake. That woman could make all of our lives extremely difficult.'

When Kirsty complains, 'How did our lives come to this?' Henry shoots her a harsh look. But now, not only are James and Kirsty trying to deal with matters of state and holding down an incredibly well paid post in Switzerland, they are also being questioned by children's social care about their treatment of Charlotte prior to the abduction.

'Look, we're not the bad guys, here,' James says firmly.

Henry has other ideas about that.

Fortunately for them, Derek and the lawyer have prepared all possible answers to the accusatory tone of the questions Children's Social Care begin to fling at the Ashmans. When it transpires that Children's Social Care now wish to interview the boys, too, Kirsty tries to put her foot down.

Kirsty and James have never been in a situation where they have so little power or control. And it makes it all the worse that it's coming from a woman who represents everything they despise in the world.

The Ashmans are not in a good place.

Whatever else she might be, Kate is efficient with paperwork, and Charlotte's foster care referral is written and ready to be distributed while she is still recovering in the private healthcare facility. It is carefully sent through a number of local authorities in different parts of the country – nowhere near the Ashman's home or Hickman's School.

The further away the better.

And then the waiting game begins.

No one picks up the referral, despite it going to five local authorities and 15 independent fostering agencies. There is a national crisis of diminishing foster carers, and a 30% shortfall this year alone. There are just not enough foster carers to go round, and Charlotte is not an attractive proposition. No one is jumping up and down to take on a 14-year-old girl who self-harms, is on medication and has been involved with the wrong people.

So until a foster placement can be found, Charlotte is placed in an unregulated home.

Henry and his brothers are not shy about reminding their parents what has happened to their little sister.

'Shall we plan a family holiday this summer? Oh no, we can't. Because we've just done everything that Skinny Man has said without question. And we aren't actually a family anymore. *One* of your *children* is in *care*!'

PART THREE

Charlotte

I

Kate, Charlotte's social worker, might once have been described as a woman who took no prisoners, but age now gives her the air of a woman from a bygone era, when things were done a little differently. She managed to retire once from the profession, but was persuaded back part-time because the local authority was so short staffed. 'I very *nearly* escaped!' she jokes, rearranging the Palestinian scarf. She describes herself as being 'at her best in the 70s and 80s' and makes no secret of the fact that she cut her activist teeth on Greenham Common. She has strong political views, some of which might make Jeremy Corbyn look a bit centrist. Around her neck she wears an LGBTQ+ lanyard ribbon, and perhaps, with hindsight, being assigned to Charlotte, the daughter of a moderate right-wing MP, was never going to be a match made in heaven.

Charlotte actually rather likes Kate. At least she listens. Or appears to. And knows what she's talking about. She has the same tendency towards kindness as Sarah, but with a steelier rod, and a more realistic understanding of the world. There are things she can say to Kate that she wouldn't dream of saying to anyone else. She sees straight away how much this woman might rub her father up the wrong way; which, right now, feels like a bonus. Liking her feels like another tiny little act of rebellion.

Charlotte is still young and vulnerable, in spite of everything she's been through, and she's never really encountered anyone quite like Kate before.

Kate doesn't hold back from letting James and Kirsty know her thoughts on every subject, whether it be political or care related. She has nothing to lose. She is already receiving her pension. This gig provides extra money that she doesn't really need. She now works Tuesday, Wednesday and Thursday mornings, signs off at lunchtime, and is selective about her caseload. Kate lives frugally in a small house with hardly any overheads, her two children long gone and living with their own families.

Kate has years of experience at pulling information out of children and their parents, so when she decides to ask Charlotte about her family, Charlotte doesn't stand a chance. Not only is Charlotte still adjusting to her meds after the sudden withdrawal when she was being trafficked, but perhaps unsurprisingly, she has a rather large downer on her family, particularly her mother, right now. Without knowing what she's doing, she inadvertently gives Kate and her manager a whole profile of emotional neglect. Charlotte's story is one of her parents continuously failing to meet her needs.

Charlotte discusses the pet name 'Whoopsie' and the little epithet which always follows, 'our little mistake'.

Kate is sympathetic to Charlotte's revelations. 'You poor, poor child. That must have been truly awful.'

She concludes in her written report that she thinks this alone constitutes a form of child abuse.

'You were desperate for your mother's love and attention, and it never materialised. Your experiences were shitty. You're probably only just beginning to realise how hurt you really feel about your past,' Kate tells her.

It sounds as if Kate genuinely understands. From that perspective, Charlotte is happy to talk about her mother and father, but she will not talk about Avril or the gang members. They instilled a level of fear into her that she would find difficult to describe. She knows that if she ever revealed anything, even gave the slightest hint of what was going on to anyone, they would hunt her down and kill her along with her family.

Despite Kate being an old hippy, who Charlotte assumes will continue to offer a soft, kind approach during her recovery, her rod of steel dominates.

'Charlotte, what you need to understand is that you've been involved in a crime. There are plenty of questions left unanswered. You still won't explain the cash which was found inside your teddy bear. You're clearly scared of someone or something,' Kate says, 'but you won't tell us what that thing is. That suggests guilt. If you won't tell me, then I can't help you.'

It's true, Charlotte is scared. She is scared of Avril, and Kate is turning out to be pretty scary too. Where she found her nice in the beginning, she is realising that Kate's actually quite tough.

'The police think that you are one of the criminals here. And I'm starting to think that they might be right. I think a spot of time in a secure unit will help put you off crime,' Kate decides. 'Unless there's anything else I don't know about what was going on before the abduction.'

Given Charlotte's silence over her time at the chicken farm, the sex acts that she is still not calling 'rape', even to herself, the way she has hidden the amount of hard-core Class A drugs she was consuming, not to mention covering up her involvement in Country Lines drug running, perhaps Kate's conclusions aren't surprising.

But they are hurtful. She can't think of herself as a criminal, too.

If she could talk about her time at the chicken farm, then perhaps the post-traumatic stress disorder she is suffering from might be diagnosed. Instead, Kate believes that Charlotte has simply chosen to behave badly.

'It seems to me that all this is just a rebellion against your privilege and super-successful parents.'

Everyone is getting it wrong, all of them. All Charlotte wants is to be at home with her family and for all this to go away. Instead she is being punished. She is always being punished. She was punished as a child for loving her mother too much, by her mother always leaving. She was punished for her poor progress at school by being taken away from her friends and sent to Hickman's. She was punished for loving Danny by being sent to the chicken farm. She was punished for the chicken farm by being taken to the shed. Suddenly it seems to her as if it has all been a cycle of punishment. Everything she's been through.

She bursts into tears.

'The overwrought emotions of a spoilt child,' Kate mutters. And, diagnosis duly made, Kate is keen to move Charlotte from the luxury private healthcare provision into the first available care home as soon as she possibly can.

'Getting you away from all this and giving you time to think about what's happened and your role in it, is exactly what you need.'

Great. A taste of medicine to cure Charlotte's 'criminal aspirations' is just the ticket, it seems. How has Charlotte become the villain here? Even the law that's meant to protect people from modern slavery has worked against her. She doesn't remember much from her history lessons, but she does know that England has a history of enslaving people. Who would have guessed that foreigners could come to England and enslave their children. Not her father, that's for sure. He didn't see that one coming.

When a care home space at the Well Being Centre becomes available, and Charlotte is deemed well enough to travel, the move takes place.

Kate takes Charlotte to her temporary new home. Her car is an old Volvo that she's had since forever. Inside, it smells of dogs and stale food items. When Charlotte closes the door its inside compartment is jammed with wrappers and half-drunk smoothie bottles. It's actually revolting, and not far off the disgusting condition of the car that was driven by the Albanian gang men who took her to the shed.

People's lives cling to the insides of their cars, and Kate's life seems as far away from Charlotte's as the gang's. Charlotte is full of conflicting feelings. Kate listens to Radio 4, which her mum used to listen to when she was home, and it reminds her of those rare days when the Ashmans felt like a family. When her mum listened to the Archers while she cooked a roast dinner and James would sharpen the carving knife and large fork ready to slice up a huge joint of meat. Back when the world hadn't tilted off its axis. Charlotte has these memories, and they remind her that the only thing she has ever wanted is to just be at home with her mum.

The secure unit is marketed as a 'Well Being Centre' which sounds a little bit like she might be going to a spa, but when they arrive, it is a modern building in pale brick situated between a housing estate and a business centre. It is soulless.

Once inside, things don't get any better. It operates, as far as Charlotte is concerned, like a prison, which is probably exactly why Kate has chosen it.

Her room has sloping walls and a toilet and shower which open into the area where the bed is. The bed looks as comfortable as a table. This is way worse than school.

Charlotte feels let down again. She has opened up to Kate, trusted her. In her position as social worker, Kate should have been on her side.

No one has any clue about how I'm feeling, Charlotte thinks. *No one cares what I've been through. If they did, they wouldn't have put me here.*

Charlotte hates adults, she decides. They're all mad.

Life in the Well Being Centre is dull and full of routine.

Kate comes to visit Charlotte twice a week, on Tuesday and Wednesday, the days she works directly with her small caseload. Thursday is the day she does her paperwork. She has only agreed to do this work on the basis that she is able to manage it without taking any work home with her.

For the other five days of the week, Charlotte is basically left to the Well Being Centre. Her mum hasn't even come to visit her here. Once things were 'settled' as her mum put it, she wasted no time in jumping on the first plane back to Switzerland.

It's the same old story. Christ, what would she have to do to get them to really sit up and take notice of her?

Her dad is busy, as he always is. Fire-fighting something at work and banging on endlessly about pushing the new bill on terrorism through. She's partly to blame for its delay, seeing as no actual terrorist group had come forward. Her brothers have gone back to their lives of university and training, and only Henry has expressed an interest in visiting her since the move to the Well Being Centre, but it needs to be passed by Kate before he gets permission.

'Your brother's been in touch,' Kate tells her. 'He wants to know if he can come and take you out for a coffee?'

'And can he?'

'We need to assess whether or not he presents a risk to you.'

'Of course he's not a risk to me. If anything, he's a good influence.'

'Hmmm. He's charming, I'll give him that.'

It's a couple of weeks before the permission is granted.

'And remember, it's only for two hours,' Kate warns.

Charlotte, who generally finds it difficult to muster excitement about anything these days, is actually looking forward to his visit. She waits for him to arrive, along with Abdul, her key worker at the centre, in the optimistically named communal 'lounge'.

Henry is on time, as he always is. He is so dependable. They wait while he's buzzed through. If he's shocked to see how thin she has become, he makes a good fist of not showing it. She's done her best to cover up the fresh cuts on her arms and neck. She's surprised to see that he's dressed in more casual clothes than she would have expected. He's wearing a sweatshirt that looks more like something Danny might wear, and less like a posh kid. Danny. She hasn't thought about him in a long time. Was he where it all started? It's difficult to unravel the story in her head now.

'Hey Sis,' Henry says.

Before they are allowed to depart, Abdul chats to Henry. Charlotte has to listen to the humiliating details once again. How she is still settling in and because of her history and the risk of her cutting she is in the 'secure' part of the centre which means that they've had to remove many of her possessions.

She is grateful to her big brother for maintaining his poker face.

'Now, what's the plan?' Abdul asks. 'Where are you two heading to?'

'Nando's?' Henry offers, as a question to his sister.

She nods, grateful again that he's made a good choice. It will be nice to hang out with her brother and eat some fast food. Anything will be better than the shit they serve in this place.

'Two hours,' Abdul reminds them. As if Charlotte could forget.

Henry leads them outside and opens the car door of the passenger side for Charlotte. 'I haven't seen this before, is it new?' Charlotte asks.

'It is, and I paid for it myself,' Henry says proudly. 'It's a Mazda, an MX-5. Second-hand. I don't think Dad's seen it yet.'

The day is fine enough to have the roof down. A hint of warmth in the late spring sunshine.

Conversation is stilted to start with. Charlotte has forgotten how to interact with people. Plus, they have to shout at each other with the roof of the Mazda down.

'Did you drive up this morning?'

'Actually, I drove up last night and stayed in a Travelodge on the edge of a business park just out of town.'

'Travelodge? You're slumming it, aren't you?'

'I did it so I could nip into town before I saw you. I've bought you a present.'

'For me? What is it?'

'Look in the glove compartment.'

Charlotte reaches into the bag that has been placed there and looks inside.

'A phone?'

'Yep, one they don't know about, so you can contact me whenever you need to. I know the social worker took your last one away.'

'You'll get into trouble if they find out,' Charlotte says. 'You know that? I never knew that my big brother was such a rebel.'

'I'm not, and I probably should have consulted someone, you're right. But, frankly, our parents, that school and this mad social worker have fucked everything up so much that I don't care anymore.'

'Thanks.'

'Look, I know you're not going to tell me anything, and I understand that it's complicated which is why you can't speak about it, but I know there's more to all this than you're letting on. I have no idea how a 14-year-old girl gets her mitts on a grand's worth of cash and part of me doesn't want to know.'

Charlotte bristles. Of course he *would* spoil it by bringing all that up. 'So leave it then. I promise you, it's better that you don't know. And you're right. I really don't want to talk about it. Let's talk about something else. Anything.'

He whitters on about the weather and other nonsense for a while, words that she allows to wash over her. It's nice just to hear his voice. He talks about his training and what they've covered so far. He has been learning about hostage situations and negotiations. 'As the negotiator you need to gain control of the situation, by creating one-to-one talks with the perpetrator. You need to explore the feelings that are underlying the demands.'

Maybe she can trust Henry. Maybe he might be the person that she can really unburden herself to. She's not making any demands, but perhaps he could be the one to finally understand her feelings.

Henry parks the car and they walk to Nando's. It feels nice when he takes her arm so that they can walk along together. Once he's ordered their food and they're settled in their seats, he relaxes a little more, becoming more normal again.

'God, what is that place like, Sis? Just knowing that you're somewhere like this hurts!'

'Thanks. You know you're not helping by saying that.'

'Sorry.'

'But it's bloody horrible. Probably worse than prison. They don't take their bloody eyes off you. I'm surprised I'm allowed to go to the toilet by myself. But there isn't even a cubicle in the room. Even when I'm on my own, it doesn't feel private.'

'Sounds horrible. Possibly worse than my Travelodge,' Henry jokes. 'But seriously. Is there anything I can do to make it better?'

'Probably not. But you could try chatting to them about my meds. I'm not on anything at the moment and they won't listen to me when I tell them that I should be. But then, who does listen to a 14-year-old girl?'

'I'll take it up with Abdul,' Henry promises.

He helps her set up the new phone while they wait. Charlotte is happier once the food arrives, and feels better once she's munched her way through a couple of flame-grilled juicy wings.

After lunch they walk around the shops and Henry tries to buy her more things, to cheer her up. He takes her to Marks & Spencer and gets her a pile of treats that fills a carrier bag: chocolate, Percy Pig sweets, shortbreads, all the things she loves.

Again, she thinks, she could confide in Henry. He's trying so hard to be kind and to help her. Perhaps he would know what to do and what to say. But then she has a reality check. If her social worker, with all her years of training, can't help her, how can her brother? She just can't bring herself to do it. She can't say out loud the shameful things that happened to her at Hickman's, at the chicken house and at the shed.

But when he asks her a direct question, 'Charlotte, look at me. Were you involved in County Lines? Yes or no?' she nods. He's not as daft as he looks, this brother of hers.

'In that case, I understand why you won't speak about it.'

She looks at him. How could he possibly understand?

'Unlikely as it may seem, I know enough about gang structures and their modus operandi from my training. They're not unlike terrorist groups – and, actually, military organisations, when it comes down to it. The ethos, morals and funding are different, obviously, but there is a huge overlap in the way they operate. I get it.'

All too soon, the two hours are nearly up and they are heading back to the centre. As they drive back, Charlotte's mood darkens and she becomes quiet again. It has been good to be 'normal', even for a couple of hours.

'I'm not far away,' Henry promises. 'And don't forget to hide that phone so you can get in touch whenever you want.'

Charlotte smiles. 'Thank you.'

She puts the phone down her trousers and inside her pants. She does it without thinking, but the frown that Henry gives means that he's noticed the practised way she performed the manouevre. He will know that she's done it before and it will add to his concerns.

She begins to walk through the car park then bends down to do up her laces. He walks her to the reception area.

'Can I see Charlotte back to her room?' he asks.

'I'm afraid that's not possible,' the receptionist explains.

Two youngish men sporting grey tracksuits and bright

lanyards appear, announcing their arrival with the tell-tale buzz through the security door.

'Hope you've had a good afternoon. Thank you for bringing Charlotte back safely and on time,' one says.

'We're here to take Charlotte back to her room,' the other adds.

Charlotte raises her eyes to heaven and then shares a look with her brother as if to say, see, I told you it was awful.

Abdul appears in reception. Seizing his opportunity before Charlotte disappears, Henry says, 'Oh, that's good timing. Can I have a quick word about Charlotte's medication?'

Abdul frowns and looks confused for a moment, then asks the receptionist to bring up Charlotte's notes on her computer. 'Can you go back to the page before?' he asks the receptionist. He scrutinises the screen to check the notes.

'May I?' he says, taking hold of the mouse. He makes another face as he scrolls up and down.

'Nope, there's nothing on here about meds.'

Henry rolls his eyes and explains that she was on meds in the last place because of the trauma and the withdrawal since she was abducted. She'll be struggling without them. She's had to go cold turkey and that's not very good for her. Why is nobody joining up the dots here? Sorry to be speaking for you, Charlotte.'

Abdul seizes on what he's just said. 'Abducted? What do you mean "abducted"?'

Henry gives his sister an apologetic look and closes down the conversation. 'Don't worry. Not your fault. I'll chase it up with our family GP. I think that was the last place we got a prescription sorted out.'

Perhaps he's finally beginning to understand how difficult life is for her here. He says, 'Leave it with me, Charlotte. I'll call Mum. I'll sort it. Take care of yourself, kid.'

Charlotte can hear the sound of the Mazda's engine driving away. The familiar, horrible feeling of being deserted returns.

And no medication. How can these people not communicate properly about her needs? She was allowed to have them in the previous place. She went through withdrawal once while she was in the shed. Now she's going through it again. Both times have been unplanned. Again she feels out of control. It's down to circumstances out of her hands.

She waits for the two men to leave her room.

She goes to the washing area, takes down the towel that has been left for her, shakes it out and sits on her bed. She reaches down to her trainer and fishes out a sharp shard of glass that was in the carpark when she walked in. She lifts her top and starts to cut, each movement bringing relief.

She slices through flesh until she thinks she must be close to bone.

Then she passes out.

II

When she comes to, several hours later, nothing in her world has changed, except that it has got dark.

Two more weeks pass. To Charlotte, stuck inside the Well Being Centre that seems to have no sense of concern for her wellbeing whatsoever, the fortnight feels like an eternity.

Whenever she asks how long she'll be here, the answer is always the same. 'Until a suitable family can be found for you.'

What 'a suitable family' translates to is one that isn't freaked out by the chaos of her referral. She knows this because she heard Abdul talking to one of the other care workers about it, but also gossiping about her abduction, like he was enjoying the sensational nature of it, picking through the bones of her life.

'Crazy story, huh? And none of it was in her records. I mean, that's mad, isn't it?'

She hates being the subject of idle gossip, chit chat in corridors. Especially when the guy Abdul is talking to seems unduly interested in her story.

She feels like she wants to vomit when the other man says, 'Is she The Cutting Girl? I've heard of her!'

None of this will ever go away.

The care worker in question, Sammy, according to his lanyard, approaches her in the evening, evidently having done a little bit more research into her identity.

'We have mutual friends,' Sammy explains, with a sly grin. 'I've been told to remind you of your connections and to be ready for work again as soon as you get out of here. You'll be discharged soon, and I'll be responsible for making sure that you get to your next location. All part of the service, The Cutting Girl.'

Charlotte closes her eyes. How is it that she can never be safe? How is it that the gang can get to her, even in here? This guy is a *care worker* for fuck's sake. Another person who should be looking out for her. Where are the adults that she can trust?

As if reading her mind, he tells her that the gang are everywhere. 'Don't look surprised. It happens all the time. The local authority who fund the Well Being Centre are only too happy to make use of the extra value of a cheap worker who's willing to go the extra mile.'

'How do you get away with it? How do you keep your job here if I disappear?'

'It's easy. I just tell them that you ran off.'

She accepts the miserable truth of his statement without question. With Charlotte's history, who is going to think otherwise?

'You know Dardan?' she asks.

'I know *of* him,' the guy says. 'Different gang. But we're in alliance. I'm on your side.'

As a parting shot, he reminds her that she needs to remain 'keeping your mouth shut. You know way too much.'

As if she needed reminding.

When she wakes up the next day, the care worker comes to her room again. He gives her a burner phone and tells her to wait for instructions. Charlotte has no option but to obey. It feels as if they're all in on it. Everyone. The world is one big circle of gangs.

There is no way out. No one to talk to. She puts the burner phone away with Henry's, without realising that it is exactly the same make and model as the one Henry has given her. When she goes to look at them there is no obvious way that she can tell them apart; she has nothing to identify them with. It's as if the universe is playing a great big joke on her. Except that it isn't funny.

She has the urge to smash both phones up, but there is nothing to do it with. All the surfaces in her room are curved so there are no hard edges. She can't even crack the screen. The carpeted floor is soft. She's an idiot to have mixed the phones up. Now she has no way of contacting Henry. This is a nightmare. It's worse than a nightmare because you wake up from those.

A different staff member comes with medication for her to take. Henry has obviously kept to his word and insisted on the prescription. Her mood drops even further as she swallows the pills. She knows from bitter experience that she needs them, but they will mess with her head. She will want to die. She already does want to die.

To make things worse, the tiny shard of glass she found has gone. It has obviously been found and taken away at some point when she wasn't in the room. Perhaps at dinner.

The room is a prison. The Well Being Centre is a prison. Her body is a prison. Her own mind is a prison. She can't escape from any of them.

She is half asleep when a text comes in.

How are you?

That must be the phone from Henry. The one person in the world who cares about her.

When are you coming to see me again? she texts back. Then, because that sounds desperate, she adds something about her dinner, just to let him know that she is okay.

204

She feels sick once more when the reply comes in. The text says, *Just wait for instructions.* She's an idiot.

She falls asleep and, when she turns over in the night, she knocks the phone onto the floor. When she wakes, with the heavy, confused feeling that the medication always brings, she reaches for the phone that is peeping out from under her pillow. There is another message.

You okay?

She remembers the brief exchange from the previous night and texts back.

You told me to wait for instructions.

She waits for the reply. *No, I didn't, Charlotte. What's going on?*

At least she knows for sure which phone is which now.

I want to leave. Can I come home?

She can see the three dots that let her know he's composing a reply. She wants it to say, 'don't worry, I'm on my way' but knows that's impossible. Her parents would never agree. They've already given up on her.

I'll see what I can do.

Hurry up, she thinks. *Please hurry.* She has to find a way to get out of here. Before it's too late.

III

The text messages from one of the phones become Charlotte's lifeline. The text messages from the other feel like a looming death sentence.

From Henry, she learns that he has approached their parents and is confident that they will listen and do the right thing.

But our parents have never done the right thing, she texts.

He tells her that he has the moral high ground, that they know she needs to leave, that they feel guilty for everything that has happened but they are trapped between a rock and a hard place. Charlotte needs to be patient because they are now under the scrutiny and control of children's social care who, despite only having 50% of parental control under Section 20, appear to be compiling a case against the Ashmans.

Charlotte knows *that* is her fault. If only she'd never told some of the truth to that social worker. She had trusted Kate. Why had she not learned her lesson that you can't trust anyone? Kate is dangerous, she has nothing to lose. She wants to hang the Ashmans out to dry.

You need to keep safe, Sis. Keep away from anyone related to the gang. I don't want to scare you, but I think you're probably still in danger.

If only he knew the half of it.

He tells her that their parents are looking once again at private provision for her. He's told them how dangerous he thinks the Well Being Centre is. But they are anxious about costs.

They gave a bunch of money to my headteacher, Charlotte texts. *Bet they regret that.*

Henry is always reassuring, but it isn't as simple as just getting her out of there. As well as the investigation by social services, the family's financial issues are complicated. Money talks and money is not liquid right now. They are waiting on a sale from one of their properties in Oxford, some new apartments that they bought as a deal through their wealth management company. They were told that they would see a massive return, but so far, the rental is beyond what most could afford. They bought on the premise that Oxford has a huge teaching hospital and students from Dubai would be renting these luxury apartments. They have two out of the three apartments rented but are trying to sell the third one to release equity.

They've had an offer. It looks like the sale is going through, Henry tells her. *Hang in there, Sis.*

But the sale of property takes time.

And, from Charlotte's end, conditions don't improve. She tells her brother about the two men who come into her room to check on her every 15 minutes. *They stink of weed.* She tells him that she is okay, but she really isn't.

She dreads any message from the second phone. Then she gets one that makes her shudder.

Be ready at 2pm tomorrow. You're being taken to your new foster home.

The message is followed by a wink emoji.

Now there is no more time to lose. There is no more time to wait for property to sell, or for her parents to make up their minds about what to do with her. She tells Henry.

I'm coming. We'll make this stop, I promise. I've signed out for tomorrow. Whatever is going to happen, we'll sabotage it.

Now Charlotte is wracked with guilt. What if she gets her brother mixed up in something that he isn't able to handle?

Mum's received the news that they've found you a foster placement. I've told her that she has to trust me that it isn't safe. I've told her to reject the placement. I'm going to the offices of Children's Social Care first thing in the morning.

He signs off with his customary words, *Hang in there, Sis.*

But Charlotte has been hanging in there for a long time. She lies awake, in spite of the meds, imagining the nightmare ahead. She survives the night, spending most of it wishing that she was dead. But things do look brighter in the morning. Henry continues to send Charlotte updates of his progress.

He has met with Kate. He has also met with her manager. He has told them everything. They have made a plan. They have told the police.

The mixture of hope and guilt is almost unbearable. Her brother is no match for a vast criminal gang. Charlotte wants to believe, so much, that he can make it stop. But that would be the miracle of all miracles.

Another message comes.

I'm coming to get you.

Charlotte won't make the mistake of mixing up the phones again, but she is now so scared that she doesn't trust herself to believe that the message is actually from Henry. It sounds ominous.

Her bag is packed and she is ready to go. She just doesn't know who will reach her first and where she will be going.

By 1pm, with an hour to go until her scheduled departure, there is still no sign of her brother. It was stupid to think that he could save her. She has no appetite for her lunch as she resigns herself to her inevitable fate. Her mistake was in believing that things could be different.

On the dot of 2pm, Sammy appears at her door. The sly smile is back. 'Ready to go?'

Charlotte nods once, and swallows, as if she can swallow away her misery. She picks up her bag and follows Sammy to the reception area. The next few minutes are a blur.

There are two police officers waiting in reception. They read Sammy his rights. He begins shouting about the NRM register.

'The register isn't going to help you. You should have been more careful with your emails,' one tells him.

And then, the miracle of miracles, her brother is there, standing in the doorway of the centre. She stumbles into his arms.

'Come on, Sis. I'm taking you to Cornwall.'

IV

The drive is long, all the way across the country, to the family home in Cornwall. The afternoon is cloudy and there are traffic problems on some of the motorways. Charlotte doesn't care. It could go on forever. It might be cloudy overhead, but the fog has lifted from her mind, at least for now. The roof is down on the Mazda, she is with her brother, and Sammy has been arrested.

'Will it be just us when we get there?'

'No, Sis. Mum and Dad are coming. They'll probably be there before us.'

Henry tells her how their parents are actually flying under the radar of Derek.

'You never met Skinny Man. One of Dad's advisors. He was in charge when you were missing. He was like an emotionless stick insect. They're finally realising that he didn't care about us, or you. His brief was to protect the government at all costs, to manage damage. Trouble is, he caused a lot of it for you.'

It feels wonderful to be back. Charlotte wishes she could turn back time, too. The last time she was here was for the party to celebrate her mother's job. She hadn't begun at Hickman's. She was a different person. She hadn't liked herself very much then, she remembers, but she'd give anything to be able to return to being that little girl.

Charlotte is once again the centre of attention. Her mother evidently feels so guilty that Charlotte is waited on hand and foot. She brings Charlotte breakfast in bed in the morning. It will take a little bit more than breakfast in bed to persuade Charlotte to forgive her mother for ignoring her, for making her feel abandoned, for sending her away to school, for not protecting her from being raped, though that conversation has not happened. And Charlotte can't imagine it ever taking place. She wouldn't know how to begin, and Kirsty wouldn't know how to hear it.

The weather isn't great which means there is no sailing, to the relief of Charlotte.

For the first time in months, she feels like she can breathe properly. They have a lovely, gentle few days with no visitors, however the bond between Charlotte and her mother is an artificial one. They both know it, but Charlotte is only just recognising it. There is a stilted, contrived air to the polite, friendly chit chat. Perhaps that's all they can achieve. Perhaps that's what 'normal' amounts to for them.

Henry has to leave after a couple of days; he has to return to his strict training regime at Sandhurst. It's a place that doesn't appreciate lengthy family crises.

Not to mention Sophie, his girlfriend, who has been waiting patiently while Henry has been dealing with his troublesome sister. Charlotte doesn't want to imagine those conversations.

It's raining hard outside when the phone rings. It's Kate.

'Good news!' she exclaims. 'We have a placement for Charlotte.'

James puts the phone on speaker so that everyone can hear. It seems there are to be no more secrets in the Ashman family. Charlotte is to have a say in all decision-making.

'A lovely family. The Reynolds. They're down-to-earth folk, and experienced foster carers. Ron is a builder, come handy-man.'

Charlotte watches her mother's face drop. What does she expect? Experienced foster carer Ron is a surgeon and 18th in line to the throne?

Her mother's annoyance makes Charlotte like Ron already.

Kate continues, 'Angie is a nurse. They have children of their own and are waiting to adopt a little boy whom they have fostered for a while. They are up country, so it will be a bit of a drive, I'm afraid.'

'Not a problem,' James says.

Kirsty asks about education and doctors.

Kate assures her that they will find a place in the local secondary comprehensive school. There is another little flicker of excitement from Charlotte, who has wanted to go to a 'normal' school for years.

'I've emailed over the profile of the family. There are pictures of them all and of their home. Have a look.'

James flips up his laptop and opens the attachment. They all huddle around the laptop to see. A group of strangers is presented to them. A mum with shoulder-length blonde hair and pink cheeks wearing an oat-coloured jumper over jeans and wellies. Dad, Ron, is the same height as his wife, Angie. He's wearing a plaid shirt under a green fleece. In another picture is what looks like an older version of the mum and dad. The caption explains that they are the grandparents who live close by in the same village.

There are three older boys in the family.

'That's familiar,' Charlotte says.

They are all doing apprenticeships and still live at home.

212

There is a blonde boy standing next to Angie holding her hand and looking up at her. He looks very cute. They are standing in front of a lovely stone house.

'The house actually looks quite nice,' Kirsty says, after reading in the profile that the cottage has been in the family for generations. The front door is putty-coloured and there are hanging baskets on either side.

Kirsty usually hates hanging baskets and Charlotte waits for the comment. But it doesn't come. Perhaps her mother is finally dropping some of her snobbishness and realising that Charlotte might be safe there.

The Ashmans pore over the photos of the interior of the house. It looks cosy and clean and, to Charlotte's delight, there are dogs. A French bulldog and two springer spaniels that she falls instantly in love with.

There is a picture of the spare room that could become Charlotte's. Vintage bunting hangs along one wall and there is a beautiful patchwork bedspread. Angie must sew and make crafts.

Kirsty sighs and looks at her daughter. 'Well, I don't know about you, Charlotte, but I think I might want to go and live at the Reynolds' house.'

V

Decision made, Charlotte's mother reverts back to process mode, deciding to treat her daughter going into foster care the same way she has done with the children going to boarding school – by buying lots of new things to go away with.

'After all, darling, the cover story is that you are going off to study at an international school overseas.'

She stops short of packing up a trunk, and Charlotte finds herself in possession of five large, colourful laundry bags, perfectly packed full of winter coats, pyjamas, slippers and new outfits, plus art materials. Most is purchased online, and for the next few days, parcels arrive in a continual stream.

'The parcel man must think it's Christmas,' James jokes.

One of the items Kirsty has purchased is a lovely hamper from Fortnum & Mason.

'For the Reynolds, to say thank you.'

'Well, that's a lovely gesture,' Kate says, doubtfully. 'Although I'm not sure it's ever happened before in the world of fostering!'

It's agreed, after a fairly lengthy discussion, that Kate should take Charlotte up country to the Reynolds in her car. It has been quite difficult getting the Ashmans to understand how having a child in care works. It's not normal for the birth family to take the child to a new placement, then participate in a placements meeting. Even Charlotte, fully behind the move, almost begs her parents to drive up as far as they can. 'I could then transfer to Kate's car just for the last bit of the journey.'

The stench of Kate's car with its stained seat covers and stale food smells still reminds Charlotte of the gang members' car and she's anxious to avoid that. On the other hand, one-on-one time with her mother is never a delight. Charlotte chooses to sit in the back with her headphones on, thus avoiding actual conversation with her mother for the best part of four hours.

When they arrive at the service station, the designated spot for the handover, Charlotte spots Kate's car straight away. Kirsty picks up her handbag and walks to the back of the car to pull out Charlotte's bags.

'A strange way to travel,' Kate observes. 'You look like you're being chauffeured.'

Kate and Kirsty chat politely for a few minutes, while Charlotte repeats her ploy and climbs into the back of Kate's car with her headphones on. Kate looks on disapprovingly.

'Wouldn't you be happier in the front?' she asks.

But Charlotte has learnt her lesson. After confiding in Kate once, she has no wish to do so again. And anyway, Charlotte is sick to death of adults. Sometimes she can't tell the difference between the parents, social workers and schools, and the gangs and dirty weird men who she was made to have sex with. She still hasn't mentioned that. Kate would freak out if she knew about that particular chapter. There's no need to go there. She doesn't need any more reminders of that time. When she is alone in her room at night, those men's faces sometimes keep her awake. Not just their faces but their smells, their words... all of it.

Charlotte stares out of the window all the way to the Reynolds'.

It's late afternoon by the time they reach the village where the Reynolds live.

'I'm not sure exactly which house it is,' Kate says apologetically. 'The satnav is giving me several different options. I remember the colour of the door from the photo. But most of the houses seem to have putty-coloured front doors.'

'There they are.'

Ron and Angie have come out of the front door and are heading towards Kate's car, smiling and waving.

Charlotte shrinks down into her hoodie and pulls it up over her head with the headphones still on. Suddenly this is all feeling a bit strange, real and uncomfortable. She is a long way from anything familiar. And she has doubts about whether she's good enough to join this wholesome-looking family.

Kate gets out of the car and opens the back door to let Charlotte out.

'Come on Charlotte, pull down your hoodie.'

But Charlotte doesn't want to. For an old hippy, Kate isn't very laid back. Weren't hippies meant to be a bit more chilled out? Kate can be seriously uptight about stuff at times. She thinks she may be 'conservative with a small C'. Charlotte doesn't really understand what that means, but she's heard her parents say it about people.

Angie intervenes. 'Lovely to meet you, Charlotte. And your hoodie is just fine.'

Charlotte catches the wink that Angie throws at her and instantly feels better. Angie must have the measure of Kate already. Ron helps to bring the bags in, and Angie leads them inside, inviting Charlotte and Kate to settle at the kitchen table. It's a homely room, with a large, old-fashioned pine table with enough of a patina to suggest that, if it could talk, it might be able to tell a good story or two about the things that have taken place around it.

'Back in a sec,' Ron says. 'I'll just walk these bags up to your room, Charlotte.'

He thumps back down the stairs a minute later and is rubbing his hands together as he walks into the kitchen.

'Alright, then. Here we are. Have you been offered a drink?'

He has a welcoming persona that makes him instantly likeable, as does Angie.

'Where are the dogs?' Charlotte asks.

Ron explains that they are all at his mum and dad's house, a few doors up. 'We didn't want you to be overwhelmed. They can get a bit excited when they meet someone.'

Angie brings mugs of steaming tea to the table and puts down a sugar bowl and spoon next to them. The Ashmans would never have a sugar bowl. Charlotte puts two heaped spoons of sugar into the blue and white striped mug.

'That takes me back,' Kate says, holding out the mug. 'My mother had this set.'

'It's Cornishware,' Angie says. 'I've been collecting it for years.'

Charlotte has spent a great deal of time in Cornwall but has never seen it before.

'I'm from Cornwall,' she says. 'Well, not actually *from* Cornwall, but our holiday house is in Cornwall.'

'That's wonderful. I love Cornwall and I'd love to live there. It's a very special place. And of course, Cornwall is famous for its tin and pottery.'

Charlotte never knew that, either.

The Reynolds' own supervising social worker, Andrew, arrives next, coming around through the back gate and putting his arm through the backdoor, a stable door, to knock on the inside.

There are lots of friendly welcomes once more. 'Hi, come in, how are you? Tea? Kettle's just boiled.'

Charlotte already thinks she might like it here. It reminds her a little bit of Nanny and Bob's house. Andrew gets himself a seat at the table and then looks towards Charlotte.

'Hello Charlotte, it's lovely to meet you.'

Charlotte smiles and nods, and pulls her hoodie back, just a little bit.

Kate is quieter than she usually is. Perhaps she has been shrunk by all the warmth and positivity.

'Now, this next bit is going to be a bit of a chore,' Andrew says. 'There's lots of paperwork to go through, but I'll do it as quickly as I can.' He places a large folder on the table.

Angie stands up and walks to a door at the far end of the table. Behind the door is a pantry. She comes back with a tin that has parchment paper sticking out under the lid. She reaches for plates and places them on the table. Angie opens the tin to reveal lots of homemade biscuits. She puts the tin in the middle of the table and says, 'Help yourself.' Angie looks at Charlotte and smiles. She takes a plate from the pile, puts three biscuits on it and places it in front of Charlotte.

'There we are.'

This is something that Nanny would have done.

Kate is soon satisfied that all the paperwork is in order and shakes hands with Andrew as if they had just agreed on the purchase of a house.

'Is it okay if I see Charlotte's room?' she asks.

'Absolutely,' Angie beams. 'And I expect that Charlotte would like to see it, too.'

Angie walks behind Kate, then Charlotte, up to the top of the house. The room is even cosier-looking in real life than it was in the photograph. It's also larger than it seemed in the picture. There is a double bed over a thick, cream carpet, a small rug by the bed, and a little window in an alcove. The room smells of lavender, another reminder of Nanny. Kate goes towards the window.

'Nice view.'

Charlotte peeps from behind her. There are fields, woods and horses.

'Who do the horses belong to?' Kate asks.

'Oh, they're ours.'

Charlotte smiles to herself.

'Well, it all looks lovely up here,' Kate says. 'Wouldn't mind staying myself!'

Charlotte can't wait for her to leave.

When they come back downstairs, the front door is open and Andrew and Ron are chatting about vegetables and white fly. Kate heads toward the open door but turns back to look at Charlotte.

'This could be good for you. Make it work.'

It sounds almost like a threat, the way she delivers it. At the very least it seems a strange thing to say in front of everyone, and Charlotte doesn't really know what to say back. There is silence for a moment as Kate gets back into her car.

Angie waits until she's started the engine. 'Strange fish, that one,' she says, which breaks the tension once more.

Andrew gets into his car, gives them a little wave and is soon gone, too.

'Right then,' Angie looks at Charlotte. 'Let's get the dogs back so you can meet them.'

They head back into the kitchen and, almost as soon as Charlotte sits back down, in through the back door charge three very happy dogs. They bound straight over to Charlotte to say hello. Behind them are an older couple, who must be Val and George, Ron's parents.

'Hello, Charlotte, luv. It's so lovely to meet you. Welcome to our little patch of happiness here in the village. We've been looking forward to your arrival. We're Ron's mum and dad, and we live two doors up. This is Digby and Barley,' Val says, indicating the springer spaniels, 'and the bulldog is Puzzle.'

Val is holding a paper bag which she hands to Charlotte. 'I've knitted you a little something, nothing special, Just to say welcome.'

Charlotte opens the bag to see a pair of handmade bed socks, in peppermint green and pink. Lace has been knitted into the outside of the ankles to give them a frilly top, but more than that, they have been embroidered with her name. Charlotte has never seen anything like them. They're ridiculous, and she instantly treasures them.

'I'm George,' the man says. 'But you'd probably best call me Grandad. Everyone else does, whatever their relationship to me! Right, let's get you introduced to Lawrence. Give us a sec. You carry on getting to know the dogs. They seem to like you!'

A few minutes later Grandad comes back in through the kitchen with a boy in his arms. 'Here he is, and he's been dying to meet you.' Lawrence is grinning. 'Hallo Sarlott,' he says, not managing the 'ch' sound of her name properly.

Grandad puts him down and the dogs bound up to him which makes him laugh. Charlotte who has read and re-read the profile and studied the pictures that Kate sent, knows that Lawrence is a foster child who is waiting to be adopted by Angie and Ron.

'Hello Lawrence,' she says, and pulls her hoodie right back to smile at him.

He's a very winning child with his little blonde curls and he seems to be just happy to be in this house. Charlotte wonders if she can be happy here, too.

Next to the Aga is a giant wicker dog bed. Digby and Barley go to it and curl up together. Lawrence marches over to join them, while Puzzle, the bulldog, looks up expectantly at Charlotte, wagging the little curl of his tail until she invites him onto her lap. Charlotte feels happier than she has felt in a long, long time. Like arriving in the land of Oz after coming through a tornado. The trouble is, it all seems a little bit too good to be true. And she knows how that story ends. Everything about Oz is a facade.

Perhaps this will be, too.

VI

'Okay. Probably time to start thinking about dinner,' Angie says after a while.

It doesn't take long for the kitchen to be full of delicious smells and promising sounds. Onions, garlic and mince are soon frying. Ron peels a ton of potatoes and granny Val walks back in with a mound of green beans. 'Fresh from the garden. Nothing like it.'

Charlotte catches Angie looking at her, and gives her a shy smile, still stroking Puzzle. She really wants these people to like her as much as she likes them.

Perhaps it's the aroma of dinner that does it, but one by one three young men come in through the back door. They take off their boots and leave them outside, under the cover of the porch.

Charlotte suddenly realises that, once again, she is the only girl. She doesn't mind. This feels safe and familiar. Tom, Sam and Ben all say hello to Charlotte and welcome her to the family. Charlotte likes this busy kitchen, so different from the clean, clinical one at her parents' Surrey home.

'Don't feel that you have to stay down here, Charlotte,' Angie says. 'No need to be polite. I know what you teenagers are like. Go and settle into your room, get your stuff unpacked. Take Puzzle with you, if you like. I'll call you when dinner is ready.'

An hour or so later the call comes. 'Dinner! Charlotte? Boys? In you come!'

The whole family are quickly seated around the big wooden table, including Val and George, who've brought over an apple crumble for pudding. 'Made from the apples that dropped in the orchard.'

They chat about the various trials and tribulations of the days they've had, and things that are happening in the village. Tom and Ben are both doing agricultural apprenticeships; Sam is doing an engineering apprenticeship at the nearby recently-built helicopter engine plant. Charlotte is asked friendly questions that make her feel welcome and included.

'Now, while we wait for the secondary school to line up their ducks, which will probably be about a week or so, we've got some things lined up to help you learn your way around the area,' Angie says to Charlotte, when there is a lull in the conversation. 'We'll maybe start you with a dog walk. And then we'll introduce you to the horses, I reckon. I saw you looking at them.' She lands another wink in Charlotte's direction.

Charlotte eats more of the shepherd's pie and apple crumble than she's eaten of anything in months, and goes to bed listening to the background sound of chatter and life from the house. She feels safe tucked up in her little room at the top of the house. As if nothing can touch her here.

In the morning, Angie has Charlotte's medication ready with breakfast.

Breakfast, like dinner, is a flurry of people and activity. The toaster is filled and refilled, a pan is on the Aga, frying eggs and bacon, and there is a saucepan of baked beans for Lawrence, who has a dollop of them with a boiled egg and toast.

Ron smiles when he sees Charlotte's face. 'It roughage, luv.

Old Lawrence here didn't get much when he was first growing, so we're still trying to sort his tummy out. And we're winning, aren't we, Lawrence?'

Lawrence smiles and sticks his thumbs up.

After all the boys have gone, Ron goes towards the dog leads which are hanging up on a hook in the corner of the kitchen. Charlotte asks if she can go with him to take the dogs for a walk.

Ron smiles and says, 'That you can. But I rather think they're going to take you.'

He piles everything up by the dishwasher and Angie loads up the machine.

'Now, what size foot d'you take?' Ron asks Charlotte.

When Charlotte tells him she's a size six, Ron says that's lucky, and hands her a pair of newish spotty blue wellies to try. 'When we're next in town you can choose a new pair, but Angie and Val both take a six too, so you'll be alright for today.'

Before she knows it, she is following Ron and the dogs out of the backdoor and down the garden. They cross over a small ditch and make their way down to the stream where a huge swing is tied to a big old tree.

'Now, the woods are ours, and this is where we get the wood for the burners,' he explains. 'And a few of the neighbours come and help themselves.'

'Can I come on my own here one day with the dogs?' Charlotte asks.

Ron beams. 'Too right, you can. You can come tomorrow if you like. I'll show you where you can go. There's a short loop, and a long one. If you do the full loop it's a good hour and a half's walk.'

When they return from the walk, Angie offers to introduce her to the horses. Charlotte has always wanted to ride, ever since she was a young child. Her mother can ride but has never thought to let Charlotte have lessons, they were always too busy. Angie promises to teach her, in exchange for help with mucking out.

And so a new pattern establishes itself in Charlotte's life in the first week. Each morning, straight after breakfast, Charlotte takes the dogs out to the woods and along the fields. The dogs know the route like the back of their paws, so there's no danger of getting lost, even if she takes a little variation. Charlotte is soon learning her way around the village and surrounds, or perhaps the dogs are leading her home and letting her think she's taking them. Either way, they always manage to find their way home. In the afternoon, Angie takes her for a riding lesson. Charlotte spends a great deal of time out in the open air as a result and it doesn't take long for the colour to show in her cheeks, nor for Angie and Ron to point it out.

'That's better. You don't look so much like you'd blow over in the first puff of wind,' Angie says.

Charlotte is determined to 'make this work' as Kate put it so threateningly, and makes an effort to get to know everyone. Within a few days, she feels more at home than she ever did at the Well Being Centre.

'If ever a place had the wrong name,' she tells Angie when she talks to her about what it was like there. She's careful about what she shares, though. She learnt her lesson by telling Kate too much. She also doesn't want the Reynolds to judge her, or find out what kind of a girl they've really let into their house. She can't help but blame herself for many of the things that have happened to her; not yet willing to see herself as a victim of exploitation. She feels ashamed, as if once they find out about her past they might send her away.

She settles into the routine of life with the Reynolds very quickly. At the weekend, Angie and Val drive her into 'the big town' to buy bits for school on Monday. While they are mooching about, Charlotte spots a rucksack that she likes the look of. It's totally different from anything she's had before. An orange waxed cotton that she thinks would be good for school. She doesn't know if she can ask for it. Have her parents given the Reynolds some money to look after her? How does this all work? She goes back to it and picks it up again, looking at it longingly, but the price tag is steep and the Reynolds don't seem to have an abundance of money. Everything is home-grown or homemade and nothing is flashy. She walks away from it. Perhaps she could ask her parents for the money and come back for it next week.

When they arrive back at home and are unpacking, Charlotte spots the rucksack in a bag. 'There you go,' Val says. 'We saw you looking at it. Angie and I split the cost and bought it for you.'

'I liked it, too,' Angie says. 'Good choice. Bit different. Good on you for going your own way.'

'Thank you,' Charlotte whispers, slightly overwhelmed. Not by the generosity of the gift, she's well used to having money spent on her; but by the care that they've taken to notice.

On Monday, they take a quick tour around the school at which Charlotte is due to start. It's the same school that all three boys attended before they took up their apprenticeships. Although the village is small, there are 1,000 students on roll, bussed in from all the rural areas. Charlotte is welcomed in and buddied up with Flo, a feisty redhead who seems to know everyone.

Flo introduces Charlotte to most of the students in the year and, by the end of the week, she has friends in each of her classes, and offers to go out at the weekend. Each day after school, Charlotte sits by the wicker dog bed with Puzzle while Lawrence sits in it with Digby and Barley. Angie chatters away. The radio is on most of the time and Angie sings along when music she likes comes on. After dinner, Charlotte goes to her room to do her homework. Another new target is to stay on top of the schoolwork. It's hard to join mid-year, but the teachers are sympathetic to that and it's easier to hide in a class of 30 than it is in a class of 12 or 15.

After an hour or so in her room, she's called down for TV and hot chocolate and a homemade biscuit or three. This has become her favourite part of the day. Everyone piles into the snug sitting room and watches TV together. Sometimes a film, sometimes a murder mystery, sometimes a comedy. Angie usually picks up her knitting. Lawrence sits next to her and leans on her arm, sucking his thumb. No one asks her about her past and no one comments on the visible scars on her arms and neck. Alone in her room, Charlotte battles to fight the compulsion and self-soothing of cutting. She wants to slow down and reduce it, although the idea of stopping seems impossible. But she doesn't want to frighten her foster family. She is mindful to only use the blades from her pencil sharpener, and to keep the small towel, that she needs to wipe away the blood, hidden at the back of her wardrobe. She knows that Angie has seen her scars, and Angie is no fool.

After two weeks, this feels comfortable enough to call home. Now that she's at school she can't have a riding lesson every day, but she can wander down to see the horses. She also finds new ways to occupy herself.

George has a shed out the back of the house. Charlotte begins to spend a lot of time in there with him. It's a fascinating place. He has a bench and woodturning tools. He likes to make furniture and he carves owls and other birds and animals that he sells at the local garden centre and markets.

'It was a bit of fun that turned into a hobby and passion and then a bit of a business,' he tells her.

He teaches Charlotte to carve, starting with a little bit of whittling and a small knife. She finds it hilarious at first, that someone is handing her a sharp object; at the Well Being Centre all sharp objects were removed and Sarah was vigilant at Hickman's. She thinks about using the knife on her skin, how delicious it would feel. But she uses it on the small piece of timber, just as George shows her. She can't believe it when her first little creature, an owl, emerges from the wood.

'You've got an eye for it,' George comments. 'He looks like he has real personality, that one,' and Charlotte feels an unusual feeling: pride in something she's done.

The Cutting Girl is reinventing herself. She helps George make things at the weekends. He always has Radio 2 playing in the background, which she would have dismissed in her previous life, but she's never really listened to it properly before. It's actually quite good. They discuss opinions and events and Charlotte feels part of a wider world as a result. Val pops in with hot drinks and cake and admires what Charlotte is working on.

'Happen you could make a bit of money if you wanted to turn them into keyrings,' George says. 'You could sell them at the markets along with my stuff.'

Charlotte sets about getting her first bit of 'stock' together. She quickly progresses from carving owls to quirky cats, which she paints in bright colours, and when she gets to a dozen she gives them to George. The whole batch sells in a single market day.

'Like hot cakes,' George says. 'Much better than my stuff,' he chuckles. 'I've never sold out in a day.'

Charlotte has a few attached to her orange wax rucksack and some of the girls at school ask for them, too.

In the evenings, Angie starts her off with a piece of knitting in front of the TV, casting on for her and getting her to do a simple stocking-stitch. When she's mastered that, Val teaches her to crochet, beginning with little squares and rounds that they decide are coasters.

'I'll teach you to sew when there's a bit of room at the table,' Val adds.

Sewing involves needles. Needles that are sharp and tempting. Again, Charlotte resists the temptation to stash one away. The pencil sharpener blade and the towel are still in her wardrobe. Their first project is a tote bag. Charlotte had no idea that people made these things. She loves that she can make them. She's never been told that she's good at anything before, only that she's failing at maths or English or science. It's quite a revelation.

Charlotte comes back to her room to get changed out of her uniform one afternoon, only to find the pink towel washed and neatly folded in her wardrobe, all the blood stains gone. A tea towel has been placed on top of it, and a pile of J-cloths.

She goes cold. The towel was encrusted in weeks' worth of blood staunched from cuts. She knows that Angie sees everything, but this is a very clear acknowledgement that she knows exactly what's going on. Charlotte is mortified. She waits for the summons to an awkward conversation that evening, but it doesn't come. For the first time, it seems, she doesn't have to explain herself.

'Ben's wardrobe was overstuffed and tilting forward, so I've gone round attaching all the wardrobes to the walls with ties this afternoon,' Ron says at the dining table. 'A safety measure.'

Which explains how he must have found the towel. It's such a Ron thing to do. Charlotte can't look him in the eye.

Sam comes in later that week with a cut between his thumb and forefinger. 'Couldn't get the distributor cap off the Ferguson,' he says, 'so I tore the webbing of my thumb trying to wrench it. I'm an idiot.'

'Here, use a J-cloth, or a teatowel. They don't give off any fluff that can get in a cut,' Angie says, reaching down for a clean one to pass to him. 'Better than a towel,' she says, looking for a moment in Charlotte's direction, just long enough to check that Charlotte has registered it.

Charlotte has heard loud and clear. It's so thoughtful that it makes her want to cry. Bizarrely, perhaps, it also makes her resolve to try even harder not to use what has evidently been provided for her. But she finds herself alone in her room less and less, outside of bedtime. There is always something happening, something to do. Angie is teaching her to cook. It's something else Charlotte has never really done much of before. With Violet, the housekeeper in their Surrey home, taking responsibility for meals, there never seemed to be any point.

'Don't know what they teach them in those public schools,' Charlotte overhears Angie scoff to Val one day with a tut. 'Not life skills, that's for sure.'

And they're probably right, Charlotte thinks. She's definitely learned more here. Charlotte pores over Val's cook books, especially the Hamlyn All Colour Cook Book, written by a very young Mary Berry. She makes trifles, scones and stews that are all praised by the family.

Charlotte sends lots of pictures to her family of her craft

work, her cooking, her gardening skills and walks with the dogs, especially Puzzle, who has been granted special permission to sleep on her bed, something that would never be allowed back at the Ashmans' houses.

That's wonderful, her father writes and gives a thumbs-up emoji to lots of her pictures. Her mother is less enthusiastic about her creations and sometimes makes less than kind remarks about the Reynolds and their way of life.

Don't worry, Henry assures her. *She's just jealous. She feels guilty about it all.*

Henry also tells her, *You're looking good, Sis. Very healthy and wholesome!*

Charlotte has put on a bit of weight in all the right places and her skin is much better. She feels so much healthier than she did during the drug-addled chicken-shed days.

More importantly, there has been less cutting of flesh. Knives and needles are used for more creative purposes.

VII

Despite not being an academic high-achiever, Charlotte actually seems to be doing well in some subjects at school: namely art, Ddesign & technology, and food technology. She's also flying along in modern foreign languages. She has been learning French and German since she was at primary school and has had the opportunity to practise on family skiing holidays in the past. Compared to some of her fellow students, she seems practically fluent, which gives her great kudos in the classroom. It feels rather odd to be able to help other students when they don't understand something.

Flo's introductions have enabled her to make friends with some of the local girls who live in and close to the village. They go around to each other's houses, and everyone knows each other; the Reynolds family are certainly very well known, and Charlotte is welcomed everywhere she goes. It's an interesting contrast with her real family, who were also very well-known. Bizarrely, it feels as if there is a more genuine respect for the Reynolds than for the Ashmans.

With each day that passes, Charlotte feels less like an outsider, and less like someone could pull all of this away from her in a second.

Ron and George take her into their woods and teach her forestry skills; they even let her cut down a tree. She takes a selfie with the shy Ron and George in the woods, showing the tree she has cut down and sends it to her family WhatsApp. Henry replies with *Awesome*. Her other brothers tease her about being a lumberjack. Her father sends his characteristic thumbs-up emoji and *That's my girl*. There is nothing from Kirsty.

Why can't she just be pleased for me? Charlotte texts to her older brother.

Henry phones her in the evening to say that their mother is feeling bitter about the whole thing. She thinks the family you're living with are 'fucking plebs'. He does such a good impression of Kirsty that Charlotte can't help but laugh, even though the words are cruel.

Spurred on, Henry continues in his mother's voice. 'I have much higher expectations for our daughter than forestry school and cake making and selling those stupid little wooden trinkets at shit markets. Don't you care, James, that our daughter is being turned into a pleb?'

'Ouch. She doesn't really say all that, does she?'

'Well, perhaps I'm laying it on a bit thick, but you know what she's like. Don't worry, Dad tells her off and defends you. And genuinely, I think she's jealous of the relationship you have with your foster carers. I'm sure she feels inadequate as a mother because she didn't actually mother her daughter. She paid others to do it. And that has cost her dearly in so many ways. Anyway, I think your trinkets are marvellous. What are you going to make me for my birthday?'

Her brother sounds so wise and grown up. He's the one she misses the most.

Meanwhile Charlotte continues to flourish. The social work reports say she is 'thriving'. Again, it's not a word that's ever been used to describe her before.

233

The only blot is the fact that County Lines are in the area. She keeps her head down when she is out and about with her new friends in town and at school if she thinks gang members are nearby. She knows the signs. She knows the look. That's why she chose a rusty orange waxed rucksack: so as not to be mistaken for County Lines kids, or as a potential target. She looks like a happy girl who loves art and crafts, who comes from a loving home where there are adults looking after her. Which is what she is. And who she wants to continue to be. The type of bag that a County Lines kid wears is like a badge in a complex pecking order. When she worked for Avril and her gang she had a black Nike rucksack that never went near a gym.

She takes care to keep her scars covered. Now that summer is here, Angie has made a safe, private space for her in the garden where she can sunbathe (with a high factor sunscreen of course) to help fade the scars. Angie has a way of making this happen without it feeling judgemental. It's the same with the medication. It's matter-of-fact, but with attention to the detail of what's needed.

The older boys introduce Charlotte and her friends to wild swimming in the river nearby. The family can't afford a summer holiday, but the little wild swimming trips with picnics feel better than any expensive foreign trip she's had. Tom and Sam, the oldest brothers, both have girlfriends, but that doesn't stop them hanging out with Charlotte and Lawrence over the summer holidays. She never feels left out.

At harvest time, they help a nearby farmer and family friend, and it's all hands to the fields. There's a real spirit of camaraderie in helping to bring the harvest in.

'Proper country girl now,' Ron says.

It's true. She loves being outside. Best of all is the fact that she is able to ride. With Angie's expert tutelage she has made excellent progress and Angie now trusts Charlotte enough to be safe and ride out on her own.

A tanned, healthy, smiling child sends new pictures to the Ashmans' family chat. James tells her that she looks beautiful.

Again there is no comment from her mother.

She's being her usual unreasonable self, Henry says. *Ignore it.*

But it's difficult to ignore. Why can't her mother just say something nice? Would it be so hard? Why can't she enjoy the fact that Charlotte is doing something – riding – that her mum does too? It would be nice to share something.

When she starts to feel herself wobble, she tries to remind herself that she doesn't need her mum's approval.

Maybe we could ride together sometime? she texts privately to her mother.

Charlotte can see that Kirsty has read the message, but there is still no response.

Well, fuck it, thinks Charlotte. I don't need her.

But Kirsty has done something towards getting them together; she has privately been in contact with Kate to arrange contact with Charlotte. Once it's been agreed, a message does come through. *Shall we meet for lunch?*

You and Dad? Charlotte replies.

No, just me. Dad's busy.

Charlotte decides it doesn't mean anything and she shouldn't be too pleased about it, but can't help feeling excited as she looks forward to the date.

Kirsty has chosen a gastro pub that also has private rooms. It has a wonderful menu and a Michelin Star. Angie and Ron are tied up with work the day Kirsty arranges for it to happen, during the half-term, so Val and George agree to drive Charlotte over there.

Kirsty is already waiting when they arrive. She is smartly dressed, as she always is. The pub has a long gravel drive leading up to it and then parking to one side, and Kirsty stands at the large entrance doors as George's red Citroen Picasso winds its way along.

Charlotte has also dressed carefully: blue jeans and clean white trainers, a blue denim jacket and her distinctive orange rucksack. She gets out of the car and runs up to meet her mother, while George and Val walk behind more slowly.

'Don't you look… well,' Kirsty says. Somehow the pause seems to indicate 'fat', or at least that's how Charlotte interprets it. For some reason, a fresh faced and healthy Charlotte seems to annoy her mother, and she finds herself wanting to apologise for the way she looks.

George and Val walk towards Kirsty, who stretches out her arm to shake their hands. Kirsty is smiling like a dignitary on ceremonial duty. Kirsty wraps her arms around Charlotte who suddenly finds herself a little ill at ease with this theatrical display. George steps back and makes polite chat and Val confirms the time that they are meeting back in the same spot: in six hours.

'You have a lovely time, now,' Val says as they turn to leave. She hovers as if she wants to say something else, but George pulls her away.

Kirsty and Charlotte sit down to have lunch. Despite Charlotte having enjoyed a hearty breakfast this morning, she has developed quite an appetite, which she knows is as a result of all the fresh air and good living. She has also taken the dogs out and been riding before they left this morning.

Kirsty orders, without asking Charlotte, a charcuterie board to share to start with. Having the decision made for her annoys Charlotte, but then she reasons with herself that actually, a sharing board is nice.

She tucks into it, while her mother picks away at the odd morsel.

'I'm spending a lot of time at the gym,' her mother says, 'and running.' Rather than a statement of fact, it sounds like a dig at Charlotte who has a mouthful of food and is unable to answer for a second.

For her main course, Charlotte has a gourmet burger with truffle fries, and Kirsty has a salad. Charlotte tries not to feel guilty about it. And actually, her mum does seem to be making more of an effort. She asks lots of questions about every detail of her life at the Reynolds' house, although Charlotte can't help noticing that she sometimes grimaces at the answers, like when Charlotte tells her about her friends from school and having sleepovers where they watch films and eat Domino's.

Once Charlotte launches into a description of all the different things she likes about her current life, there is no stopping her and it becomes a monologue. How every morning she walks Lawrence to the chicken coop to collect eggs for breakfast. How Angie makes muffins every weekday morning for breakfast and a full English cooked breakfast at weekends. How she has created a shrine to Taylor Swift in her new bedroom.

Her mother seems to be looking at something on her phone while they're speaking. Is she actually Googling 'Taylor Swift'? How can anyone be on the planet and not know who she is. Only her mother.

Eventually her mother interrupts and steers the conversation back to the past: all their fun holidays abroad and their adventures, like the time a few years ago when they went on safari in Kenya. They chat about all the locations and people that they remember from the trip.

'We're thinking of the Caribbean this year for a holiday. How do you feel about that?' her mother asks.

'Yes! That would be amazing!' Charlotte agrees, buoyed by the memories of good times. While Charlotte is poring over the dessert menu which Kirsty has very pointedly put down, Charlotte can feel the tug of war rope pulling inside her alongside the olive branches being waved by her mother.

Kirsty has another surprise for Charlotte.

'Do you remember my friend Alexandra? From university?'

Charlotte doesn't remember Alexandra, but then she must have been introduced to hundreds of her parents' friends and acquaintances over the years.

'We were at med school together, and then Alexandra went off to set up a private health care business. She does rather well. I only thought of her, darling, because of you suddenly getting into riding! We used to ride together. Alexandra's father was a hedge funder, one of the seven who own most of the veterinary practices in England. Super rich, had racehorses and also looked after horses for other wealthy owners because his stables had such a good reputation. I used to love staying with her before I met your father!'

Charlotte isn't interested in racehorses or super rich hedge funders, but it's nice that her mother is making an effort to connect with her, even if Charlotte can't get a word in edgeways.

'Well, we reconnected recently. Alexandra invited me to stay for a long weekend. She lives near Winchester on a very impressive estate. We went fox hunting which I haven't done for years. It was very exciting. Anyway, darling, there was another one of our friends there, a trustee at an all-girls boarding school.'

Her mother names a well-known school.

'Anyway, to cut a long story short, I was chatting about you and your situation, and she thinks she can get you in.'

'Oh, right.'

Charlotte has a horror of going back to boarding school. The idea of being cooped up again makes her heart sink. Not just cooped up, but stuck with hundreds of girls with whom she has nothing in common, and every aspect of life controlled again. What a contrast to the freedom she enjoys at the Reynolds' and the warm welcome every afternoon when she returns home from a school where she is finally making a success of things. The whole thing makes her feel sick. Not to mention the threat of the same things that happened last time.

'I don't know if I want to. I mean, I…' she trails off. She desperately doesn't want to sound ungrateful, because she knows that the boarding school will be very expensive, and Henry has kept her informed about some of the financial juggling the family have continued to have to do.

'No worries, darling. It was just an idea.' Her mother changes the subject.

Charlotte breathes a quiet sigh of relief as her mother quickly moves on. Eventually they leave and drive into the nearby town. There are many lovely shops. Kirsty furnishes Charlotte with almost everything she looks at. Hoodies, new trainers, jewellery and room scents for her bedroom.

'Darling, you deserve it after everything that's happened. If I can't treat my own 14-year-old daughter while she's away…'

Charlotte cuts her off, 'Soon to be 15!'

'Exactly!'

For the first time that she can remember, perhaps in years, she has fun with her mother.

They return to the pub in advance of the appointed meeting time, and George and Val's faithful red Picasso is already in position as Charlotte and Kirsty wind along the gravel drive.

'Well, isn't that a lot of bags!' Val says. 'Have you had a nice day?'

'Delightful!' Kirsty says, before Charlotte has a chance to answer.

Charlotte nods, because, actually, she really has. She felt a little trepidation this morning, but there was no need, it has genuinely been good to see her mother.

'Well, that's wonderful, but we'd better get going. It will be dinner time soon and I expect you'll be hungry after all that shopping.'

'What's for dinner, Val?' Charlotte asks.

'Cottage pie and carrots tonight.'

'Oh great, I love that,' Charlotte says.

There are the usual, superficial, 'lovely to meet yous' liberally sprinkled by her mother at George and Val, before Charlotte and Kirsty share a hug. It feels good to be in her mother's arms. Charlotte walks to the car and puts her bags in the boot. She chats all the way home about a holiday to the Caribbean and proper riding lessons, only stopping when she sees Val's usually smiling mouth settle into a tight-lipped line and realises that she might be being a little bit insensitive.

'Sorry, Val. I didn't mean that there was anything wrong with Angie's riding lessons, or our summer. I love it with you guys.'

Val nods. 'I know, luv. We just move in very different worlds I think.'

VIII

As soon as Charlotte arrives home she throws her bags in her room and runs back downstairs to lie on the floor and be licked and jumped on by the spaniels and Puzzle, her darling.

After dinner she goes over to say goodnight to the horses and vows not to mention 'proper' riding lessons again. In the morning she makes a point of going out with Val first thing to help her collect the eggs from the hens and doesn't complain about how muddy the coop is.

But when she overhears Val at the gate say to Angie, 'I don't trust Kirsty. She's up herself,' she is horrified and wonders why she needs to feel apologetic for spending time with her own mother. She also had no idea that Val could speak like that about anyone. She's usually so kind and never has a bad word to say.

She tries to put it out of her mind.

At parents' consultation evening up at the school, Ron and Angie talk with all the teachers, and Charlotte blushes with pride to hear them sing her praises one after another. It's the first time she's ever been present at a parents' evening. Unlike her previous schools, no one dwells on the fact that she isn't an academic high achiever. She is asked about her future and she talks about training to be a nurse, or possibly taking her woodwork further. The whole evening unfolds into a positive and optimistic experience.

Charlotte finds a new game to play with Lawrence. She has started seeing animals in clouds and faces in knots of wood. The house has stripped wooden doors and furniture everywhere that expose dark, dry knots that Charlotte enjoys staring at. It becomes her thing and, when she shows Lawrence, they cut up address labels and write names for each knot-face. George thinks this is brilliant and helps Charlotte to photograph the knot-faces, showing her how to adjust the depth of field to take shots in micro close-up. He encourages her to turn them into characters and create a narrative for their adventures.

Together they self-publish a simple illustrated book and do a run of 50 copies at the local printers. Charlotte gives each of the Reynolds a copy, and they make a great show of getting her to sign them, just like a proper author. She sends everyone in her family a copy. Henry is enchanted by it, and James thinks *it's the best children's book I've ever seen*, but, as ever, nothing from Kirsty. The lunch and shopping trip was evidently a one-off. Her mother has no interest in her.

We're fed up with her negativity, too, Henry confides. *It isn't just you.*

As the season begins to change and Charlotte spends more time indoors, she finds herself having more time alone with Angie. Their closeness grows, and Charlotte begins to open up a little about what happened when she was at Hickman's.

Angie is interested in talking about whether she thinks she might be gay. 'I've noticed the way that you like spending time with Ben, Sam and Tom, but you don't have any other male friends.'

'I'm used to brothers.'

Angie also reminds her about the time they were out together and a youngish man had evidently noticed Charlotte and thought she was attractive, but Charlotte didn't want to engage with him.

'It's complicated,' Charlotte admits. Her friends discuss boys a lot, but Charlotte doesn't get involved.

Angie also broaches the subject of drugs.

'Yeah, been there, done that.'

'I don't want to pry, luv, it's none of my business. I won't push you. But you know that I'm here if you ever want to talk about anything. You're not the first child to join this family and, trust me, we've heard it all.'

Charlotte smiles. She isn't ready. She might never be. And whatever Angie says, Charlotte doesn't believe that she really knows about County Lines and sex rings. For now, she just enjoys spending time in the family and trying to feel comfortable in her own skin.

One of George's projects is making a large toy box for Lawrence, and Charlotte is helping him with the design and construction over a couple of weeks. He also asks her to draft out the words 'Lawrence's Toy Box' on the front.

She carefully chooses a typeface and traces it onto the box.

George encourages her to paint the box as well as do the lettering, and the finished job is beautiful.

'You've done a wonderful job of that,' George tells her.

She photographs it and sends it to her family WhatsApp, along with a picture of Lawrence by the box with George in the background, cleaning his brush on a rag and smiling.

Henry phones her in the evening.

'You won't believe it, but Mum now thinks the Reynolds want to adopt you as well as Lawrence. She's losing the plot. I asked her what her fucking problem was.'

'You swore at our mother.'

'She deserved it.'

Good old Henry. He always has her back.

'She said that you were becoming too attached to them. And that you're easy to manipulate which was obvious from your stupid involvement with a bunch of rednecks selling drugs and getting caught up with people trafficking,' Henry continues.

Charlotte shivers. It was weakness. She was manipulated. Her mother is right.

'She thinks that the whole Reynolds family are groomers, brainwashing you into not loving your real family. I nearly told her she was having a mental breakdown!'

'Yeah,' Charlotte says, but the conversation takes the wind out of her sails…

The Reynolds' eldest son, Tom, is getting ready to fly the nest. He and his girlfriend have found a little cottage to rent which is affordable and nearer to Tom's work. He finished his apprenticeship in the summer and is now on good money. His girlfriend has a job as a chef in the restaurant which is attached to a National Trust House that's not far from their new home. So, Angie and Ron have gathered pots and pans and bedding to help get them started, along with some furniture from the barn. Val has made them a double quilt in blues and whites, which Tom and his girlfriend are thrilled to bits with George has been around the new cottage and garden making sure everything works and has given the inside a lick of paint for them. He's also used his pick-up to take some plant tubs from their own garden to put outside the front door, 'so it feels more like home'.

All the Reynolds love the gardens and plants; they all know how to garden, and even Charlotte now knows the difference between a plant and a weed.

'If there is more green than flower, pull it out, it's a weed,' is George's sage advice.

On the day Tom is moving out Angie is unsettled.

'Oh, don't worry about me, luv. I'm sad, but I'm happy at the same time,' she explains to Charlotte.

They all pitch in to help with the move, including Lawrence. George empties out some of the boxes without letting Lawrence see and then gets Lawrence to 'help' him lift them. 'Because, I'm big and strong, Sarlot,' Lawrence tells her.

At the end of the hard work, Ron drives to the fish'n'chip shop and buys everyone dinner. They sit together on the spare chairs and on the floor, laughing and drinking tea. When they've finished eating, Val gathers up all the rubbish into a bin bag, 'to sort out later'. Charlotte has put a shift in today, and feels her place on a footstool in the midst of the chaos is firmly deserved. She looks around, grateful to be so fully entrenched in the love and kindness of the Reynolds.

'Would you do that for me?' she asks Ron and Angie on the drive home.

'Of course we would, luv,' they say, almost in unison.

Her mother's harsh words temporarily forgotten, Charlotte feels a warm glow inside.

IX

Lawrence's social worker, Petra, arrives unexpectedly. 'Just doing a spot-check to make sure that Lawrence is being looked after as well as Charlotte is.'

Angie is confused. 'What do you mean, *as well as Charlotte is*? How do you know how well Charlotte is doing?' Kate is Charlotte's social worker, Petra is Lawrence's, and Andrew is the family's supervising social worker. They don't usually have anything to do with each other.

'So, what have you been doing, Lawrence?' Petra asks him.

Lawrence tells her how he helped Tom to move house and carry the heavy boxes.

Petra checks the house for photographs of Lawrence, of which there are many. There is also plenty of Lawrence's artwork and photos on the fridge.

'I'm not stupid,' Angie says to Petra. 'Something's going on here. We're at the stage of finalising the adoption paperwork before it goes to court. What on earth makes you think that Lawrence isn't getting much attention? Because that's what you're thinking for some reason, isn't it?'

Petra looks embarrassed. 'I just needed a little bit more information for my report.'

Angie is fuming and vents to Charlotte when the social worker has gone. 'Now, where has all that come from – out of nowhere!'

Charlotte feels protective of Angie, and outraged on her behalf. The care she has received while she has been staying with the Reynolds has been amazing. She couldn't have wished for a nicer family home to be invited into. Why would anyone doubt that? Once again, she fumes, authorities think they know better and get it all wrong.

Henry continues to keep Charlotte abreast of family news. The big bill on terrorism looks like it will go through Parliament, finally, and all the signs are that it will be successful, so their father is a little more relaxed. Financially, things are a little better: they have some money from the sale of the apartment in Oxford and Kirsty sold a small house from her own portfolio, without consulting James, which caused a bit of a row. Kirsty has had a couple of meetings with Kate; has Charlotte heard about that?

No, Charlotte has not. Perhaps her mother is planning to organise another contact visit for the two of them. It has been a while since the last one.

'She seems much more positive about the Reynolds these days. She was really down on them at one point, but now she talks about how they've really helped you get back onto your feet after all the dramas at Hickman's.'

'Yes, they have. They're all wonderful. They've been so amazing.'

'I think everyone can see that. Apparently even our mother, now!'

Apparently, Hickman's is clearly a terrible school and Kirsty and James regret sending her there so much.

'I bet they do.'

'She's also asked us all to check our diaries, because she's trying to organise a family holiday with all of us together again.

I'm doing everything I can to get the time off because I haven't seen you in so long.'

'I don't think she's mentioned that to Angie, yet,' Charlotte says, determined to be cautious in her optimism.

'Ed and Oli are up for it, too.'

'Well, that sounds great. I think she'll need to get permission from Kate though.'

'Perhaps that's what they were meeting about.'

The contact arrangement comes through. The same venue as before, only this time her father will be there, too.

Val half closes her eyes and says, 'Take care luv. That family of yours, I'm not sure they know how to look after a Charlotte quite like we do, eh?'

This time when they arrive in George's Picasso, her mother is dressed even more expensively: head-to-toe Chanel, and her hair is immaculate. Angie has come with George today, rather than Val, and Charlotte looks at them side-by-side, her two 'mothers'. Angie is fresh-faced without a trace of make-up, while her mother is immaculately made up. Angie looks frumpy and unkempt in a checked shirt over New Look jeans and non-branded trainers. They really do look like they come from different planets, or are different species. Charlotte knows only too well how much her mother will be judging Angie for her clothes, and feels more than a little protective of her foster mum.

She is delighted to see her father, though; it has been a good while since they've seen each other in real life and not FaceTime. James is wearing a pale blue open collared shirt and pinky-red fine cords with a mustard yellow jumper thrown around his shoulders. He walks towards George and reaches out his hand to shake George's, assuming that he is Ron.

'No daddy, this is George – grandad,' Charlotte explains.

James covers the little *faux pas* instantly with a charming and skilful apology. He's so good at handling any social situation, but it still makes Charlotte feel uneasy.

He holds out a hand to Angie, too, who smiles and thanks them both so much, as they all stand for a moment a little awkwardly in the entrance of the gastro pub.

'Darling, how are you?' her mother asks, and throws her arms around Charlotte, who isn't expecting such an effusive greeting and takes a step backwards, mainly in an effort not to fall over.

George and Angie agree a time for collection then drive off. For a fleeting moment, Charlotte wishes they could all sit down to lunch together, then realises how ridiculous that would actually be.

Inside, Kirsty makes sure they have been given a quiet table in the corner. Menus are passed around and drinks ordered. The waiter politely informs Charlotte that, 'Unfortunately we don't have Coke or Pepsi, but we do have some locally-made organic cola.' Whatever that might be.

Still, they enjoy a long, lazy lunch punctuated by lots of stories from James. He talks about his recent visit to the White House and how they lost one of the French visitors, who somehow took the wrong turn and ended up in the president's private quarters. They talk about the two-week holiday in the Caribbean and how much the boys are looking forward to it.

'None of us can wait for us all to be together as a family again.'

Charlotte looks for some edge to the words, but her mother seems to be sincere.

Then Kirsty reaches into her bag and pulls out the latest iPhone in brand-new packaging. 'Darling, this is for you. An early birthday present. Yours must be quite old now. Time for the latest model.'

Charlotte is thrilled! She has been hankering after a new phone, but wouldn't dream of saying so to Ron and Angie, because she knows what they cost and that the family aren't rich. She has overheard them talking about money and never wants to ask for anything extra. James has bought Charlotte a new iPad and laptop, 'to help you with all the wonderful craft projects you're working on, and a little bit of homework'.

It is incredibly generous, and Charlotte thanks them and tells them that.

'Well, hopefully we're not just helping you out, but also helping out the Reynolds. After everything they've done for you they don't need to be forking out more. We know how expensive teenagers can be,' James says, with a wink.

After lunch, there is more shopping. 'You only want me for my money,' James jokes as he is cajoled by his wife into spending a fortune on new clothes for his daughter.

When it is time to collect Charlotte, this time Ron and Val arrive.

'Oh, I'm getting to meet everyone, today; I feel like I'm under scrutiny,' James jokes. 'I hope we pass muster,' he says with a chuckle as they all shake hands.

'Well, I'm not sure that's all going to fit in the car,' Val says, disapprovingly as she takes in all the bags of shopping and presents. 'Ron, we should have brought the pick-up to move that lot.'

'Oh, she's a card, isn't she,' James says, and Charlotte thinks it's funny, too.

Charlotte is tired on the way back, and closes her eyes. Val must think she's actually nodded off, because Charlotte hears her whisper to Ron that she suspects that Charlotte might have been a bit anxious, 'because Mrs A is a bit, you know'.

You know what? Charlotte thinks. She doesn't have to wait long because a moment later Val says, 'I don't like her one little bit. She's a stuck-up cow.'

Charlotte is shocked by her comment, and even more so when Ron seems to concur. 'Hhmmm, I'm not sure I'd trust that one, something's not quite all there if you ask me.'

'No it bloody isn't, Ron. No it bloody isn't.'

X

With less than three weeks to go until Christmas, Lawrence is very excited. Charlotte cannot help but feel the same. At school, Charlotte has joined the choir with her friends and has spent several evenings performing in old people's homes. She's found it surprisingly good fun and has enjoyed watching the old folk sing and smile. She is planning to meet up with some of the girls at the weekend for some Christmas shopping. She really wants to choose some thoughtful gifts for all the Reynolds family, to add to the animal family that she has been carving.

Angie is resisting the children's pleas to put up the decorations inside, but does relent and allow them to start to decorate outside. George and Ron put up tons of lights and decorations, mainly for Lawrence's benefit, but it is enjoyed by the whole village, especially the little herd of reindeer in the front garden.

Kate comes for her monthly visit with two pieces of news. The first is that she is leaving and going back to her retirement. Charlotte is pleased about this, she has never quite forgiven Kate for allowing her to be banished to the Well Being Centre with the medieval idea that staying in an unregulated secure unit would basically teach her a lesson.

But the second is the bombshell: Charlotte is to leave the care system. She is no longer going to be on their books. After an in-depth review it has been decided that Charlotte is ready to go back to her family and to their choice of school.

Angie slumps down in her kitchen chair. 'What? Let me get this straight. You mean Charlotte's not actually going home, she's going back to school, to boarding school?'

Charlotte bursts into tears. She sobs and sobs. 'I don't want to go. I want to stay here. No, please don't take me away. Please don't.' She is beside herself, not just at the thought of leaving but at the betrayal of her mother. She told her mother she didn't want to go back to boarding school. She told her!

Angie waves her hand across the kitchen table in short, brisk movements, as though she can somehow cut through the news.

'When exactly was this decided? *How* was it decided? How has that decision been reached without consultation with us?'

Charlotte is still crying, her head in her hands.

Val, passing by the backdoor on her way down to the hen coop, looks in. 'Is everything alright? Has something happened?'

Angie blurts it out. 'They're taking Charlotte away. They're sending her back to bloody boarding school.'

Val sits down too, putting the empty cardboard egg box on the table.

She looks at Kate with venom. 'Why? She's doing so well. She's so happy here. We think of her as one of our own. How can you possibly even think about doing this?'

Kate puts her hands on the table. 'Look, I know this is hard but it's out of my hands. Mrs Ashman has made a very generous offer to the local authority, who were, it has to be said, in some financial trouble, as most authorities are. So we weren't very well able to refuse.'

'I knew it! That bloody woman! Don't tell me, it was her who got Petra checking up on Lawrence, too, wasn't it?'

Kate shrugs in a gesture of defeat.

'She's Charlotte's mother and she has a great deal of power.'

'Don't I get a say in this?' Charlotte cries out.

Kate goes on to outline what will happen next, as if Charlotte hasn't spoken. 'Charlotte will be collected from here on the 22nd December, ready to spend Christmas with her family in the Caribbean for two weeks, then back ready for school on the 6th January where Charlotte will become a boarder at St Margaret's School for Girls.'

Angie breathes out as she pulls the written plan towards her.

Val folds her arms and sits back in the chair. 'So we don't even get to spend Christmas with Charlotte. Thank you very much, Mrs A.'

Charlotte is still reeling. She genuinely didn't know this was coming. She had no idea that her mother was planning for her to return to boarding school. She stands up and shouts out, 'Fucking bitch!' to no one and everyone and runs out of the kitchen. She stands behind the door, breathing fast.

The conversation continues without her. Val turns towards Kate. 'So, Kate, you're happy with this, are you?'

'Like I just told Angie. It's not up to me.'

'Well, I've heard you speak out with some strong views and opinions since we've known you. Why the quiet now? What's really going on, Kate?'

Kate taps her dry fingers against the tabletop, then says, 'As I keep trying to explain, it's not up to me. The truth is, I haven't exactly retired for a second time. I have been, let's see now, what's the phrase? Ah yes: let go. This is the last case I work.'

Val evidently isn't satisfied with her response. 'So you're just going to walk away from this, are you? You know as well as us that it was boarding school and all that nonsense with drugs and those bad men that got her here, so why on earth is she going back?'

Kate loosens her tongue further. 'It's down to money. The Ashmans are funding the school and, I don't know, but I think the Ashmans are not the sort of people to have their children in care.'

Charlotte can hear Val's voice in response. 'Kate, you know as well as I do that those private schools can be just another version of being in care, but without the love and family that that girl deserves and needs.'

Kate sighs. 'I'm done with the system, Val. It's broken. There are rules for some and not others. All I know is, money talks. Especially when our local authority is bankrupt.'

'Is it now? Well that was stupid. Who would have thought a council would be allowed to go bankrupt?' Val is incredulous.

Her parents sold her out at Hickman's with a donation to the school. Now they're doing the same to a local authority. Charlotte can barely believe it. She breathes even harder through her gritted teeth. The level of betrayal. How dare they?

The rest of the day and evening is a dark time for the Reynolds family and for Charlotte. It's difficult to know who is more devastated, Charlotte herself or the family.

Tom and his girlfriend come over for the evening to show support and join in the family's painful experience.

Charlotte has been crying all day long, until she has no tears left, only shuddering, heaving, dry sobs that erupt from inside her without warning.

After dinner, Angie and Charlotte sit on the sofa. Charlotte puts her head on Angie's lap whilst Angie strokes her hair.

Charlotte's tears might have dried up, but Angie's spill down into Charlotte's hair. Even Ron and George have shed a tear.

George has brought a couple of bars of chocolate around but nobody really wants to eat them.

Val's mouth chews away. It's a very angry mouth.

Back in her room at bedtime, Charlotte's devastation is replaced by fear. She knows only too well what it will be like when she goes back to boarding school. She feels as if she is being sent back to the war zone.

If she tells someone what really went on last time, would they stop it? She knows it's impossible. If people found out, it would destroy her dad's career and her family's reputation. Also, Henry might never look at her in the same way again and she couldn't bear that.

But how does she know that it's going to be safe? The new, more resourceful Charlotte begins to do her homework. What's this school even like? She looks St Margaret's up on her new laptop. It's a long, long way away from Hickman's. A good start. Bloody Hickman's is still going! The website boasts a new gym that has been named 'Ashes'. Close enough to Ashman's, and sporty enough to suggest cricket. So Martin still took the money then. Nice. Back to St Margaret's. It's all girls, so that might be better; no dodgy boys at least. What are their rules? How strict are they? She never wants to go out on Saturdays. Never again.

For the first time since she moved here, Charlotte struggles to get to sleep.

She spends the next few days fully processing the news. She is going to have to say goodbye to her friends at school, and in the village. She is going to have to say goodbye to the horses and the dogs. She is going to have to say goodbye to the Reynolds. She is going to have to say goodbye to her weekends with George, her afternoons with Angie, her cuddles with Lawrence. Just the thought of it all makes her cry.

If only there was a way to change it. But no one says no to Kirsty.

The day of departure arrives. Leaving the Reynolds is one of the saddest days of Charlotte's life, no question. Kate, who seems to have been brought out of retirement for the purpose, collects her from the house and informs the Reynolds that they must delete Charlotte's phone contacts and all social media; they must cut all contact with Charlotte.

Angie is raging once more. 'Why? Is it not enough that she leaves our home? Why does she have to be cut out of our life?'

'It's come from the top, and it's non-negotiable. Charlotte will be safe and well looked after in the new school. Having complicated attachments will not be good for her and won't help her move forward.'

'Come on, Kate. You know that's not true. The best thing for Charlotte is to have people who genuinely love and care about her still in her life!'

Kate looks down at the papers before sliding them across the table. 'Not in this case, it seems.'

There is a legal document insisting on total severance.

'Lawyers and posh old school networks keeping a vulnerable child away from the one thing that's good for her,' Val sneers.

Angie ignores the papers and ignores the boiling kettle. It seems that Kate isn't going to get the cup of tea that was offered to her.

'It's a violation. That's what it is. They'd rather hurt their own daughter, who is happy and safe; upset her all over again, move her and put her among more strangers, just because her mother can't cope with seeing and knowing that her daughter is happy – or "in care".'

Angie mutters something under her breath that sounds to Charlotte suspiciously like 'that bitch'.

So Charlotte can't even tell Lawrence that she'll write to him and draw him knot-face pictures, because that would be a lie.

And then in a blur of goodbyes and more tears, Charlotte is bustled into Kate's car and her time at the Reynolds is over. The closing of the car door before they drive away feels like the slam of a prison cell.

PART FOUR

Charlotte

I

In her final role as a social worker, Kate drives Charlotte all the way to the Cornwall family holiday home, delivering Charlotte for Christmas as if she's an Amazon parcel.

Charlotte manages to spend the entire journey with her headphones on and has minimal conversation with Kate, who no longer bothers trying to impress upon Charlotte the importance of manners and the appropriate social etiquette for being a passenger in her car.

When they arrive, Charlotte feels nothing as she meets her mother again. The old numbness has returned.

'I took the liberty of packing you some clothes,' Kirsty explains. They are all new, all expensive and all chosen for her by her mother who knows less and less about who Charlotte is.

'But I have clothes,' Charlotte says.

Even though they are all clean and Angie helped her to pack them, Kirsty is keen to wash Charlotte's old clothes. 'New Look and Primark? Really? I'm not sure you'll be needing *these* any more, darling. I think we can do a little bit better than that!' She expresses further disdain at the chunky hand-knitted jumpers made by Val and Angie.

When Charlotte is unpacking and gets to the knitted bed socks with the lacy tops and the embroidered name on the ankles, her mother holds them up with pinched fingers as if they were covered in sick and swings for the bin.

'No!' Charlotte pulls them out of her mother's fingers and puts them in her pocket. It is a tiny victory, but Charlotte doesn't feel like she has much fight left in her. She is tired from the journey and emotionally broken from the goodbyes. She already misses the Reynolds family, the hustle and bustle, the laughter, the calls of 'Where are my pants?' 'Dinner's ready'! 'Char! Puzzle be a good boy.' All the sounds that she has come to love.

Here in Cornwall, the family dogs are in kennels rather than in the house. It's the usual Ashman way of paying others to look after their family. The boys haven't arrived yet. Charlotte knows that they are coming back for the glamorous holiday and chance of winter sun, not to spend time with the family. And Charlotte doesn't blame them because what kind of a family are they really? Living with the Reynolds has shown Charlotte what a family life can be like. Her own family is hollow and pretentious and completely led by ambition and money. And Charlotte is under no illusion that the end of her placement was entirely driven by her mother.

True to their promise to Kate, she hasn't heard from any of the Reynolds. She keeps checking her phone, but nothing. She does find a card in the bottom of one bag, the bag that has all her craft bits in. Along with the card is a long, flat box with a bow around it and a small label attached. Charlotte quickly covers them up so that her mother doesn't see.

She waits for her mother to finish fussing around and

criticising her clothing and to go downstairs with all the washing that doesn't need washing. The fact that there is no staff in the Cornwall house is amusing, because Kirsty doesn't really 'do' domestic chores. Normally she would expect each child to do their own washing, but this time she is keen to do it for Charlotte. Maybe it's a weird show of being maternal or simply to be nosy. Who knows?

Charlotte sits with the box for a few minutes before opening it. The label is in Angie's handwriting and reads *Charlotte, we all love you and miss you and wish you a very happy Christmas. You will always be in our hearts.*

Well, it isn't Christmas yet, but she can't wait any longer. She carefully unwraps the box and lifts the lid. Inside is a silver heart locket on a delicate chain. When she opens the locket there are tiny pictures of the Reynolds family, one on either side of the heart in two group shots. The adults on the inside of the lid part and all the boys on the right with the dogs. She smiles and stares at their tiny faces. It's a perfect gift and so thoughtful. She puts the chain around her neck and hides it under her jumper, the rainbow jumper that Val made her because, without ever pushing things or making a big deal about it, Angie has guessed that Charlotte is gay. Everything that has been good in her life is in that locket and Kirsty will never get her hands on it; Charlotte will make sure of that.

The Caribbean is vibrant and colourful and festive – and yet the holiday atmosphere is pained and distant. They sit together at dinner beneath palm trees at the outdoor tables of the main restaurant in their luxury resort. They are surrounded by the wealthy and privileged and a few famous faces. It should be fun, but it isn't. James and Kirsty strive for jollity, but it all feels forced and empty. Nobody says it outright, but it feels like the end of an era for the Ashman family. The boys all have other lives and partners now, but are all aggrieved with Kirsty for the way she has behaved about Charlotte. Charlotte envies her brothers and the fact that they have all effectively flown the nest, no longer under the power and jurisdiction of their mother.

They even occasionally dare to challenge James on his politics. Oliver has joined the Green Party in the last few months and tried to call his father out on various aspects of policy. Charlotte no longer wears swimwear that hides her cuts. It's part choice and part necessity; her mother forgot when she bought the expensive designer beachwear. Charlotte's ultimate act of rebellion is to sit on the sunbeds near her family in skimpy bikinis that reveal her pain: large, crude, ugly scars that criss-cross her torso.

The scars aren't just a reminder of her former self, they also make Charlotte think about Avril. Avril who used to control so much of her life. Avril taught her how to cut in places that the teachers and her parents wouldn't be able to see. Avril, who even told her that she needed to be careful about how The Cutting Girl attacked herself because, 'one day, Charlotte, you might need to get a proper job. And no one will want to employ someone who is so obviously damaged.'

It's interesting to observe the effect her body has on other people. Some walk by and notice and immediately look the other way – perhaps so they don't have to think about the reality of what it might mean. Kirsty, James and her brothers have all been forced to come to terms with the significance of these scars in their own way. For Henry, it's shame and anger, and that causes Charlotte more pain. Perhaps for the first time, Charlotte really owns her scars. Making them public is a form of acknowledgement.

All through the holiday, Charlotte longs to be back with the Reynolds. She would give anything to swap sitting on a sun lounger for sitting in the dog basket with Puzzle and little Lawrence. Charlotte is very careful to keep the locket away from her mother's gaze. She is well aware that if her mother discovers its existence it will only make matters worse. She will wait until she has been delivered to the school to untuck the heart from her clothes and wear it proudly on the outside.

A silver heart that symbolises love and hope.

'Have you heard from Angie? Or anyone?' Kirsty asks.

'No, I haven't,' Charlotte answers truthfully, not wanting to provoke her mother by adding the words she wants to: *I know you're checking up, because you instructed them not to.*

After a few days, the holiday vibe really begins to drag. There is tacit agreement that this isn't just the end of an era, it's the end of the road for trying to fix this family. Somehow they survive the last few days. There is polite, strained conversation at the airport as they wait for their flight to London, then back to their Surrey home, then off they will all go again to their wider lives. Everyone, apart from Charlotte, is staring at their phones. Charlotte looks out of the plane window as they descend for landing, bracing herself for the next chapter. The next bloody nightmare. She really doesn't want to go back into the boarding school system. The whole idea of it makes her feel sick. When she was little, all she ever wanted was to be at home with Nanny and Bob. Living with the Reynolds was as close to that dream as she could have got. Better, even.

She looks at each member of her family in turn, studying them. She saves her mother until last. There is her bony chest and shoulders, her red hair pulled up by an expensive, tortoise-shell hair claw. Her gold earrings shine in the sunlight.

She wears a fresh, white, linen shirt that drapes stylishly over her straw-coloured linen trousers. Her toenails are painted dark red and coordinate perfectly with her mink-coloured sandals. As always, she looks amazing. Like something from between the covers of a classy magazine. But it's an illusion. Charlotte smiles to herself when she pulls down her boatneck top as far as possible to reveal the scars on her shoulders and upper arms. She knows her mother will feel humiliated by this. When they are disembarking and going through passport control, Charlotte makes sure she stands next to her mother as much as she can, inviting people to make their judgements.

The goodbyes are quick, the boys keen to scoot back to their various locations. Each of her brothers gives Charlotte a hug and they each offer positive slogans.

'Keep your chin up, Sis,' Edward says.

'Here if you need,' Oliver says.

Henry asks Charlotte if she still has the phone he gave her. She shakes her head. 'I never thought I'd need it again.'

He sighs.

James and Kirsty drive Charlotte to her new school. Her parents are both experts at putting on a brave face, but it's clear to Charlotte that her father is not happy about the decision that was 'cooked up behind my back'.

Money tensions are still in evidence, in spite of the expensive trip they've just been on. James seems cross that Kirsty has used the money from her property sale to fund the boarding school. 'I just think that, in the present circumstance, it would have been better for the money to be reinvested. Given the last year in government, I'm not even sure if my role as an MP will be tenable after the next election.'

'Write your memoirs, then,' Kirsty snaps.

'I'm not famous enough to write a biography,' he says. 'I've started to look around for something else. I wouldn't mind heading up a charity of some sort. There are a number that would suit my profile and experience.'

Not to mention the future image of himself that he desires to cultivate.

'Army veterans?' Kirsty offers.

'I've been thinking about that. But there has been some rather negative publicity around corruption with a few of the existing charities.' He carries on explaining how his PR person has suggested a children's charity. Being CEO of a children's charity would help his political career if he ever decided to step back in via another route. 'All of which goes to explain why I'm angry about the money and the underhand way it was all handled. Investments need to be carefully managed because we don't know what's going to happen, what lies around the corner.'

Charlotte sits in the back of the 4x4 with her headphones on, tuning in and out of their conversation. Her mum has packed everything for school. Charlotte has done nothing apart from load up a few Reynolds-related items into the orange waxed rucksack that seems to offend her mother. So much so that it's definitely a keeper. Her hand-painted cat faces are still dangling from the strap fastenings, looking a little new age and, what with Ollie moving towards Green politics, this is probably a bit much for the Ashman image. She's seen the way her mother looks at them. The hand-knitted socks are in her rucksack, along with Gertie and Fred. Val repaired Fred for Charlotte. It's a silly toy, but it means a lot, despite the memory of having over £1,000 stuffed in his body back in the dark days. It reminds her of Kirst. She never really valued Kirst as much as she should have at the time. But even though she knows she probably seemed ungrateful to her friend, she is still very fond of Fred. Charlotte wonders whatever happened to that money. Did the police just take it?

After a couple of hours of driving, they stop off at a gastro pub. Of course they do, her mother wouldn't stomach stopping in motorway services. Charlotte barely says a word through the meal. Another last supper.

Eventually they arrive at the school. Charlotte has seen pictures of it on the website, but she is a little daunted by the scale of the buildings in reality. It's a place that looks like it has a lot of history. The main building was built from stone in the 1600s. She only knows this because her mother wouldn't stop banging on about the building and the facilities at lunch. It has hamstone windows cut in beautiful circles and arches with old, diamond-lead glasswork. It's huge and reminds her of cathedrals in France.

'Very impressive. It was once a monastery, you know,' Kirsty says.

Next to it is a larger, black and glass state-of-the-art building that has been carefully landscaped to try to blend the ancient with the modern. The new building is the arts block. Next to that are the dorms. Each year group has their own house, and these are more Scandinavian-looking in design.

'The three different types of architecture work remarkably well together, don't you think?' Kirsty says.

Charlotte couldn't care less about the fucking architecture, or the way there are 'visual tie-ins through shape, colour and materials' or whatever it is that her mother is wittering on about. She just needs to survive it for the remaining two terms of Year 10, and then two more plus exams in Year 11. That's how she's rationalised it to herself. Terms. She can survive four and a bit terms. Surely. That's all it is.

One thing Charlotte does notice is that it looks incredibly expensive. A big step up from Hickman's that's for sure. Kirsty has so far kept pretty quiet about how much this is going to cost. Perhaps she's breaking down the remaining number of terms just as Charlotte is.

'It looks perfect, doesn't it darling? I think you'll be very happy here.'

Charlotte is still miserable, but now she's also fearful. Not about starting somewhere new. God knows she's done that enough over the last few years. No, she's fearful about safety. As if reading her mind, Kirsty says, 'The levels of security and safeguarding here are exemplary. They're going to take very good care of you.'

The principal, Laura Downey, comes out to meet them as they stand in the entrance hall. Charlotte is the only new student today. Principal Downey shakes all of their hands. Charlotte smiles but doesn't mean it. The principal thanks Kirsty for her generous donation; James looks horrified. Charlotte scoffs as she thinks about the 'Ashes' gym. Money talks and it can certainly walk, mostly away for Kirsty. So, her parents, or at least her mother, has donated money to broker a deal to get Charlotte in. Who'd have thought?

While they have tea in her office, Kirsty humiliates Charlotte by giving the principal a tight brief to, basically, not let Charlotte do anything. She doesn't reference her prior history – does the school even know about that? Instead, she makes it seem as if the Ashmans simply have very old-fashioned views about how girls should grow up. This is so at odds with her mother's real philosophy that it's laughable. Nevertheless, it is agreed that

Charlotte can go on trips and outings that are supervised by staff, but under no circumstances is she to spend any time on her own outside the campus. 'We've picked this school specifically because it is a ladies college,' and her mother, 'wants Charlotte to become a lady as well as reach her potential.'

Yeah, right.

Principal Downey assures them that she 'runs a pretty tight ship.' She talks eloquently about the wrap-around care they have planned for Charlotte to keep her safe and bring her learning up to speed. She shares her educational philosophy of high expectations for all the girls and waves her hand to indicate the many photographs of alumni that adorn the walls. Her parents ooh and aah appropriately over the most well-known of the names. There are a lot of overseas girls at St Margaret's, Principal Downey explains. They come from all corners of the globe: from Hong Kong, Mexico, Thailand, Japan, Malaysia, China, Spain, Germany, France and of course the UK. This place is awash in money and with that comes high security. Charlotte will not be able to become involved with locals nor will there be any drug culture allowed within the school. There is a zero-tolerance policy.

Charlotte already hates this place. She longs for her tatty old school in the Reynolds' village, with her friends, and teachers that were fun and who encouraged her to be herself. Every girl here looks like a clone in their uniform. There is no individuality. In casual clothes they look like fashion shoots in a magazine, expensive and stylish. Charlotte's new clothes are exactly the same; Kirsty has paid attention and done her homework. At least from that point of view Charlotte will fit right in.

But her mother has also bought eyes and ears. She can do nothing without her mother knowing. Every penny she spends is to be accounted for. Her phone will be checked to see who she's had contact with. Her mother is particularly insistent that she has no contact with the Reynolds. How can she not see that they are not a problem? It's as if her mother somehow sees a harmless, loving family as more of a threat than County Lines and gangs.

After James and Kirsty leave, to embark on what will, no doubt, be a fairly frosty car journey home, Charlotte is escorted to her room by one of the senior prefects, so she can unpack. The new school term begins tomorrow. Charlotte has to share a large room with three other girls and is a little overwhelmed by this. But at the same time, she laughs to herself. She knows that her mum will have paid a fortune, but for what, exactly? The bedrooms are painted white and decked out in IKEA furniture. To be fair, they are clean and modern, and there are little communal areas in each corridor which Charlotte has already decided she will have no interest in. She's not hanging out with anyone. She is going to be a loner. That's a conscious decision. She doesn't want any part of this.

She will simply endure it, somehow, alone.

II

The school has umpteen rules and expectations which kill Charlotte's recently found freedom. At the Reynolds' she had the run of the fields and woods, the adventures of every dog walk with Puzzle and the springer spaniels, and the joy of riding in the open air. Here she is always being watched, and written about – all the girls are, but especially Charlotte because her mother has paid extra for micro-management, believing it to be the best way to keep her wayward daughter away from trouble. The problem is that rather than feeling safe, it just feels oppressive.

At the end of each week Charlotte has to sit down with her pastoral adviser, Miss Shambrook; each year group has its own pastoral adviser. They meet with each girl at the same time each week, and spread them out through the week so that there are appointments with girls every night. Charlotte's is at the end of the week, the second to last appointment on a Friday. When she asks why, Miss Shambrook tells her that it's because, for some reason, the pastoral lead thought they would reverse the alphabet.

'Girls whose surnames start with the early letters of the alphabet have been used to going first for everything since they were in primary school, so now they go last.'

Great. It makes Charlotte feel like she's part of some weird social experiment.

Instead of asking Charlotte about how she feels, the session is constructed around going through all of the observations and comments that her various teachers have written. Miss Shambrook is young and doesn't seem to know what she's doing. It feels critical and punitive. Charlotte is more astute than she was a year and a half ago and can see through some of the systems. The pastoral adviser isn't really interested in Charlotte. This is more about self-protectionism. Everything that is written about her is to tick a box and protect their jobs and the school's reputation. Perhaps they don't even realise this is what they're doing. Maybe they really believe they're helping. As far as Charlotte is concerned, it's all bollocks.

They don't know her.

Charlotte's self-imposed isolation means that *nobody* knows her here. She keeps herself aloof from the other girls. As the new girl, mid-year, she is on the back foot; friendship groups have already been formed. Some of the nicer girls try to befriend her, but Charlotte keeps them at a distance and they quickly give up. They're either too emotionally young and annoying, or a snitch. There is no one to relate to. And, although it's her choice to set herself apart, the price she pays is loneliness.

Used to all the exercise and outdoor life, Charlotte still eats the same kinds of portions that she did at the Reynolds', and is repulsed by the fat that she feels appearing on her body. She works out a way to deal with that, though; she can make herself sick after a big meal.

When Charlotte looks around, she does see girls who might be described as 'thriving', but they are girls who know their futures, who know who they are and where they want to get to. Girls that someone like Kirsty would be proud of. Charlotte doesn't fit the mould. If she analyses it, she'd say the school is like some sort of very expensive boot camp in which she just feels like an outsider who is trapped. There is nothing homely about her IKEA dormitory. The uniformity is a world away from her cosy room at the Reynolds', with its warmth and its patchwork quilt and its rug.

Charlotte begins to reduce her food intake. It's one of the only things she feels that she can control. But 'they' are monitoring that too and her eating comes under scrutiny. The school has created a culture of lofty snitches; girls report on each other to the staff.

Charlotte steals a lightbulb out of the store room and takes it to her room where she smashes it and uses the thin shards to cut herself.

As before, she is careful. She is an old hand at this. She does it while sitting on her knees by the bath, catching the blood with toilet roll or letting it drop into the bath where she can wash it away.

It lets out some of her inner pain. It gives her relief.

She hates it at St Margaret's Ladies College. She has a lot of time to think. Her mum has placed her here to punish her for loving the Reynolds family, for fitting in with the people she called 'plebs'. It's unbearable.

But, despite being all about control, Charlotte discovers that there are girls here taking drugs and getting away with it. The principal is naive if she thinks it's not happening. Dealers love private schools, as Charlotte knows only too well; the kids always have money and are desperate to rebel. The thing is, they're not very good at knowing when to stop. How many kids in the private system develop addictions? A number that would shock her mother, that's for sure. How much translates into their adult world? What happens when the kids grow up and move into their cool jobs in the music industry or the arts or the media world? She knows her brother Oliver is smoking a lot of weed. What would their father think of that?

The world she is back in seems to be all about denial and lies.

While she was living with the Reynolds it was all about truth, and tangible things. Making, creating, getting your hands dirty. It was the happiest time of Charlotte's life and the experience of living with them has made it very hard to do *this*.

When Friday comes around again, she sits with her pastoral adviser, a recent graduate who doesn't even have a teaching qualification, Charlotte discovers.

Miss Shambrook reads from her notes. 'Charlotte, yesterday you chose chilli for dinner and no pudding, and you drank two glasses of water.'

This level of scrutiny seems so pointless and petty, and it's killing her. She hasn't even been here for half a term yet. It had seemed possible that she could survive the time if she counted it out in weeks, but now she doesn't even think she can do that.

But again, when she looks around, she can see that the control seems to work for some of the girls. Some of the international students, in particular, thrive on this level of control towards them. It means that they don't have to think, they just do as they're told.

Charlotte's pastoral adviser clearly hates her job. Miss Shambrook graduated from university and is earning some money before she goes off travelling. She has a family connection to the school which is how she got the job in the first place. Apparently, there is no skill or experience needed in working with young people. Charlotte has noticed over the last month that her notes are becoming shorter and repetitive. Everything starts with, 'Charlotte, you have worked hard in X subject this week and should be congratulated for…'

It's their way at the school. It's meant to feel like a personal letter to the girls, but it doesn't. Instead, it's patronising and bossy and makes Charlotte want to change her name. She is sick of seeing it and hearing it.

The lead pastoral adviser announces that there will be interviews for two new advisers as Miss Shambrook and another member of the team are leaving at half-term. Charlotte is not surprised. It's so boring and meaningless. It's just a way of creating accurate logs for insurance that's being dressed up as care. That's why it's a graduate's job; no one stays very long.

The cutting becomes more frequent.

Charlotte's weight is dropping and the clothes she chooses become baggier to disguise it. Every time she goes out to the shops she is accompanied by a chaperone, a member of staff. She can spend her money, the money Kirsty gives her, but everything has to be accounted for. Receipts are kept and a careful ledger is completed. There is no way of spending a single penny without her mother knowing exactly where it has gone. Apparently, this is to help students to 'learn effective money management skills' but, of course, it's just another form of oppressive control.

Charlotte wears her rainbow jumper underneath a huge black hoodie, along with baggy bottoms. There is no nod to fashion when you're developing an eating disorder.

Charlotte asks if she can go back on meds. Angie had, in consultation with their local GP, gradually reduced Charlotte's medication and then phased it out completely, but now she needs some scaffolding to help her through each lonely, controlled day. There are things to do and some of the teachers are lovely, as are some of the girls, but Charlotte is locked into a mindset that she hates and can feel its destructive power. She has regular family meetings online with her parents. Her father tries to engage but is always late, time is short and he has no idea who his daughter really is anyway.

Her mother accidentally, or possibly on purpose – who knows – drops the 'Whoopsie' bomb during one of their conversations. Charlotte gets up and walks away from the laptop.

Days run into weeks. She has tried texting Angie, but nothing has come back.

Perhaps all the love she felt in the Reynolds household was fake, too? They obviously didn't care about her if they can dump her so easily.

It's Wednesday morning, a drizzly day. Charlotte and her art class are going out for the morning to do some sketching in the gardens of a local National Trust property and, as they climb aboard the coach, there is a glimpse of sun from behind a cloud.

It's a tiny moment of epiphany: she really needs to be outside more. She needs to get away from *here*. In the gardens, she finds a spot alone and manages to get caught up in a shrub as she clambers through foliage. Her cover story is that she's checking out some fungi as a proposed subject for her artwork, but the truth is that she's looking for magic mushrooms to alleviate the boredom. Because her money has to be accounted for so closely, she can't join the girls from her art class who buy pingers, the little tabs of MDMA, from the local dealers in the lane outside school. She has to rely on natural, free drugs to get off her head and try to have a break from this bloody place. But there aren't any, so she returns empty-handed and only receives a curt instruction to sort out her hair before she returns to school.

'We can't have one of our own looking like that!'

There is a degree of urgency to get back to school, since the morning art class has overrun a little and a few girls need to be back pronto. They've been chosen to show the graduate pastoral candidates around the school before their interviews in the afternoon. The little suck-ups. Charlotte hasn't been selected. Why would she be? Another thing she has been left out of.

The girls are in their regulation dark blue and grey uniforms. They all look smart – and identical. Some of the selected girls are already lining up by the main front door as the coach draws up. The deputy principal brings out a line of young women, ready for their tour. Charlotte gives a loud yawn while looking out of the coach window. One of the graduate candidates looks a little familiar. She frowns and takes a closer look. Then her stomach tightens and she feels sick.

It's Avril.

But it can't be. Avril must have been arrested after everything that happened? Musn't she?

III

The lunch break gives Charlotte the opportunity to take a closer look. She hides behind shelves in the library as the train of graduates walk through, led by one of the St Margaret's girls who is busy pointing out things and explaining where everything is. She peers through a gap in the shelf. The girl has Avril's colouring and Avril's accent. Her name badge says 'Isabelle' and Charlotte overhears her saying that she is Italian. On the coach, she'd managed to convince herself that she was mistaken. She was right, this isn't Avril, but it's someone very like her. Charlotte doesn't believe that she's Italian. She must be Albanian, like Avril. Charlotte finds herself shaking. This is terrible. What if she's connected to a gang? Is it too far-fetched to think that? Charlotte struggles to think rationally. She just knows that she can't go through any of that ever again. Seeing this girl, so like Avril, feels like being in a waking nightmare. Perhaps there really is no escape. Perhaps she is destined to be pulled back into County Lines and sex work.

Is it just a coincidence that this girl is here with her strange accent? Her father always says that there is no such thing as a coincidence.

Charlotte feels terrified. She can't control her breathing. She feels like she might pass out, here in the library.

It feels as if the predator has come to get her.

Back in her room, after the final lesson of the day, Charlotte cuts herself: deeper than she ever has before, right into the flesh of her forearm, all the way through the flesh as far as she can go until she meets the resistance of bone. Oh, yes. Yes. Then she panics again and cleans it all up. She has a few big plasters stashed away that she puts on her arm and rolls down her sleeve to cover it up.

Isabelle gets the job. Of course she does. She starts the following Monday. The good news, if there is any such thing, is that Isabelle is not appointed as the pastoral adviser for Charlotte's year group. Charlotte can try and ignore the fact that she is here and will not have to have anything to do with her.

Charlotte has a bit of a fever and genuinely feels unwell. She is checked on by the school nurse and house parent, neither of whom think to check her arms for cuts. She thinks the deep cut has become infected, but can't tell them that.

They decide that Charlotte has a temperature and should take some paracetamol, stay in bed and rest. Part of her fever is fear. Charlotte still doesn't know if Isabelle knows that she is at this school. The not-knowing is awful. Charlotte just wants to run.

By the end of the week, cocaine and weed are already available in the school. Isabelle – it must be her – has evidently recruited her network of 'clean skins'. Charlotte remembers how Avril talked about the way the gang had deliberately targeted private schools. She is certain that's what is happening again here.

She manages to blag some weed and coke from a girl she knows through art, who is in the year below her; the year group for which, coincidentally, Isabelle now has pastoral responsibility.

Charlotte manages to stay away from Isabelle. There is no need for her to have anything to do with her year group, but Charlotte knows, deep down, that it's only a matter of time. Sooner or later their paths will cross.

Charlotte is right. It doesn't take long. Nine days. Charlotte is sitting in the communal lounge in her house, by herself, when she looks up and sees Isabelle.

'Hello, Charlotte, are you ready for work?'

Charlotte sighs. 'What do you mean?' she says, although she knows the answer to that question.

'I think you know what I mean.'

Charlotte's right hand goes instinctively to the place on her left arm where the infected wound still festers underneath her sleeve.

Isabelle notices the movement and smirks.

'I think you and I could help one another.'

No, no, no. This cannot be happening again.

'You could help me recruit,' Isabelle says, lifting the sleeve of Charlotte's school blazer. 'Ouch.'

'It's fine,' Charlotte says, snatching her arm away.

'I see you, *Charlotte*. I know who you are.'

Maybe Isabelle does know who Charlotte is. Maybe she just recognises Charlotte's fragility and sees an easy target. Whoever Isabelle is, Charlotte feels as if she has been backed into a corner. Charlotte stands up. It takes all her powers of self-control to say, 'Excuse me, I have a lesson I need to get to.'

Back in her room, Charlotte responds the only way she knows how: she prepares her rucksack, packing a change of clothes, and then she cuts herself.

Deep into the other arm.

Deep into the flesh of her thighs.

When she reaches a point where it becomes too much, she manages to get herself to the house parent who calls an ambulance.

Charlotte is taken to hospital. She is patched up and put on antibiotics. Perhaps it won't be long until Isabelle, or someone else from the gang, comes to the hospital. She doesn't have much time.

Straight after breakfast and the doctor's ward round, she legs it out of the hospital. She has no money and knows better than to use her card. Where she really wants to go is to the Reynolds, but they have let her go and will have moved on by now. Besides, she doesn't want to bring all this nightmare onto them. All she knows is that she has to keep moving. If she stops, she will be found. She has a vague plan to aim for Cornwall. Her parents will not be there and she knows where the key is kept. She can hide out there for a bit. But it doesn't much matter where she ends up.

She'll find a way to get hold of some cash; she's nothing if not resourceful.

She no longer cares what happens to her.

IV

When the alarm is raised by the hospital about their missing patient who is a vulnerable minor, several things happen in different places.

Firstly, several police officers descend upon St Margaret's School and Principal Downey is obliged to let them search Charlotte's possessions to see if they can discover anything that might give a clue to her whereabouts.

Charlotte's parents are informed of her disappearance.

'For Christ's sake. Not again!' Is James' reaction.

Of course, this time there is no suggestion that she has been abducted. The assumption is that she's run away because she's involved in criminal activity. Given her previous history, it's the obvious reasoning.

Kirsty doesn't take the news well.

'Darling, don't blame the school. I'm sure they've done everything they can to keep her safe,' James says.

'I'm not blaming the bloody school,' Kirsty growls. 'I'm blaming our idiot daughter. What the hell has she got herself involved in now?'

'We musn't jump to any conclusions,' James says.

'Oh, yes? Don't tell me you aren't already worrying about the headlines in your constituency when the news breaks, as it inevitably will.'

'I think her safety should be our first priority.'

'But she isn't taking her own safety seriously. She's chosen this. She's run away. We've done everything we possibly can for her and yet she just throws it back in our faces! She's a bad child through and through.'

'I'll let the boys know,' James says, reaching for his phone.

'No, don't do that. There's no need to let the boys know just yet. We don't want them to worry, or for Henry to interfere again.'

So the Ashmans do nothing.

Charlotte is listed as a missing person.

It isn't until 10 days later that another call is made; this time by Social Services to Angie Reynolds. Charlotte's case isn't a high priority, but one of the police officers who was called to St Margaret's has been in touch in case there has been any contact between Charlotte and her former foster care family. The enquiry has been passed to a member of the social services team at the local authority who has no knowledge of Charlotte, or Kate. 'I'm ever so sorry to bother you, but I'm just checking to find out if you happen to have heard from,' she pauses, 'bear with me, a Charlotte Ashman recently?'

'No, of course I haven't. You told us not to and made us delete her number from our phones so we couldn't.'

'Okay, thanks very much. As I say, I was just asked to check.'

'Hang on a minute. Why are you asking us? Has something happened to her? Is she okay? Where is she?'

Angie isn't able to gather much information other than that she seems to have run away from school and there is police involvement because she's involved in drugs. As soon as she gets off the phone she shares the news with Ron, George and Val, trying to shield Lawrence from as much as possible. They're all horribly concerned about where she is and what might have happened to her.

George then triumphantly pipes up, 'I know something that may help to find her. I put one of those air tags in her rucksack. You know, the orange one she really liked. If she's got that with her, we might be able to see where she is.'

'What do you mean, you put an 'air tag' in it? What's an air tag when it's at home?'

'I was listening to Jeremy Vine on the radio. He was talking about how he lost his keys but managed to cycle across London and find them because he put an air tag on the key ring, I thought what a good idea it was, and it was just after I got my iPhone, so I was all teched up. Deep down I was always worried about Charlotte. We never really knew what she had been involved in, did we?'

Angie says, 'That's brilliant, Dad. Where's your iPhone?'

While they are searching the phone, Val is amazed. 'How on earth did you set it up?'

'Same way I do with everything else,' George says. 'I watched a tutorial on YouTube.'

Ben and Sam, the IT wizards, take over and use the 'Find My' app and there it is: Charlotte's tag.

'She's in Birmingham!'

'Let's do it,' Ron says to George. 'I'll get the car.'

'I'm bloody coming too,' Val says. 'Give me a second to get some blankets, drinks and food. That poor child.'

V

Three of the Reynolds head to the nearest supermarket petrol station, fill the tank of George's red Picasso and begin the long drive to Birmingham. Meanwhile, Angie calls the police to get hold of someone who knows what's going on, seeing as the council offices are closed and no one wastes their time with the out of hours teams. It takes Angie several hours to finally speak to someone in the right police department, by which time the other Reynolds are closing in on the rucksack's tracker.

At a few minutes before midnight, George announces that he is getting a bit tired. 'Do you fancy taking over for a bit, Ron? I'm normally tucked up in me bed by now. I'm not sure I've been out this late in years.'

Val is in the back. 'Both of you wind down your windows and drink the black coffee I've brought in this flask.'

George finds a suitable spot to pull over so that Ron can take over. George checks his phone to see exactly where the Air Tag is. An arrow tells them to drive to Stourbridge Canal.

'We're very close now,' George says, glaring at the screen. They park the car and get out. In the early hours of the morning it doesn't feel like a very welcoming place to be.

'Give that here, George.' Ron takes hold of the phone.

Val grabs a blanket and a bag.

'Do you really want to cart all that with us?' George asks.

'I don't know what I'm going to need yet, do I?' Val replies.

They walk in darkness towards where the screen says the air tag is and begin calling out.

'Charlotte?'

'Charlie, luv?'

'Charlotte, sweetheart, where are you?'

They keep walking very slowly. They look behind every bin, and peer down every alleyway. They check behind cars, George using the torch on his iPhone to light the way.

'I feel like a bit more money spent on street lighting here wouldn't go amiss,' Ron says.

They make slow progress, because, according to the tracker, she should be here. But there's no sign.

All of a sudden, Val shouts out. 'Look! It's her bag. She's got to be around here somewhere.' She lifts up the orange rucksack. 'Charlotte, luv. It's Val. Are you there?'

She keeps calling out to Charlotte, as do the men.

'I'll look over here,' Ron says. 'You two go up that path.'

Val opens up Charlotte's rucksack as they walk. The first thing she pulls out is the knitted bed socks she made for Charlotte all those months ago.

'George, look at this. The poor child, the poor, poor girl. Look, it's her socks.'

George looks and keeps calling as they move along a footpath.

From out of the darkness comes the sound of Ron's voice. 'Get off her, you dirty bastard, get off!'

They turn around quickly and follow the direction of his voice. Ron has a man by the throat against a wall.

'You disgusting bastard. She's a child. Get out of here or I'll call the police!'

Charlotte is lying on the floor, crying.

VI

Charlotte is in some kind of dream. She must be. It can't really be Val on her knees next to her, hugging her. What would she be doing out here, miles from where they live in the middle of the night?

'Oh, Charlotte, my beautiful girl, what's happened to you?'

And that sounds like Ron's voice.

Suddenly, Charlotte is being hugged very tightly. A blanket is being put around her.

'Dear child, you're all skin and bone,' the woman with Val's voice says.

The man who looks like Ron has his hand on his lower back and the other on his forehead. He sighs and sighs.

Charlotte is very unwell. She is sore around her mouth and on her face. Her arm hurts. Everything hurts. She doesn't know where she is or what's going on. She is cold and wet and filthy dirty. They mustn't see her like this.

But Val and Ron lift her up and take her to the car.

George is there, too, on the phone. 'We've got her, Angie. She's safe. Hang on a minute, I'll put you on loudspeaker.'

Angie explains that, eventually, after she got through to the police, and managed to access the right department for 'missing persons', she was told that Charlotte had been missing for a week and a half, after running off from the hospital.

'Apparently, they're sending a patrol car to look for her because I said you'd found a signal on the air tag thingy.'

Val is fussing over Charlotte's seat belt, clicking her in as if she is Lawrence's age. 'Let's take her home, but first we take her to our hospital, then those idiots are less likely to come and get her and take her back to that school.'

Val holds Charlotte for the next few hours as they drive back home. Ron and George talk quietly in the front about roads and hospital parking. The sound of the radio is soothing background noise, though it has to be re-tuned each time they pass through a new county.

It is light by the time they arrive at the hospital. Charlotte is shivering, despite being wrapped in the blanket. Ron and George have taken turns to drive with the windows open. Val seems to have nodded off. Ron parks at the front of A&E and drops them off while he goes to park.

There is only one other person in the waiting room. 'Definitely the right time to come to A&E,' Val remarks. 'Make a note of that.'

It doesn't take long for Charlotte to be called forward to the triage room. Val goes in with her, a supportive arm around Charlotte.

'Well, I've seen you looking better, my girl,' Val says with the shake of her head.

Charlotte is too tired and broken to give anything more than monosyllabic answers to the nurse who asks her questions. Charlotte wonders why Val is crying.

When the triage is done, they return to the waiting area. Charlotte struggles to walk. She feels so weak. When they are seated once more she leans her head against Val, who makes the best pillow.

Val still seems to be crying, and has a tissue to blot her tears.

George asks the receptionist if they can have a wheelchair.

It's another half an hour or so before a doctor comes through the double doors and calls Charlotte's name. First of all, he wants to know who the party of adults is.

Charlotte doesn't speak while they explain that they are her old foster carers. They tell him the story of how she has been missing for 10 days and they only managed to find her because George had put an air tag in her rucksack. The doctor smiles and asks why Charlotte is no longer living with them now.

'Because my mother is a stuck-up dick,' Charlotte says, with her eyes half-closed.

No one answers her.

'Would you like me to come in with you, luv?' Val asks her as the doctor indicates the way to the consulting room.

Charlotte nods. She never wants to be on her own again.

Ron and George sit outside in the corridor while Charlotte is being assessed and having her observations done. It seems to take a long time. She is weighed, measured, has her blood pressure done and some bloods taken. The doctor is concerned about her wounds and her levels of hydration.

'We'll admit you, at least for the next day or two. You're dehydrated and need to be on a drip. We want to get some antibiotics into your system to get the infections from your cuts under control.'

'But we'll stay with you,' Val says. 'If that's okay with the hospital.'

Charlotte is taken to a ward. George sits with her while Ron drives Val into town to get a pair of pyjamas, some toiletries and some new underwear. Val returns with a teddy bear as well as the necessities.

Charlotte stays in for two nights, the Reynolds on visiting rotation. They bring her Taylor Swift books and magazines. Sometimes Charlotte puts her hand to her neck to make sure that the silver loveheart locket is still there.

Val takes her clothes home to wash, and repairs the pulls and rips in her rainbow jumper. She brings it back to the hospital along with new leggings and a hoodie from New Look, plus some trainers.

'No need to put those filthy things back on. We'll just get rid.'

The medical staff liaise with the local authority social services team and with Charlotte's parents throughout her stay. Whenever Charlotte is asked, she makes it quite clear that she wants to stay with the Reynolds. With her parent's permission, and with the agreement of the social services team, she is discharged to their home. When she arrives at the gate, Ben and Sam have put up some bunting outside the front door and Lawrence is jumping up and down with excitement. Puzzle makes a beeline for Charlotte when he sees her. He squeaks and yaps and will not leave her alone.

Inside, everything is just as she remembers it. There is the wicker dog bed with Digby and Barley. There is her favourite kitchen chair. There are the knot-face characters in the door, smiling. She is led to the sofa and her old quilt is put over her. Everyone fusses around her and nothing is too much trouble. They put the TV on and it could almost be like she has never been gone.

Lawrence has lots of questions.

'Why did you leave us? Where have you been? Why is your face sore? How did you hurt your arms?'

Angie moves him to the armchair. 'That's a lot of questions

for one person to be thinking about. Let's wait until Charlotte is feeling better.'

But Charlotte is already feeling better. She feels safe and happy to be amongst everything that is warm and familiar. There is the smell of stew and dumplings from the kitchen, layering over the other smell of baking cakes and, from having no appetite whatsoever, Charlotte suddenly feels ravenous.

'We'll soon have you back to your old self,' Val tells her. And, when they are alone and no one else can hear, Val whispers, 'You don't need to worry about anything here, you know that.' She puts her hand on Charlotte's arm. 'You're not the first woman who's had to resort to giving blow jobs for money.'

It's unbearable that Val knows, and that she said the words out loud, but it's reassuring at the same time. Charlotte is shocked by her worldliness but it takes away some of her shame.

Charlotte is definitely home.

VII

The police, having spoken to Charlotte briefly in hospital are anxious to interview her in more detail as soon as possible. There are also procedures to follow with the social workers.

'I've tried my best to put them off until Monday,' Angie says, but they're having none of it. They want to talk to you so that they can close your case. Best get it over with?'

Charlotte nods.

The police want to come around after dinner, at 7pm. When they knock on the door, Lawrence, Ben and Sam are sent off to their rooms. Val stays in the kitchen, tidying up and making Lawrence's packed lunch, and hanging around to be on standby in case they want a witness statement. Ron and George are out putting the animals away.

Angie shows them through to the sitting room and asks the two police officers if they would like a drink, which they do. One talks to their radio while the younger, female police officer sits in a chair facing Charlotte. Angie brings the cups in.

Charlotte knows she still looks rough. She hasn't had a shower yet, and even though her clothes are clean, underneath she feels disgusting.

'How are you, Charlotte?' the officer asks.

Charlotte looks at Angie and Angie smiles back, both resisting any sarcastic answers.

'Can we start by going back to your previous hospital visit, from St Margaret's? What happened to you to make you leave the hospital and go missing?'

Charlotte looks down at her lap and is silent.

Val comes in, sits down on the sofa next to Charlotte and takes her hand. 'Look at me. Now, come on love, you're a good girl, a brave girl and you've done nothing wrong, we know that, and we all want to help you.'

With Val holding her hand, Charlotte talks about seeing Avril or Isabelle or whoever the hell she really is, and starts to cry.

'She wanted me to go back to work for her again. I just couldn't do it. I was scared and just wanted to be away from her.'

Charlotte has to explain that Isabelle turned up as a graduate at an interview to become a pastoral adviser for one of the houses at St Margaret's, 'but Isabelle was Avril at Hickman's where she got students to run drugs and a few girls, like me, were forced to work at the chicken farm.'

Val keeps stroking her hand. 'It weren't a farm with chickens though, was it?'

For the very first time, Charlotte talks about the Albanians, and about having sex with men who paid the Albanians.

Angie paces around the living room with her hand in her hair at the front of her head.

The police officers alert their superiors. They weren't expecting to uncover a member of a major drug cartel and human-trafficking ring.

Val sits quietly, offering reassurance, still holding Charlotte's hand. Charlotte tells them about the New Year's Eve sex party and the little girl, the scared girl who'd been brought in from a children's home and was part of the auction.

Once she starts, she can't stop her terrible tale of being groomed, trafficked, and running drugs for the Albanians. She talks about guns and knives and local kids in County Lines and how she kept hearing the phrase, 'People behind people, behind people.'

She mentions the man Peter, who she thinks may have recognised her when he found out her real name.

'I think he might know my Dad,' she whispers.

The tears flow freely as she talks.

Nobody interrupts her. The police don't need to ask any questions. Charlotte explains why she ran from the school, her fears that Isabelle was just like Avril and connected to the Albanian gangs, and why she had to do what she could to get money. And how she knew what to do because of her time at the chicken farm.

When she runs out of words, there is a long pause.

'Am I in trouble?'

The young officer replies no, and thanks her for being so brave and helpful. The likelihood is that Isabelle was indeed connected with a drugs gang.

'The girls they tend to recruit are usually college girls who believe that coming to England will be an opportunity. Then they find themselves in debt bondage and are under threat that if they put a foot wrong their families will be hurt.'

Charlotte nods. She knows the lyrics to this particular tune.

Angie asks if Charlotte is safe here, indeed if the whole family are safe from potential gang retribution.

George reminds her that neither boarding school has their contact details.

'But these people can find you if they really want to,' the police officer says. 'So take every precaution over the next few days.'

Charlotte is suddenly terrified again. What if she has dragged this whole family into her vicious world?

The officer explains that they will be in touch again soon and makes an exit.

Val says, wisely, 'Let's keep things in perspective. I think Charlotte is the least of their problems. Let's let the police do their job.' She sits back down with Charlotte while Angie makes more tea for everyone.

Ron goes around the house, checking windows and double-locking the front door, 'because you never know and it's better to be on the safe side.'

Val has been looking at the local town's Facebook pages and seen posts about County Lines with explanations of what it is. 'It's not inner city boys from London like people talk about, it's naive local kids from the countryside.'

'Well, it might be bigger than us, but it won't stop us from looking after Charlotte,' George says.

It's all too much for Charlotte, who begins to sob.

'That's it, girl,' Val says with her arm around her. 'You let it all out. You need a damn good cry. You've been through hell, that's for sure, but you're back safe with us now.'

VIII

Over the next few days, Charlotte settles back down into her old room, and to life at the Reynolds. She is surprised to find that it has been left exactly the same.

'Well, we didn't take any other children after you left. Perhaps we knew you'd be back,' Angie says with a wink.

Angie changes the dressing on her arm, makes sure she takes her meds and keeps up her fluids, despite Charlotte's protests that she's had enough. Charlotte isn't well enough to ride yet, but she can visit the horses and take a short walk with the dogs. When she has contact with her parents, she tells them that she is happy to talk over the phone, but she isn't ready to see them just yet. They schedule a face to face meeting for a few weeks' time.

Ron spends a day fitting CCTV around the outside of the house as a precaution, 'just for peace of mind.'

The police tell them that if they are scared, or notice anything suspicious, then they should call 999 immediately.

They hear of further developments at St Margaret's School. It transpires that Isabelle never returned to work after Charlotte was taken to hospital. Following a police spot check to search a number of St Margaret's girls' lockers, a selection of drugs was discovered. Principal Downey is keen to limit any damage to the reputation of her school, and avoid bad publicity. The 'zero tolerance' policy means that the girls who were involved are automatically expelled, and she can continue to claim that they maintain the highest standards.

Charlotte's name is included in the list of expulsions.

Charlotte's mother is furious about the whole thing when she speaks to Charlotte on the phone. 'But you weren't part of the drugs thing. You were cutting yourself. And you were doing that to get away from a member of staff at the school. Are they expelling you for self-harm? If that's the case then I've got a few things to say about that.'

'Leave it, Mum. I'm not going back there anyway.'

'But you don't want to have that on your academic record, darling.'

Charlotte doesn't give a fuck about her academic record.

She speaks to Henry. The Ashmans have finally told their sons about Charlotte 'running away' and Henry is initially cross with his sister – until she tells him more of the story.

'I was in fear of my life, and for our family. I left to live. I didn't run away because I was a silly girl!'

Henry is contrite when Charlotte talks about how she has been around the men in the gang, seen their guns, and overheard their conversations – when they spoke in English – to County Lines kids and the girls at the chicken house. Just thinking about it makes her feel ill and terrified.

There are more police visits to the Reynolds' house to endure, but the case has been passed above the local team.

'Special Branch, MI5, the Police Commissioner, the National Crimes Agency, the lot!' George says. 'All for our Charlotte.'

'Yes, but none of them seems to know what the other is doing,' Val remarks, wryly.

'The police are a complicated bunch, aren't they?' Ron says.

'And they clearly don't have as much power as they should

have,' Angie says, when no arrests have been made over the last few days.

Another police officer reveals that, 'no one messes with the Albanians. They are fearless and would think nothing of throwing a child, or their parent, into the river.'

George goes a bit pale and Angie says that perhaps they shouldn't be talking that way 'in front of the child'.

Angie means Charlotte, not Lawrence, who is at school, but Charlotte is confused, since she no longer thinks of herself as a child.

Val says, 'Well, the damn police should shine a light on it then, shouldn't they? They need taking in hand, these bloody people. They get away with what they can, then they push it further and further until finally they do something that reveals what they're up to. At which point it's a bit late and can't be ignored. The police should get involved before it reaches that stage.'

Ron suspects that it's all down to a lack of resources, and most armed response units are near cities, not villages or hamlets.

'That's what I'm saying,' Val insists. 'They get away with it because they can. They should be able to track down that Avril-Isabelle girl at the very least, surely?'

The word 'corruption' is bandied about. The commissioner tells them that the fact that Albanian gangs were operating in the part of the country where Charlotte has been to school most recently is probably nothing more than a coincidence, they just target wealthy private schools where pupils often have no immediate family support.

The next job is to sort out Charlotte's meds properly. She is on and off them too regularly to be doing her any good, and Angie can see she needs some scaffolding right now, 'to help you cope with this madness.'

The GP initially refuses to prescribe anything for Charlotte, but Angie refuses to leave without the meds. 'I happen to know that this health care group has joined the collective action, in dispute with NHS England over changes to the GP contract. I know that you're not taking on any additional work. But the local community won't be pleased to know, will they? Now, I suggest you start again with the meds, and then I won't have to start shouting about it, will I?'

When the GP still resists, Angie asks to speak to her in private. Charlotte says, 'It's okay. You can tell her.'

Angie doesn't hold back. She explains what has happened to Charlotte. She talks about her involvement with the police, the abduction, the Albanian gang, the ill-treatment in terms of children's social care, the lack of duty of care at both boarding schools and the current, complicated situation with her estranged parents.

The GP reaches for her prescription pad.

Angie starts Charlotte on the new medication immediately, 'because we know it will take a few weeks to have any effect.'

In the meantime, the Reynolds create a roster of activities to keep Charlotte busy and take it in turns to check on her at night, because that's when she relives the nightmares and wants to cut again.

That's the most dangerous time, when Charlotte becomes almost catatonic with fear and retreats into her trauma. In the absence of the professional help that she needs, they smother her with love and care.

It's the best they can do.

There is a meeting between Ron and Angie and the social workers. The outcome is that Charlotte can stay there for the time being. Angie is fuming at the way the manager frames the discussion, as though she is doing them the favour of allowing Charlotte to stay.

'But it's obviously only a short-term decision and we'll review it in the very near future.'

'We'll cross that bridge when we come to it,' Angie says, firmly.

Charlotte is re-enrolled at the local school. Although she feels a little bit stronger every day and is glad to be back with her friends, she still has days when she can't face school; when she can't get out of bed.

The social workers are keen for her to take her exams and stick to the curriculum of her age trajectory, but according to Angie, that's 'a total nonsense, given what you've been through.'

'Then why do they make me do it?' Charlotte asks.

'It's a funding issue, plain and simple – once you're over 16 you won't be getting the same funding, so it's in their interest to get you through. Never mind that it isn't what you need and isn't a sensible way to treat you.' Angie and Ron stand firm, battling with the school, while reassuring Charlotte that she can take her time and do the exams when she is ready.

Charlotte's brothers are not speaking to either of their parents.

Henry and Oliver drive over to the Reynolds' to see their sister, and are as enamoured by the Reynolds family as much as Charlotte is. They meet Tom, Sam and Ben and sit out in the back garden on the bench, while Lawrence tries to impress them with his toys. Charlotte sits among them. Grateful to have six brothers rather than three, all of whom care deeply about her.

Ron and George tend the BBQ, while Angie and Val make salads and bring out the rolls. 'No gender stereotyping to see here,' Angie laughs.

Henry and Oliver talk to Charlotte about their parents, and how things are changing. They also talk about Nanny and Bob, and Charlotte tells her brothers how much the Reynolds' home reminds her of her childhood saviours. She's carrying her plate back into the kitchen when she overhears Val talking to George.

'They're nice boys aren't they? I was wondering how they could have turned out as well as they have, given what we know of the parents, until I heard them talk about Nanny.'

It's true, Charlotte thinks. All the love and kindness she remembers came from them, not from her parents.

IX

The police remain regular visitors to the house. Different faces, different departments, sometimes uniforms, more often plain clothes. There is still no breakthrough with the case nor any arrest of gang members.

Angie pushes for mental health support for Charlotte, and the council puts her on the list for CAMHS (Children's and Adolescents' Mental Health Services) meetings. Angie sits with Charlotte in an initial assessment meeting with a CAMHS doctor and a very earnest student. They ask Charlotte if she feels sad, 'all the time, some of the time, rarely, or never?' They repeat the structure, substituting the word 'sad' for 'empty'. 'Is that all the time, some of the time, rarely, or never?'

'Do you have to talk to her like she's three years old?'

Angie complains and is banned from attending any future sessions with Charlotte. A report is written about her which uses words including 'pushy', 'over protective' and 'unhelpful'. As far as Charlotte is concerned, Angie has been one of the most helpful people she has ever met, and her pushiness and protectiveness is exactly what she needs.

Because she has been feeling better, which, given how she was found on that dark night was a pretty low bar to beat, she's dropped down the list. Not a priority. According to the CAMHS method of assessment and benchmarking, Charlotte may be entitled to some group therapy with fellow teenagers in approximately eight months' time. Angie is furious once more. 'But she's been through so much: rape, trafficking, drugs and lord knows what else!' She complains to the social worker.

It's irrelevant, because Charlotte doesn't ever want to go back. The social worker explains that there is no alternative available for Charlotte. CAMHS is a free service and they won't fund a private therapist, 'just because Charlotte didn't get on with the doctor. She needs to try harder if she wants help.'

'We'll work something out,' Angie promises. But her face is one big frown. Without asking Charlotte first, Angie phones Kirsty and James to explain that their daughter needs therapeutic support. 'An NHS pub quiz isn't going to help her.'

They agree to fund a therapist.

'I know a good one in London,' Kirsty says.

'No, that won't work,' Angie explains patiently. 'The therapist needs to be local. Charlotte can't travel to London and it can't be online. Charlotte needs to work with an actual human being in real life. It will cost £70 per session and she'll need two a week for a few weeks, then we should be able to drop it down when Charlotte starts to feel better.

'Well, can a therapist be any good if they're only £70 a session?' Kirsty is sceptical. 'My Harley Street colleague works with the Royal Family and senior politicians. Wouldn't that be better than some local shrink?'

'I think this local one will be fine,' Angie replies, tightlipped.

The 'local shrink' Angie has in mind is called Aoife. She has already met Charlotte and they clicked instantly. The down-to-earth therapist grew up in Northern Ireland and knows about gang culture from having lived in an IRA-dominated community.

It works. She shares stories with Charlotte, makes her feel better and makes her laugh. They talk about the future and how the brain works, also how the world works and why young people need to learn the skills of how to protect themselves – because gangs and terrorism are as old as the hills.

'It tends to be run by greedy men who were dropped on their heads as babies.'

Charlotte looks confused and Aoife says, 'Well, to be fair, I have no evidence of that last bit, but it could have happened. Perhaps their mummies took drugs or drank alcohol at a critical point in the foetal development. They may have unresolved mummy and daddy issues. Basically, Charlotte these people are, what we in the profession like to call, *fucked in the head.*'

Charlotte finds it refreshing that an adult in authority is finally speaking sense. She doesn't imagine the expensive Harley Street version of her therapist would use quite the same language.

'My job is to help people like you get through their crap and come out the other side. Not only to be able to live a good life, but to know how to avoid these people in the future. All children are vulnerable. If you're rich, you want to try being poor and down with the 'bro'. If you're poor, you want to grab an opportunity to become rich and look after your family. It's just how we're wired.'

Charlotte asks which one she is and Aoife laughs.

'Charlotte, you are a good kid born into a family who didn't see you. Frankly, it seems to me that they are caught up in all the crap of success: the power and money. And, when you look at it, it's no different to gangs. The desire to always have more or *something else* is the problem, and it's part of the human condition. But if we were all appreciative, and content with what we have and who we are, then none of that crap would have any oxygen and it would die out.'

Charlotte wonders if this is true, but her therapist now knows her whole story.

'Then there is the recruitment process itself. The gang's HR department whose main policy is grooming. You were groomed by the first boy who cuckooed his nan's house.'

Charlotte hasn't thought about Danny in a long, long time.

'He was probably greedy and insecure, so he needed to be the big I am. But he was being controlled by others. That young woman, Avril or Isabelle. She was working for the gang, and probably "the man"! She may even have started off in your position. She was probably being paid a lot, but couldn't display her wealth or her cover would be blown. So she was being controlled too.'

'Who is this *man*?' Charlotte asks.

'Every gang has 'the man', the boss. You can see it begin with bullies in the playgrounds at school. You would not believe how many children I work with because of bullying. Bullies are usually unhappy people transferring their misery onto people who are usually picked because of basic jealousy. My own son was bullied at school because a boy saw him walking through the park with me when he was 10 years old with his arm through mine while we chatted about this and that. It turned out that the bully's mammy was having an affair and had left home and so he resented my son having something he didn't.'

It seems strange for Aoife, as a therapist, to be talking about her own life, but actually, Charlotte is all ears.

'Everyone will have something going on, no matter what they say. Look at Hitler, even. His father was harsh and distant. He had a closer relationship with his mother, and her death from cancer when he was 17 was traumatic for him. There is always something!'

Aoife laughs. 'I'm going to tell you something. I have my own issues, too. I come from a pretty large Catholic family. As kids, we lived alongside the protestants. They were our friends, at first. Then it all changed and we couldn't speak to our friends in case we got hurt, or our family got hurt. My friends' dads and brothers were shot as traitors. My mammy was an informant for the protestants, nothing fancy. She wasn't like a big spy or anything. She carried messages to people. Like you carried drugs – she was a message mule, you were a drugs mule. None of us knew about this. She was our mam, she was an ordinary housewife. Then, one day they followed her, put her in a car and drove her to a warehouse where they shot her in the back of the head. Our tea was in the oven. It burnt, and that's the first we realised something was wrong. You realise, Charlotte, that all big crime is connected. Mainly connected by the same sorts of people who were dropped on their heads as babies,' she lightens the dark conversation with a laugh again.

It is astonishing to Charlotte that someone who has been through so much can still manage to be cheerful. Perhaps she will one day, too, though it doesn't seem possible just now.

Aoife has still more to say. 'Those Albanian fellas are tough men and women. They're fierce and would cut you or shoot you as soon as look at you. We did a tour of Italy, Sardinia and Albania for our honeymoon, me and my husband. We had the best time and ate some of the best food. They were very friendly, all the Albanians we met. All of them were lovely, but who knows? Some of them may have been dropped on their heads, and they're the ones you've got to look out for.'

'How do you know which ones have been dropped on their

heads?' Charlotte asks, thinking of Avril and how much she looked up to her in the beginning.

'You don't. So you have to be on your guard.' Aoife sighs.

'Look. We don't see all the connections. All the machinations behind the scenes. We see important figures in isolation in the media and on TV and whatnot – as if they work alone. Because that's what the ones at the very top of the tree decide to show the world, while keeping the others, those who are really responsible, hidden from view. You will usually only hear about one or two; never will you hear about all of them. But they rarely if ever work in isolation. Crime, politics, war, propaganda…'

'What's propaganda?' Charlotte interrupts to ask.

'Ah, well now. Propaganda – that's your social media now, I suppose. But that, and the news and religion are all connected by the same people. Each area has dedicated followers, the blind fools who believe in the bollocks they are told. If you look at the very top of the tree it's the people you will never see. They control the giant companies, the politicians, the armed forces, the churches and faiths. They all pretend that they know nothing when they are actually all working together. When my mammy died, I remember this man, a fat man, very fat, so you would notice him fat. Well, he was in the area before my mammy died. Then one day, when I was coming in from school, he was leaving our house. I asked my dad who he was and he said 'nobody'. But it's the nobodies who do the bidding for the people we can't see. Everything is connected, trust me. But you'll never clearly see all five things at once in the same incident: crime, politics, war, propaganda and religion. They can never afford for all five to be exposed. If they are, then down it will all tumble.'

Charlotte sighs. 'It all sounds so complicated.'

'It's so much less complicated than we think. They are basically all the same people. They need success and power because it makes them feel special. They have a lack of empathy. Ha-ha, because they were dropped on their heads as babies. They ignore consequences, they have a chip on their shoulder, they happily speak untruths, assuming everyone knows what they're thinking. That's them. They are the boss and everyone around them has to be a bloody mind reader. They have to have control, they are paranoid and suspicious and usually get rid of people who threaten them. They don't listen. Oh, and they like a title; they always need a title.'

Charlotte laughs. 'I think you've just described my mother.'

Aoife smiles. 'Have I? Well, it'll all come out in the wash.'

'So, who am I?' asks Charlotte.

'You're you. You're Charlotte. But you've also been coerced and manipulated by adults who are connected to crime, politics, war, propaganda and religion.'

Charlotte thinks for a bit. 'The gang are the crime, my dad's in politics, he has this PR team, public relations people around him, so that's propaganda, and my mum and dad were both in the army. I don't know about the religion part.'

The therapist smiles. 'What politics was your dad involved in, what was his role?'

Charlotte frowns and thinks some more. 'Oh my god, he was putting through an anti-terrorism bill, and it was something to do with religious groups.'

'There you are, and do you think this is all connected or just a coincidence?'

Charlotte takes a deep breath and blows out her cheeks. 'I don't know.'

Aoife smiles again. 'You probably never will. But it's the

famous five at play everywhere and you, my sweetie, according to the government's own description, are a mix of runner and shotter with a mix of bae thrown in.'

'I don't follow.'

'That's the gang's HR description of your jobs. Teenies are the under-10s, below the age of criminal responsibility, who carry drugs and weapons, or move parcels.'

'Yes, I've met some of those.'

'Runners and shotters are your age, 12 to15-ish, and they move drugs, sell drugs in the streets, arrange street deals, stay in 'trap' houses where drugs are sold or made.'

'Sounds familiar.'

'And the baes, or sometimes 'links' or 'baby mamas', take your pick, well, they're the girls exploited by members for sex. But the faces are those at the top or higher end of the chain, and you won't know them. Because they have limited contact with street level operations and aren't often seen or known by street level members like you.'

Charlotte absolutely loves working with Aoife. She tells Val and Angie how she is having her 'mind blown' during the sessions.

'People behind people behind people,' Charlotte whispers.

X

The Ashman family has gone their separate ways. Charlotte's brothers are living independently, Edward still in America. Charlotte chats to Henry regularly, but he has his own life to lead and a wedding to plan. James has moved over to Washington DC to help set up a US think tank, though what exactly the tank is thinking about has never been clear. Kirsty has moved to Switzerland permanently, wasting no time moving in with the owner of the private hospital once James' various affairs came to light.

The social worker calls to arrange another meeting about Charlotte's care plan, 'because obviously the arrangement we made was only temporary.'

'What if they take her away again,' Val says. 'I couldn't bear it. Charlotte needs a family.'

'And that family is us,' Val says, firmly.

So, the Reynolds decide, after much deliberation, 'Well, actually, it was three minutes in me shed,' George tells her later, that they should try to adopt Charlotte.

Angie and Ron think that it will be much safer for Charlotte if she is able to change her surname, but they've no way of knowing whether Charlotte's parents and the social services people will agree or not.

The time and place of the meeting is agreed; the first part of it takes place in the afternoon while Charlotte is still at school. In attendance are the social worker, the social work manager who will chair the meeting, someone from 'wellbeing' and another man who is introduced as an auditor from the department.

Ron and Angie are nervous. They've prepared their presentation of why they think that they should adopt Charlotte – if indeed that is what Charlotte wants. They can't ask her yet because they don't want to get her hopes up. They've planned to talk about everything they think they can offer Charlotte, and all the benefits for her, if she legally becomes part of their family.

The big pine table in the kitchen has been recently waxed, and the attendees of the meeting gather around it. The introductions are soon made. 'It seems a bit strange introducing meself in me own kitchen,' Ron says.

Angie, sitting next to him, gives him a little nudge in the ribs.

The manager thanks Ron and Angie for all their hard work and the progress that has been made with Charlotte who is beginning to show signs of feeling much better. 'Which is a credit to you, after all she's been through.'

Before the Reynolds have a chance to share their plan, out of the blue, the manager says, 'We'd like to discuss with you the possibility of adoption as a way forward of looking after Charlotte.'

The man from auditing, a rather strange-looking man, very tall and thin and grey, pushes forward a document that offers a weekly allowance to look after Charlotte until she is 18 years old. 'And, when she reaches 21 years, she'll receive a trust fund that has caveats to receive further funding until she is 30 years old.'

He pauses. 'There is also an allowance for you, the Reynolds family, in recognition of the work you have done and will continue to do for Charlotte after this challenging time. We'd only ask you to consider giving Charlotte your surname, "Reynolds", so that she's free of the Ashman surname.'

'Well, we were going to suggest it ourselves. And we'd do it for free,' Angie says, 'wouldn't we, Ron?'

'Yes, of course we would. We love her,' he says, simply. 'We're assuming her parents are OK with all of this, then?'

The thin, grey man whose name they didn't catch smiles. 'It's best, I think, if it's done this way.'

They agree to talk to Charlotte when she comes in about the idea and, if she's in agreement, 'then we can propose this as a formal arrangement from today and set the various legal aspects in motion,' the thin, grey man says, before announcing that he has to leave. He stands up, taking his black leather messenger bag with him.

As Charlotte comes up the drive to the back gate on her way home from school, she sees a very tall man come out of the front door. She watches him get into a silver car and drive off. She's a little perplexed, because he seems vaguely familiar, though she can't think where she might have seen him before.

Ron and Angie come to the door, beaming.

'Come here and sit with us a minute, would you, luv?' Ron says, indicating the bench table next to the barbecue.

'What's going on?' Charlotte asks, worriedly.

Angie takes her hand. 'Would you like to officially become our child, for us to adopt you, I mean?'

Charlotte's hands fly to the locket at her neck as she tries to soak in the words.

'Yes, I would. Are you serious? Is this real?'

They walk back into the kitchen to be met by an expectant

social worker and her colleagues, who clap their hands together when Ron shouts, 'She said yes!'

He runs round to George and Val who have been waiting anxiously on the outcome of the meeting.

'Well then, Chinese take-away and ice cream tonight, to celebrate welcoming Charlotte into our family properly,' George says as he comes through the door.

As Charlotte is falling asleep later that night, beneath the handmade quilt, warm and happy, she suddenly remembers where she's seen the man before. It was at her parents' Surrey home and he was in a meeting with her father.

'Skinny Man,' she whispers.

Afterword

Charlotte got lucky in the end, but so many don't. Too many girls are cut adrift, or simply go missing – sometimes for good. The National Police Chiefs' Council (NPCC) estimates that 1,900 children went missing in 2021/22, specifically due to County Lines.

This is nothing new. Fagan from *Oliver Twist* was using children for criminal acts like pick-pocketing. Given what was happening in Victorian Britain, exploited children were probably moving opium and, no doubt, being sexually exploited.

They always are.

As a human race we have always exploited children. Just look at the biblical references to the sacrifice of children.

County Lines is more shocking and horrific because of the layers of organisation that lie behind it. There are over 6,000 County Lines in operation in the UK according to 2024 data. The lines are the phone lines: connections, the WhatsApp groups, the pings and vibrations of messages from drug addicts, middle class professionals, single mums, people with disabilities, or people who are in pain physically or emotionally; plus those who are bored and those who want to party. Who knows why? But drugs are there. They always have been, it's just that now demand is through the roof. The main gangs are from cities but rural gangs have grown exponentially.

Too many children are involved in County Lines, too many

children are being exploited, sexually and financially. No children being exploited is my preferred number. If we track images of children used throughout art history, we see so much abuse, neglect and sexualisation.

The only period in art that I think celebrated children was the Renaissance. A good example is Raphael's two well-nourished angels, the two little cherubs resting on their arms looking upwards, from the Sistine Madonna, popularised on calendars, bags, cushions and trays. But if you look at contemporary images of children they are repeatedly over-sexualised. There is a piece of work by the Chapman Brothers called 'Fuck face'; it's a little boy with a penis for a nose. I worry that we have lost our love and respect for children and childhood. We stick children in front of screens and large corporations make as much money out of children as they can. And so many are forced into slavery and a dystopic life.

Gangs from other countries have set up shop along with the owners of other businesses. You know the ones I'm talking about. Those empty shops on the high streets that suddenly become occupied with barbers, nail bars and kebab shops. How many are there for the purpose that the name says over the door? How many barbers can a town need? New chairs, Porsches and 4x4s parked outside and hardly any customers. The kind of businesses that are good for laundering money.

The mums and families of children caught up in County Lines end up having to work for them too. Car boot sales are a good place to wash the money, along with local, friendly little sweet shops and post offices. They're not bad people, they're scared people. The drug need and problem is now so great that it is unlikely that the police or government, whichever is in power, can get a handle on it.

County Lines runs a successful business model based on fear. Key findings within the latest NPCC assessment reveal that the County Lines threat has become more localised, with 'internal' lines (not crossing different police force borders but staying within one area) increasing by 232%, year-on-year. This represents a shift in organisation. The regular structural changes are another reason it is hard to break: they are good and switching and moving.

People may not be who we think they are, and certainly not who we might hope them to be. You will probably see the people at the top of these organisations dining out in fancy restaurants with their families. Just because they have children doesn't mean they will be kinder to other people's children. That's not how it goes. Joseph Goebbals had six children and that didn't stop him murdering thousands of Jewish children. He finally murdered his own as Nazi Germany faced defeat.

But what's new is the awakening that girls are a big part of County Lines enterprise. They are easier to hide in plain sight. Girls can be violently controlled and sexually abused. I know; I've fostered a few. The County Lines PR team have been really successful at presenting themselves as boys in hoodies. TV and film still push out this stereotype and, of course, we see them everywhere. But the majority of boys in hoodies will have nothing whatsoever to do with County Lines.

However, let's not lock up our daughters.

Instead, let's shine the light on what's going on, notice it, and learn how they operate to keep our children safe.

Louise Allen, March 2025

Acknowledgements

Thank you to my good friends, for your continued support and faith in me and my work. You know that for me there is only one way to 'say it' - with honesty and conviction.

My wonderful family, who are growing-up and can see for themselves what a strange world we offer children. I'm grateful for your counsel. Lloyd, my husband, who I have known since art school many years ago; my sons, Jackson and Vincent; my foster girls Maisie and Chloe and my step-daughters, Poppy and Millie, now grown with girls of their own.

To my incredible comrade, Theresa Gooda, who never ceases to amaze me; as well as working with me she is an incredible poet. To Jane Graham-Maw, my very special agent who is relentless with her pursuit of quality and standards. To Jo Sollis, my brilliant editor, and her wonderful team. To Claire Brown, who creates PR magic and is always a delight. To Catherine Lloyd, Alexandra Plowman and Karen Furse, who had first eyes on the manuscript and who are so generous with their time and their insights.

Mostly, I want to thank you, my readers, to whom I am eternally grateful. Without your love and support, I would not be here.